A New Theory of
Human Rights

A New Theory of Human Rights

New Materialism and Zoroastrianism

Alison Assiter

ROWMAN & LITTLEFIELD
Lanham • Boulder • New York • London

Rowman & Littlefield
4501 Forbes Boulevard, Suite 200, Lanham, Maryland 20706, USA
With additional offices in Boulder, New York, Toronto (Canada), and Plymouth (UK)
www.rowman.com

British Library Cataloguing in Publication Data

A catalogue record for this book is available from the British Library

ISBN: HB 978-1-5381-4629-3

Library of Congress Cataloging-in-Publication Data

Names: Assiter, Alison, author.
Title: A New Theory of Human Rights : New Materialism and Zoroastrianism / Alison Assiter.
Description: Lanham : Rowman & Littlefield, 2021. | Series: Czech theological perspectives | Includes bibliographical references and index.
Identifiers: LCCN 2020044160 (print) | LCCN 2020044161 (ebook) | ISBN 9781538146293 (cloth) | ISBN 9781538146309 (epub)
Subjects: LCSH: Human rights. | Philosophical anthropology. | Universals (Philosophy) | Feminism. | Materialism.
Classification: LCC JC571 .A7837 2021 (print) | LCC JC571 (ebook) | DDC 323—dc23
LC record available at https://lccn.loc.gov/2020044160
LC ebook record available at https://lccn.loc.gov/2020044161

Contents

Acknowledgements

I would like to thank the various readers of the manuscript who gave me really helpful feed-back on an early version of the text. They will know who they are. I'd also like to thank Frankie Mace and the production team at Rowman & Littlefield. Dagmar Wilhelm also read several chapters and made some useful comments. I would also like to thank the Feminist Dissent collective for their support and help with formulating my ideas on human rights and my friends and family who have given me support and love. Jane Adams deserves thanks for her beautiful drawing of Cyrus the Great, that appears on the cover of the book.

Most of all, I have to thank my partner (wife, he would say, although we are not legally married in the UK) for encouraging me to understand and think differently about the world, for encouraging me to learn Farsi and for enabling me to recognise the great and significant ancient cultures there are outside my own European heritage.

Introduction

Re-Thinking Human Rights in Light of New Materialism

بنی‌آدم اعضای یک پیکرند

که در آفرینش ز یک گوهرند

چو عضوی به‌درد آورَد روزگار

دگر عضوها را نماند قرار

تو کز محنت دیگران بی‌غمی

نشاید که نامت نهند آدمی

Bani aadam aazaye yek digarand
ke dar aafarinesh ze yek gooharand
cho ozvi be dard aavarad roozegaar
degar ozvhaa raa namaanad gharaar
to kaz mehnate digaraan bi ghami
nashaayad ke naamat nahand aadami

Rhyming translation by M. Aryanpoor:

Human beings are members of a whole,
 In creation of one essence and soul.
If one member is afflicted with pain,
Other members uneasy will remain.
If you've no sympathy for human pain,
The name of human you cannot retain![1]

In 1992, Fukuyama wrote his famous book *The End of History and the Last Man*[2] where he argued, drawing on Kojeve's reading of Hegel, among other influences, that liberal democracy would represent the end of history.[3]

His proclamation was that the world of the future would contain only liberal democracies and no other political form.

Critics, Derrida for example, claimed that Fukuyama was no defender of liberalism but he was rather a right-wing ideologue who was worried about Marxism. Fukuyama was, indeed, a 'neo-Conservative'; a right-wing thinker, working for the Rand Corporation.[4]

Whatever the politics of Fukuyama, his thesis became very influential around the time of the fall of the Berlin Wall and the collapse of communism in Eastern Europe, and his work was widely read and reported. But we are in very different political circumstances today in 2019–2020.

I began writing this *Introduction* in the late summer of 2019.Then, as I wrote, the summer in the UK was just drawing to a close and Boris Johnson had prorogued Parliament in a development that was provoking the reaction that it was 'unprecedented'.

I didn't think, when I was growing up in the 1950s and 1960s in the shadow of the Second World War and participating in movements that looked for alternative ways of living, that I would see, in my lifetime, the rise of a new form of far-right populism. Bolsonaro, Trump, Modi, and Orban among others, all, in their different ways, deride the notion of a human right or the obligation to protect precious land, as 'establishment' and misguided. In this respect they share with some who purport to be on the opposite side, the religious fundamentalists in Saudi Arabia or Iran, for example, a disregard for the concept of a human right. Indeed, some of the former draw on a form of Christian, or Hindu, fundamentalism. Given this setting, one would have hoped that there would be a robust defence of the notion of a right, at least as a precondition for making deeper changes in the world, from the left of the political spectrum.

However, rather than this, there is a strange alliance between left- and right-wing on this issue. In this book I will aim to respond to the left-wing critique of the idea of a right. The left has also ridiculed the underpinning concept of a right – the notion of universal humanity.

The left critics of the concept of a right deride it as 'Enlightenment' inspired and Eurocentric; as 'western', racist and sexist. This is merely a selection of the critical comments about the concept of a 'right' from the left of the political spectrum. The concept has also been critiqued as biased in favour of imperialist and colonial powers. In its turn, this critique is inspired by a theoretical position that is postmodern, postcolonial and that dismisses its opponents as reductionist, dualist and essentialist.

I am turning to look again at this Introduction in April 2020, when we are just beginning our third week of lockdown due to the coronavirus outbreak. I cannot and should not claim to be able to say much about this. But I would like to make three comments: there are many indications of the sense of 'community' – local, regional and global – that this pandemic has unearthed. There are also reports of rises in racism and the pandemic obviously affects poor people across the world economically and socially in more extreme ways than those who are better off. But there are also risks that pertain to the subject matter of this book.

In the *New Statesman* of 20–26 March 2020, Ross Douthat wrote: 'But even more than terrorism and the Iraq War, the financial crisis of 2008 and the Eurozone stalemate, Brexit and the election of Donald Trump in 2016, the pandemic of 2020 promises to stall globalisation, harden borders, freeze economies, and push the dream of liberal progress ever further into history's rear view mirror'.[5]

In just one nation, Hungary, for example, police powers have been introduced with no time limit and independent journalists could face jail. In another very sad case, the Chinese government has announced, during the pandemic, that it is not bound by Article 22 of the Basic Law relating to Hong Kong. This article states that the Chinese government is not allowed to interfere in the internal affairs of Hong Kong. This is at a time when Hong Kong was controlling its own epidemic effectively but at the same time arrested and put pro-democracy activists on trial.[6]

Moreover, to quote another source: 'The far right in America has received the coronavirus pandemic in much the same manner as any other event: with disinformation, conspiracies and scapegoating. Many seem to see it as a significant opportunity, whether it is for financial gain, recruiting new followers, or both. The delayed and much criticized response to coronavirus by the Trump administration has helped talking about how to use the crisis to recruit people to terroristic white supremacy.[7]

One final example is that there is evidence, at the end of May 2020, that women's rights are being eroded during the pandemic. A survey conducted for a group in Spain found that '80% of the 12,600 women who responded were struggling to balance teleworking with childcare'. In Valencia, a study showed that mothers were the ones 'ensuring children kept up with online classes and homework during the lockdown'.[8]

So there are real fears for human rights during and following this pandemic. However, to reiterate an earlier comment, there is also cause for hope. In the UK, in May 2020, an alliance of Labour Party members, trades unionists and others has drawn up plans for an 'environmental revolution' on a par with the radical changes brought in by the Attlee government after the Second World War.[9] The Black Lives Matter protests taking place during the pandemic, where thousands of people, globally, risked their health to protest about the death of George Floyd at the hands of police in Minnesota,[10] have shone the spotlight on racism and killings of BAME people in the United States and elsewhere in an unprecedented fashion. In the city in which I work, Bristol, UK, the statue of Edward Colston, a seventeenth-century figure who was celebrated in the city for his 'philanthropy' but who made his money from trading in African slaves, was forcibly removed by demonstrators. This toppling of a hugely controversial statue will no doubt have lasting symbolic significance. The demonstrations were enabled partly by the poignant slogan 'I can't breathe' uttered by Floyd, as police kneeled on his neck and reflected in the feelings of those seriously ill from COVID-19.

In this book I will set out to defend an unpopular 'essentialist' and 'universalist' theory both of universal humanity and of universal womanhood. I will set this defence in the context of an elaboration of my own version of a 'new materialist' position. This is a recent fashionable expression but my inspirations are Schelling, Kierkegaard and also Andrew Collier and Mary Midgley. The first part of the book will defend this materialist metaphysical position against various opponents. The specific focus on defending human rights will occupy the second half of the book. It will deploy the metaphysical position defended in the first half of the book as its underpinning metaphysic.

I would like to note, at the outset, that I myself, along with others who labelled themselves feminist, at the time, including, for one Juliet Mitchell,[11] would not have seen the need, in the 1970s, and indeed even later, to defend the concept of a right. Equal rights, as we saw them then, were essentially liberal and bourgeois. As Juliet Mitchell argued, writing in 1987, the principle of equal rights for all, while being based on a universal conception of humanity, arises and connects with capitalism, which depends on individuals selling their labour power for a profit. I have also argued, myself, in the past, that the concept of a right connects with an individualist metaphysic that I did not and continue not to want to accept. I believe, and I will argue this in what follows, however, that it is possible to disentangle a concept of a right, which arises from the needs of all, from its legal, its individualistic and its capitalistic clothing. In its essence, the concept appeals to the notion of justice within a community and the community will be all human beings. While the legal expression of the concept of a right does at times link with capitalism, this, I will suggest, does not, in the present context of a challenge to the concept from those who would deny justice to all, detract from its importance.

In this Introduction I will sketch one key political and theoretical position I will be challenging and I will note my various disagreements with it.

The position on which I will focus here is one that is inspired by postmodernism. I choose to focus on this particular perspective because it is one that has become so influential on the left that, in certain forms, it is taken to be obviously true. The focus here will be on feminism, but the postmodern-influenced perspective on which it draws has influenced some of the key critics of the concept of a human right whose work I will evaluate later on in the book.

In one example of a position that is taken to be obviously true, postmodern-influenced feminists challenged all forms of universalising thinking. They claimed that many of the views that purported to be universally true of humans in general and of women as a group were in fact true only for humans or of women of particular classes, races and cultures. Abortion on demand, for example, was not a demand that those women undergoing forced contraception could relate to. Postmodern feminists, then, following the critics of universal humanity, suggested that early feminists unconsciously and falsely universalised from their own perspectives. From this it was concluded therefore that there are no 'essential' or 'universal' characteristics of women. This is the first claim that is taken for granted by many on the left, that I will challenge in this book.

Postmodern feminists further argued that feminist theory must be 'explicitly historical' and 'non universalist'[12] and they derided universal theories as 'essentialist and mono-causal'. The word 'essentialism' became, following them and others, basically a term of abuse. I will argue, in this book, for a biologically based materialist essentialism that, rather than being mono-causal, will derive from a perspective that favours a materialist powers–based ontology.

I go along with critics who reject certain types of universalising theory for falsely universalising features of the theorists' own 'era, society, culture, class, sexual orientation, and ethnic or racial group'. However, I will challenge the claim that universalising theories need do this and I will also question the Lyotardian-inspired view, given in his classic text on the subject,[13] that such theories need be 'foundationalist' or derived from the Enlightenment with its falsely optimistic faith in progress.

One central figure who writes from a related tradition to that of postmodernism is Judith Butler, although she herself is influenced by a range of philosophical positions that make her perspective distinct from theirs. For her, there is no such thing as a pre-discursive, natural body, and she critiques the view that there is as 'reductive' and 'essentialist'. The form of essentialism I will defend will be one that is not reductive. I will, however, defend a 'pre-discursive' natural body. Indeed, this claim seems to me to be vital in the contemporary world, with the threats we are facing to the natural world and the natural human body as part of that world.

Butler critiques feminists' use of the category 'woman' as falsely essentialising a notion that is historically and culturally formed, and that, indeed, skates over significant differences among women. For her, such a view artificially creates a boundary between 'woman' and 'what is not woman' that may have been drawn in the wrong[14] place and in a fashion that is biased against one group specifically. For Butler, in her famous and influential book, *Gender Trouble*, 'compulsory heterosexuality' produces and genders all bodies.[15] The category of universal oppression of women, she argues in Foucauldian vein, prevents us from noticing the ubiquity of power and the way in which it constructs and constrains subjects in multiple and intersecting ways. Foucault argued, in *The History of Sexuality* that scientific and juridical discursive structures produced the category and the actuality of sex. Butler uses this argument to make a point about the category and the apparently natural entity 'woman'. Woman, according to her, is not a natural being; rather she has been constructed by discursive processes that set out to portray her as natural. Any theorisation of woman as a natural biological being is castigated in a fashion that has become ubiquitous in the literature, as reductive and 'essentialist', or as an unfortunate 'totalisation' of feminist thinking. This is not, it should be noted, a simple claim to the effect that speaking subjects construct the self, but it is rather a more subtle view to the effect that there are, in Karen Barad's words, 'unexamined'[16] habits of mind that give language more power in shaping the ways in which we represent the world, and, in this case, gender and sex.

Following Butler's magisterial work, it has become a cardinal sin to attempt any form of defence of 'essentialism'. In her later work Butler does revise her view somewhat, but only after it had influenced thinking on the left in deep and abiding ways.

While, in this book, I will critique much that has been taken for granted in the literature that Butler inspired, there is one central claim of hers that I will accept. Indeed, my contention will be, in part, that she has underplayed the possibility of the opposition accepting some elements of her theses while critiquing others. The sense in which I concur with Butler lies in her critique of the metaphysics of the subject – the human subject – as a particular type of substance. According to her, this subject is not an inert entity, but rather it is produced by certain discursive constructions. For her, conceptualisations of the body are produced by normative scientific discourses. This leads effectively to the view that the body is not a pre-given substance but it is rather an effect of productive power. In this book I will concur with her critique of the body as an inert substance.[17] But instead of suggesting that this body is an effect of scientific and other normative discourses, I will argue, rather that it is an effect of biological powers and processes, 'souls', in Aristotle's sense, or powers that can 'actualise' themselves in a range of types of living bodies, including plants and animals. So I would want to extend the range of types of body, beyond those recognised by Butler, that are produced by powers. I would want the notion of 'body' to cover plants and animals as well as humans. I will contest the assertion made by Butler, that the powers that produce these bodies are wholly discursive in form. Rather, I will argue that these powers include some that are biological. Indeed, there is a 'new materialist' tradition with which I am sympathetic, that critiques the assumption made in much of the literature that is influenced by Butler's position, that focusing on the biological dimension of the body implies dualism and reductionism.

For Butler, in *Bodies that Matter*,[18] 'performativity' is equated with the power of discourse to produce bodies. Norms of gender continually work on bodies to bring about constructions of womanhood that are heteronormative. In their turn, in a thesis that becomes crucial for the work of Saba Mahmood that I will discuss in this book, the bodies themselves continue this process of productively effecting this heteronormative construction. Women who fail to fit the normative construction are effectively excluded; they are effectively non-existent.

I accept, then, the Butler-inspired thesis that bodies are partly the effects of powers. However, it is odd, for me, that the biological powers – the power of our genetic makeup and our chromosomes, to take two biological powers – should be excluded from the productive forces that contribute to creating the bodies that we become. Butler's focus purely on normative discursive powers seems to lead to a form of reductionism that is akin, in certain respects, to the form she strongly rejects. To deny the natural body and to assume that such a body is an inert, passive substance seems out of tune with her overall philosophical position. Karen Barad, in her article on *Post-Humanist Performativity* quotes, at the outset, one Steve Shaviro who makes a telling point:

> Where did we ever get the strange idea that nature—as opposed to culture—is ahistorical and timeless? We are far too impressed by our own cleverness and self-consciousness. . . . We need to stop telling ourselves the same old anthropocentric bedtime stories.[19]

Barad herself writes:

> Language has been granted too much power. The linguistic turn, the semiotic turn, the interpretative turn, the cultural turn: it seems that at every turn lately every 'thing' – even materiality – is turned into a matter of language or some other form of cultural representation.[20]

Indeed, the present pandemic, to refer to it once more, has forced us to recognise the significance of our own biological bodies, our immune systems and our chromosomal makeup to take two examples.

In Butler's work, famously, the distinction between sex and gender is an illusion because sex is as much an effect of power as gender. By contrast, as Elizabeth Grosz has noted, human beings are two. This biological fact, along with others, such as the importance, for all of us, of the living natural world from which we emerged, is, I will argue, a vital one that we must defend at our peril.

In this book, I will defend a form of 'new materialism'. It will be my own form that is inspired by the works of Schelling and Kierkegaard. I will begin with a defence of a metaphysical position. I will then move to defend a perspective on human rights that will derive from this materialist metaphysical outlook.

In the first three chapters of the book, I will defend a form of 'new' materialism. This will be akin to the views of others who have been given this label, but it will be my own distinctive position. I will begin, in chapter 1, with a defence of 'realist' materialism, against some key opponents, including positivist-inspired opponents of the position. I would like not simply, then, to assert the realist materialist position, but to defend it against its major opponents. Realism is important for me since it is compatible with a Darwinian-inspired perspective to the effect that humans emerged from a reality that preceded us. I should note, however, at the outset, that realism is a philosophical position that takes many guises.

The form I would like to defend owes something to its idealist contrary. It will not be a 'naïve' form of realism and it is important to me to challenge the way in which certain linguistic structures, such as the subject-predicate grammatical form, implicitly suggest metaphysical positions, such as constructivism or naïve forms of realism.

In chapter 2, I will outline the philosophical precursors, including Spinoza, Schelling and Bergson, as well as some contemporary biologists, who influenced my form of new materialism. I will outline my version of this theory. This derives from a reading of Kierkegaard as offering a view of the natural world as akin to a birthing body, containing powers and capacities that continually shape the specific form taken by individual biological bodies. Freedom, I will suggest, emerged in each human from a nature that pre-existed them.

Moving to chapter 3: here I will offer a defence of my position, suggesting that it allows one to account for a key moral question – the possibility of humans committing evil, which the major opposing theory – that of Kant – cannot explain. I will also suggest, in this chapter, that the metaphysical position I am developing provides a foundation for some distinctive and important moral issues – the defence of future humans, and the defence of the natural world.

That will conclude the foundational section of the book. In chapter 4, I will move to outline and defend universalism and essentialism, both significant claims for the defence of human rights. The form of essentialism I will develop will derive from the metaphysical position outlined earlier in the book.

Finally, in the last four chapters of the book I will defend the notion of a right. Chapter 5 will offer a possible account of the origin of the concept that fits with the materialist metaphysics of the first section. Most people – defenders and critics – take for granted that the concept derives from the European Enlightenment. However, I will suggest that there is another possible account of the origin that derives from Aristotle and from a much earlier period – the Zoroastrian Persian Empire. These two sources, I will suggest, broadly lie within the materialist perspective outlined in earlier chapters. My suggestion, here, is that this perspective may not be the only source for the concept of a right, but it ought not to be ignored as a possible story, as it commonly is. I continue in that chapter, by beginning my response to some common recent critics of the concept of a right.

I then move, in chapter 6, to begin considering some critics of the concept and set about offering some detailed responses to some key points.

Chapters 7 and 8 focus on the work of a theorist who was taught and inspired by Judith Butler, Saba Mahmood. Mahmood adopts a broadly similar outlook to Butler, but her critical focus, rather than being on the constructive power of compulsory heterosexuality, is on the normative force of the concept of a right, in adversely shaping views about minority religious groups, such as the Copts, on the one hand, and on would-be pious Muslim women, on the other. In these two final chapters I will offer a critique of her work and a defence of the concept – human rights – that she critiques.

NOTES

1. Bani Adam, Poem by Saadi Shirai, a Medieval Persian poet. It appears on a Persian carpet in the UN building.

2. The article *The End of History* (see footnote 2) preceded the book *The End of History and the Last Man* (London: Penguin, 1992) by three years.

3. Francis Fukuyama, "The End of History?," *The National Interest* 16 (1989): 3–18, ISSN:0884-9382, JSTOR:24027184.

4. https://www.theguardian.com/books/2014/mar/21/bring-back-ideology-fuku yama-end-history-25-years-on, accessed on April 6, 2020.

5. Ross Douthat, "On How the Zombie Liberal Order might Survive an Age of Disease and Climate Change," *New Statesman* 20–26 (March 2020): 24–28.

6. See, for one source, *The Guardian*, Ilaria Maria Sala, "Covid-19 was a Chance for a Reset in Hong Kong. Instead, the Crackdown Continues," May 4, 2020.

7. https://www.theguardian.com/world/2020/mar/19/america-far-right-corona virus-outbreak-trump-alex-jones.

8. Ashifa Kasam, Kate Connolly, Kim Willsher, and Rory Carroll, "Lockdown Threat to Women's Rights in UK Replicated in Mainland Europe," *The Guardian*, May 29, 2020, 16.

9. See *Guardian UK Report*, May 1, 2020.

10. https://www.bbc.co.uk/news/world-us-canada-52961599.

11. Juliett Mitchell, *Women and Equality, in Feminism and Equality*, ed. Anne Phillips (Oxford: Blackwell, 1987).

12. Fraser and Nicholson 1990, 19–38.

13. Jean-Francois Lyotard, *The Postmodern Condition A Report Knowledge* (Manchester: Manchester University Press, 1984), n (1979).

14. Michel Foucault, *The History of Sexuality* (Paris: Éditions Gallimard, 1976).

15. Judith Butler, *Gender Trouble: Feminism and the Subversion of Identity* (New York, NY: Routledge, 1990).

16. Karen Barad, "Post-Humanist Performativity: Toward an Understanding of How Matter Comes to Matter," *Signs: Journal of Women in Culture and Society* 28, no. 3 (2003): 802.

17. It is important, and this point has been made to me by Fiona Ellis, to note that there are conceptions of 'substance' that do not regard it as inert. Aristotle's view of it, for example, is different from those who see it as a passive, inert 'thing'.

18. Judith Butler, *Bodies that Matter* (New York, NY: Routledge, 1993).

19. Shaviro 1997.

20. Barad, "Post-Humanist Performativity."

Chapter 1

Some Defences of Realist Materialism

Recently there have been, respectively, revivals of materialism, on the one hand, and realism, on the other. In its contemporary revived form, materialism is neither reductive nor static. Materialism, wearing its new clothes, is differentiated both from mechanical materialisms, and, ostensibly also, from all idealisms.[1] Drawing on a diverse range of thinkers, from Spinoza, through Hobbes (read in new ways), Diderot, Bergson, Merleau-Ponty, Marx, Simone de Beauvoir and many more, materialism, in this new tradition, is dynamic and non-reductive. Rick Dolphijn and Iris van der Tuin testify to its complexity when they wrote, in 2012: 'New materialism' or 'neo-materialism' is such a new metaphysics. A plethora of contemporary scholars from heterogeneous backgrounds have, since the late 1990s up until now, been producing (re-readings that together work towards its actualisation).[2]

Some 'new materialists', Jane Bennett, for example, draw on a 'vitalist' tradition to suggest that artefacts commonly regarded as lifeless and inert – like a power blackout, for example, or like obesity – are in fact animated and constituted in part by means of a 'life force' or, to use Bergson's words, an 'élan vital'. Seeds, embryos, and personalities are all organic wholes and therefore there is 'an isomorphism between physical and civilisational' orders.[3] In my book, *Kierkegaard, Eve and Metaphors of Birth*,[4] I defended a particular version of new materialism, one based on Gaia theory and a reading of Kierkegaard, inspired by Schelling, as offering a picture of the universe as a living being, analogous to a birthing body. Rather than emphasising the 'body' however, my focus was on the universe as living and as comprising powers and capacities.

One version of new materialism draws on a phenomenological tradition that with Merleau-Ponty, on the one hand, and Simone de Beauvoir, on the other, emphasises an embodied subjectivity that dispenses with the commonplace

1

assumption in much of the empiricist tradition, namely that experience is basically visual. Instead their primary focus is on 'lived experience' – embodied experience that engages with a living and vital form of reality. Both the experiences of humans and of non-humans, on this perspective, consist in some form of 'lived' experience. To quote Diana Coole on Merleau-Ponty: 'The task of a phenomenology of perception is to rediscover that "vital communication with the world" which precedes yet is taken for granted by the physicists 'freezing of being".'[5] According to her, Merleau-Ponty's task is to 'explain a generative, self-transformative and creative materiality, without relying on any metaphysical invocation of mysterious, immaterial forces or agencies'.[6] Some other new materialists, though, might be quite happy with invoking such forces as underlying or giving rise to material things.

For a significant figure in this tradition, Rosi Braidotti, for example, 'social discourses about "life" are often taken as indicating a return of real bodies and real materiality; an ontology of presence after so much post-modernist deconstruction'. I refer to this return of a neorealist practice of bodily materialism as *matter-ialism* or radical neo-materialism.[7]

I would like to defend a realist form of new materialism. The self is born from a reality that pre-exists it. This reality, contrary to some idealism claims, would continue to exist if all humanity disappeared. As Roy Bhaskar once put it,[8] 'The tides would still turn and … metals conduct electricity in the way that they do … (even if) there were no humans to hear or see them'.[9]

In this opening chapter, I will defend the thesis that there is a reality that is 'outside' the domain of the subject, however this subject is construed, and in whichever manner that domain of reality is conceptualised. Most 'new materialists' would contest the realist claim in that bald form, for both subject and object, for us, consist in lived, active processes that affect and are affected by other such processes. However, it seems important for me, if the position is to lay claim to being genuinely materialist, that the view that there is a reality outside the human is upheld. I will defend a view that this 'reality' consists in interactive and emergent processes that manifest as 'things' such as minerals, plants and rocks, but also as ideas like numbers. Reality, then, on this perspective, will not be 'seen all at once' but will rather be in a constant process of change. 'Things' manifest themselves as the results of potencies and potentialities to come into existence. These potencies constitute a form of unfolding or freedom that, I will argue, is ubiquitous in the world.

I endorse the words of Karen Barad, who sets out a 'materialist, naturalist, and post-humanist elaboration – that allows matter its due as an active participant in the world's becoming, in its ongoing intra-activity'.[10]

Furthermore, to quote Rosemary Hennessey: 'A rigorous materialist theory of the body cannot stop with the assertion that the body is always discursively constructed. It also needs to explain how the discursive construction of the body is related to non-discursive practices in ways that vary widely from one social formation to another'.[11]

I would like to use the word 'processual systems' to describe entities ranging from humans through other living beings, including bacteria, to non-living material entities. This conveys the idea of each system engaging and interacting with every other. Some systems, on the view, will 'emerge' from others. In Darwinian fashion, I will suggest, humans emerged from a reality that preceded them, and it is this that constitutes for me, the key realist claim.

In this respect, I go along with the speculative realist, Meillassoux,[12] for whom the view that there is a reality 'outside' the human is the prime realist or materialist claim. His view lies in contrast to that of many epistemologists, primarily Kant, who argues, by contrast, that the subject constructs reality. For Kant, the world, including the forms of space and time, are constructions made by the self.

Meillassoux stresses that the earth existed long before the emergence of the human life form. As Lovelock puts it: 'Our cosmos is 13.8 billion years old. Our planet was formed 4.5 billion years ago and life began 3.7 billion years ago. Our species *Homo sapiens*, is just over 300,000 years old.'[13] So there is a temporal as well as a spatial aspect to realism. The species that is able to comprehend vital materialism emerged late in the evolution of the cosmos.

For most of the recent materialists, although few of them spell this out, one of the key thinkers of the opposing tradition is Descartes. The latter distinguishes 'thinking substance' from 'extended substance'. Matter – in extension – comprises simple parts, externally related to one another. Matter, for Descartes, as Diana Coole has put it, is devoid of interiority or ontological depth.[14]

In this book, I would like to expand on the thesis of my previous book – the idea that the universe is analogous to a birthing body. One important feature of such a notion is that like we ourselves, the universe came into being – it can be construed as the result of a capacity or a power to be produced. In turn, this potential to come into existence is replicated throughout the living world so that each 'thing' is the result of a process of change and it also has the potential to become something other. Human subjects are implicated in this dynamic process so subjects are not 'outside' the world, looking on it. Rather subjects are shaped by processes external to them and, in turn, they contribute to producing other material processes and systems. This does not mean, of course, that we humans cannot speak of 'things'. As Bergson recognised, it is important, for some purposes, including forms of scientific experimentation, that we 'freeze' the world in a moment of time and see it as comprising things.[15]

In this first chapter, I would like to ask a second-order question: 'Why should anyone accept a materialist or realist position?' It is all very well to state the contrary position and to describe and illustrate a contrasting view. However, it is important to attempt to 'convert' those who adopt the contrary view. One significant attempt to do something analogous is Fiona Ellis.[16] I would like, in this opening chapter, to offer a different set of reasons why one ought to believe in some kind of materialist or realist position. It seems important to me to attempt to be fair to the 'non-new-materialist' position and to try to defend materialism against this contrary view. There is a risk, otherwise, of speaking in incommensurable frameworks and of the two sides failing to hear one another.

The major non-realist positions I will consider in this chapter, are first Descartes's idealism, second positivism and finally Kant's transcendental idealism, although some other non-realist theories – postmodernism, for example – will be touched on. Karen Barad has noted that the postmodern-inspired theorists mentioned in the Introduction to this work have replaced the 'representationism' of positivism with a notion of 'performativity'. For Butler, particularly, there are 'unexamined habits of mind that grant language more power to determine our ontologies than they deserve'.[17] But this 'postmodern' position denigrates the 'performativity' of the natural.

For the non-realists, then, we cannot speak of nature in itself but only about discourses on the subject of nature. There is also, on the view of some postmodernists, a suspicion of scientific thought as irrevocably connected with political and social domination. It becomes difficult, on these assumptions, to discuss and to act upon issues such as loss of biodiversity, ecological degradation or the destruction of immune systems given that these have become mere 'discursive constructions'.

BACKGROUND DISCUSSION

Whether one adopts a materialist or an idealist perspective involves a claim about ontology. So as background to the discussion, I'll begin attempting to answer the question: 'What do we mean by ontological claims?' There are two kinds of focus as responses to this question. On the one hand, we mean claims like the following: does reality ultimately comprise just one thing or many? Is it made up of 'things' at all or rather 'processes' of some kind and can we know the answers to these questions? Does reality, ultimately, consist in experiences of some kind, or must there be something 'outside' experience that grounds it or makes it possible? Is the social world made up of individuals or does it also comprise groups? How ought we to characterise any entity we claim exists?

Those concerned with ontology might then ask the further question: Why is there something, or some process, rather than nothing at all, or no process?

What is the meaning of Being per se? This question is quite general and may be different from the answer to questions like: What does it mean to be a human being, a fish, an angel or a stone in my garden?

It is important, in offering a theory about the nature of ultimate reality, in response to the above question, to recognise one preliminary point. This is that theories about the nature of ultimate reality are probably speculative hypotheses. Since Kant's demonstration of the impossibility of proving that God exists, it has proved difficult to make claims about how reality must be. Some recent thinkers, however, have claimed that proofs like Kant's of the paradoxical nature of reasoning about ultimate reality suggest that reality must be, at its core, paradoxical. Quentin Meillassoux, for example, following Alain Badiou, has argued that we can derive from contemporary mathematics a claim to the effect that reality itself must be contingent.[18] However, Kant would reply to this that we cannot know that contemporary mathematics gets things right. We cannot make claims about existence from mathematical axioms alone. This is not at all, it is important to reiterate, to suggest that we cannot make speculative hypotheses. I will contend, in this book, that ontological claims are speculative hypotheses that can be given a strong justification but that is not to say that we can be sure that any particular ontological theory is right or true. One can derive, from contemporary biology and contemporary Cantorian mathematics, a view of the universe as in a constant process of change, as comprising potencies and powers. This picture can be given an independent justification and I will provide this but I believe that neither it nor any other position can be proven with certainty to be true.

Some recent writing on ontology has, in a true post-Kantian vein, lost the concern with the ethical alongside the belief that it is no longer possible to prove, in the manner of many pre-Kantians, the existence of God, although there are others – Badiou and Giorgio Agamben, to name but two – who link their concerns with ontology to political and ethical interests. I will suggest, in this book, that ontological questions need to be connected with political and ethical concerns and that issues in the latter domain can constitute part of the proof of the ontological claim. This might seem counterintuitive. However, I will suggest that the ontological and the ethical are connected and that there is a mutually reinforcing role linking the two. Alongside this claim, I will suggest that it is preferable to construe God or the Absolute in terms rather like those of Schelling as comprising potencies or powers to come into existence rather than in the fashion of an Absolute substance of some kind.

In this chapter I will defend a version of realist materialism in the following way. I will argue: (i) that a realist materialist position makes more ontological sense than the main opposing positions; (ii) that materialist realism offers a better theory of meaning than the alternatives; and finally, (iii) that materialist realism makes more sense epistemically than the non-realist

positions. The third of these three options will be mainly considered in relation to a discussion of the second as it is a particular epistemic position –
that of foundationalism – that is mainly used in support of a positivist and
Cartesian view of meaning.

Sometimes, in what follows, I will use the word 'thing' to describe what
is outside the human, partly because that is the word used by some of those
whose works I will consider. However, I will qualify this position where it is
important to do so. But I would also like to note, at the outset, that although
the position I will ultimately be defending sees the human as a material entity
intertwined and interacting with other material systems, it is also important
to describe human consciousness of the rest of the world. This will involve,
at times, taking a different perspective. Humans, to use Bergson's words,
'enter into' 'things', move around them and form part of them. But humans
also have an awareness or a consciousness of the world around them and
sometimes this consciousness takes on a spatial and 'frozen' form. It is difficult, as Bergson taught us, to capture 'multiplicity'.[19] 'Perception is never
a mere contact of the mind with the object present; it is impregnated with
memory-images which complete it as they interpret it'.[20] Perception then is of
duration. Yet we can conceptualise 'quantitative multiplicities' – like a flock
of sheep.[21] A certain form of 'scientific knowledge' proceeds, as he puts it, by
going around a thing, 'by relating it to other known reference points, rather
than by "entering into it"'.[22]

REALISM AND ONTOLOGY

I will begin with the first of the three options outlined on page 16. In this
section I will defend a version of transcendental realism against Kantian transcendental idealism. I will consider Bhaskar's arguments for transcendental
realism and offer my own as well. I will be considering epistemic claims
in this section and therefore I will sometimes use the words 'subject' and
'object'.

Recent defences of realism range from Meillassoux's 'grand dehors' to
Bhaskar's transcendentally real. There is, indeed, shared territory between
these two positions. Both are critical of Kant. They would also each be
implicitly critical of Descartes or of positivism as well, but, I will argue, it
is more difficult to critique Kant than it is to critique each of the latter two.

Bhaskar and Meillassoux both set out to critique a view Meillassoux labels
Kant's 'correlationism' and Bhaskar his 'empirical realism'. For Meillassoux,
much of 'pre-meta-physical' contemporary philosophy – by which he means
phenomenology and 'various currents of analytic philosophy'[23] – has lost 'the
great outdoors, the absolute outside'.[24] This metaphor, for him, conveys the

idea of a domain that is not relative to us humans, an area of reality that exists in itself whether or not anyone is thinking of it or perceiving it in any way.

By 'correlationism', Meillassoux means the view that the only reality that exists is one that is, in some sense, a construction of the subject. He writes: 'By "correlation" we mean the idea according to which we only ever have access to the correlation between thinking and being, and never to either term considered apart from the other'.[25] For Meillassoux, Kant is the paradigmatic culprit. Bhaskar expresses a similar view to that of Meillassoux. 'Empirical realism', which includes the philosophy of Kant, inappropriately denies, according to Bhaskar, the existence of the 'real' world of rocks, stars and tides.[26] This view, although neither is an 'empirical realist' would also include the perspective of Descartes, since for him, the real world only exists insofar as we can prove the existence of God, as well as that of many postmodernists.[27]

The position Bhaskar labels 'empirical realist' therefore also denies the existence of some form of the 'great outdoors'. Bhaskar calls his own form of realism, in contrast to 'empirical realism', 'critical realism' or 'transcendental realism'. For both Bhaskar and Meillassoux, then, the Kantian view that the world is derived from the forms of space and time as well as the concepts that we, as finite beings, deploy to 'create' appearances, renders natural objects like stones incapable of an existence independent from the creative powers of such limited beings as ourselves. It does not follow, on this Bhaskarian view, that stones don't interact with humans. Rather the claim is that if there were no humans, stones would continue to exist and interact with other forms of matter and with other living beings. I would like to reiterate that this is the key realist point. Nothing follows, at this point, about the nature of the interaction between humans and stones or about the connectivity between them.

By contrast to this Kantian 'correlationist' perspective, or, one might add, to the Cartesian view, then, the recent realists seek to defend a conception of Being, or the Absolute or Nature, that exists whether or not there are any beings like us, or indeed like an omnipotent God, as a Thing of some kind, to experience 'it'. But, one might respond, is this not exactly Kant's noumenal world? The contemporary realists, however, argue that the noumenal is like having your cake and simultaneously eating it. The noumenal, they lament, is for Kant both required for experience to be possible and such that we are unable to say anything about what it is. We experience the world through the spectacles of space and time. The noumenal is supposed to be outside these and yet it is also expected to play the role of grounding experience. The realists would argue that the faculty of sensibility, for Kant in the Transcendental Aesthetic, 'receives' representations and these must emanate from the noumenal, yet the noumenal is constructed in such a way that it cannot itself cause anything to happen. The noumenal cannot fulfil this function when it is outside the conditions – the principle of causation, for example – that are required for this 'grounding' to make sense.

This is, indeed, a version of an argument earlier put forward by Hegel. According to him, the Kantian 'thing in itself' is self-contradictory. It is supposed to cause sensation but it cannot do this since causation is a category of our minds. Moreover, the whole conception of an unknowable existence is self-contradictory anyway since if we know that a 'thing'[28] exists, then we have some knowledge of it, which itself therefore involves a self-contradiction.

It is also important to note that although Kant uses the word 'appearance', to describe the world we know, he famously does not intend this word to be understood in an empirically idealist manner. He explicitly distinguishes 'appearances' from their subjective counterparts – 'intuitions' and 'concepts'. 'Appearance' is the 'undetermined object of an empirical intuition'.[29] Appearances comprise matter and form. These are the 'definitional' claims about appearance. But Kant also, in several places, but specifically in the 'Refutation of Idealism' section of the first *Critique*, sets out to prove that there must be objects existing in 'space outside me',[30] in order for me to be conscious of my own existence in time. Indeed, in this section, Kant aimed to show that 'material idealism', in both its problematic and its dogmatic forms – the form of idealism which 'declares the existence of objects outside us to be either doubtful and indemonstrable or false and impossible' – is false. He shows that we could not have a sense of our own experiences in time unless there was something (or some process) outside these experiences. The consciousness of myself, he argues, which is required in order for us to think or to imagine anything at all, requires the possibility that some 'thing' exists outside me. I could not identify any of my thoughts as thoughts of redness or thoughts of fire, for example, unless something (or some process) existed outside those thoughts against which I could measure the accuracy of my claim to be thinking of redness, as opposed to yellowness, to take one example.

So Kant is, in this limited sense, already an ontological realist, and a realist about the independent existence of rocks and stones, despite the fact that the label he gives for this 'realism' is 'appearance'. He gives it this label because it is important for him that he offers grounds for any claim he makes about the world that is knowable to such limited, finite beings as ourselves. He contrasts the 'transcendental' employment of a concept, which consists in its application to things in general and 'in themselves', with its empirical employment, which consists in its application to objects of a possible experience.[31] It is a criterion of a concept's having application that we have both the 'logical form of thought in general' and the possibility of giving it an 'object to which it applies'.

Hence, it is possible to argue that equating the noumenal with the 'real' is both textually wrong and ignores the epistemic claims made by Kant. We might also argue that, contrary to Bhaskar's claim that the world of rocks and stones does not, for Kant, exist independently of the subject, that this is not true for an individual self. In general, beings like us create the conditions that make knowledge of any kind possible and these conditions actually require the relative independence of 'things outside me' from my own experiences, for Kant. To the claim that they exist absolutely independently of my experience would be to make a claim that we could never know to be true or false.

On the other hand, though, as his contemporary, Maimon[32] noted, in his critique of Kant, the notion of a 'passive outside' of experience is open to challenge. The view that there is a 'given' 'outside of us', according to Maimon suggests a passive entity outside and a passive faculty of the self. He also dislikes the word 'given' which suggests, according to him, that we have nothing but a representation, whose manner of origin in us is unknown to us. While I would not accept Maimon's view that the challenge to the distinction between 'sensibility' and 'understanding' means that everything emerges in some fashion from the subject, rather the point that Kant makes that sensibility 'receives' representations from some unknown external reality that operates through some passive causal process, is indeed open to challenge. The idea, in other words, that 'matter' is passive and that there is some unknowable thing in itself that gives rise to this passive matter is indeed open to challenge.

SOME ARGUMENTS FOR TRANSCENDENTAL REALISM

Opposing the transcendental idealism of Kant, Roy Bhaskar defends a transcendental realist materialist position. In his work, *A Realist Theory of Science,* Bhaskar offers a transcendental analysis, using a Kantian form of argument, for the conditions of the possibility of experimental activity. In this section of the chapter, I propose to outline Bhaskar's arguments for transcendental realism, assess their strength relative to the transcendental idealist arguments of Kant and then offer some alternative arguments for a realist position. Bhaskar argues that the conditions that make experimental activity possible require transcendental realism. Unless we assume a transcendental realist position, experimental activity, which is a crucial requirement for the possibility of science, would make no sense.[33]

Experimentation, then, according to Bhaskar, is a significant feature of the natural and (in some cases also) the social sciences. This is the initial premise of his argument, and he proceeds to demonstrate certain conditions that he argues are required in order for this premise to make sense. He claims (and this is the crucial feature of his 'critical' realism) that, in order for it to make sense, there must be something (or some process we might add) that is absolutely independent of humans. As he puts it: 'We can easily imagine a world similar to ours, containing the same intransitive objects of scientific knowledge but without any science to produce knowledge of them. In such a world, which has occurred and may come again, reality would be unspoken for and yet things would not cease to act and interact in all sorts of ways'.[34]

In support of this claim, Bhaskar argues that it is necessary to draw a distinction between the regularities of succession generated by scientists in an experimental context and the causal laws these regularities describe. If this distinction were not made, then we would have to draw the implausible conclusion that scientists themselves generate causal laws. This would in turn commit one to the absurd view, according to Bhaskar, that scientists themselves cause and generate the laws of nature.

In response to this, one might inquire, from a Kantian perspective: how do we know that this is the case? How can we be sure that scientists do not themselves produce the laws of nature?

Bhaskar is clear that he is deploying a broadly Kantian argument form – a transcendental argument – one that takes the form of suggesting the conditions for the possibility of X being the case. The question arises, however, whether or not this argument form carries the same weight outside its original Kantian context. Kant, in deploying this form of argument, is concerned with describing the conditions necessary for the possibility of experience. Operating in a context where Hume's discussion of causation had famously 'awoken him' from his 'dogmatic slumber', he set out to demonstrate, among other things, that if Hume's conclusions were true, then no experience would be possible at all: if the world were constantly changing, as it might be on Hume's view, then we could not even have the kind of experience that is initially presupposed by Hume. We could not, in other words, have the kind of experience that is required for us to make a claim about, for example, the sun and whether or not it will rise tomorrow. In order for us to be able to make such claims, we need to assume a relative degree of stability both in our own consciousness and in the rest of the world that contains the sun. These claims are made in various forms in the three Analogies section of the *Critique of Pure Reason*, and particularly in the Second Analogy. There, Kant argues, against Hume, that while individual causal sequences are not themselves necessary, the principle of causation must be presupposed in order for us to distinguish, among our temporally successive experiences, those that represent objective succession from those that represent objective co-existence.

I am not assessing the extent to which Kant is right about these claims. The point in question is the strength of the argument, if he is right. If he is right, then there are certain conditions that are required in order for such finite beings as ourselves to think or to have conscious experience at all. In contrast to Kant, Bhaskar appears to be making a far weaker claim. Even if we accept – a point that is controversial – that experimentation is ubiquitous in science, and even if we accept all the steps of Bhaskar's argument, we will not have produced an argument that is as strong as Kant's. It will not be as strong because describing the conditions necessary for the possibility of experience is stronger than describing the conditions necessary for experimentation in science. Denying that something is necessary for scientific experimentation to be possible has less drastic consequences than denying the conditions necessary for experience to be possible. Moreover humans could exist and function without scientific experimentation, but by definition, not without experience. The former actually requires the latter. If no experience were possible, there could be no scientific experimentation; however, it is not the case that if there were no scientific experimentation, there could be no experience.

Therefore, if we are setting out, as Bhaskar and others are, to show that transcendental realism is true and transcendental idealism false, then we require a stronger argument than the one given so far. To put the point differently, Kant, if he is right, has demonstrated the conditions necessary for the possibility of experience. Bhaskar, if he is right, has demonstrated the conditions necessary for the possibility of experimentation in science. So if we are going to produce a stronger argument for realism than this one, then it would have to demonstrate that a reality independent of humans is necessary for the possibility of experience in general.

Now Kant himself, of course, did demonstrate the necessity, in the first and second Analogies, of something existing independently of our combined sensory and conceptual states in order for us to be aware of these states. But this 'something', which he couched in terms of Newtonian substance – the 'substrate' – is not absolutely independent of humans.

A second argument offered by Bhaskar is that if scientists did indeed generate causal laws then there would be no point to their activity. The whole point of experimental activity would be lost, since scientists would be producing the laws rather than investigating them. Once more, though, the argument has not shown that the distinction between the activity of scientists in generating causal laws and the laws themselves must be made.

So, to reiterate the point above, in order for Bhaskar really to have developed an argument against Kant, he needs a stronger form of argument.

A Bhaskarian realist, however, has a counterclaim. She might say that, on a Kantian form of argument, investigation of the world would be impossible

unless this world existed independently of the investigator. She could elaborate this point by generalising it beyond the domain of experimentation (which
is at the very least a practice that, as noted, takes place only in a limited sphere
of human existence). So she could argue that, if the Kantian assumption
were true, that the world of trees, fields, rocks, planets and stars were only
a construct of the human forms of experience, through the human frame of
time, space and causation, then these things would fail to fulfil the conditions
Kant requires of them. Kant requires that something exists independently
of the consciousness of an individual self, in order for this consciousness to
make sense to the self. So if the tree in my garden were purely a construct of
my sense experience combined with my conceptual apparatus, then it would
strictly fail to exist independently of me, and thus it would fail to meet the
criteria laid down by Kant for the elements of my stream of consciousness
making sense.

A Kantian retort to this, though, might be that all that is needed is a relative degree of independence from the elements of my consciousness and that,
although ultimately the forms of space and time are forms of my intuition and
thus constructed by me, they are also a priori forms and thus independent of
a particular individual experience of mine.

To be sure, in support of a Bhaskarian conclusion, albeit using a different
argument from those he offers, one could argue that the very conception of
substance Kant himself develops in the first Analogy is actually a conception
that requires a form of realism that is stronger than any he actually wants to
hold. A permanent substance, existing throughout time and space, is not the
kind of substance that is possible according to the spatial and temporal frame
developed by Kant in the Transcendental Aesthetic. It has a degree of reality
that is independent of the a priori forms of intuition.

So one might develop an argument that is not restricted in the fashion adumbrated by Bhaskar, and that leads to the conclusion that there must be some
entities that exist independently of the spatio-temporal frame of such beings
as ourselves. The argument would not be restricted, as is that of Bhaskar, to
that of laying down the conditions necessary for scientific experimentation to
make sense since the latter argument is, as noted already, a weaker form of
argument than is required to generate the desired conclusion. We could argue
that, for example, in order for the spatio-temporal conditions that we deploy
to construct experience to make sense, there must be something permanent
or some relatively permanent or ongoing process against which we engage in
this construction for otherwise we would be spinning in a void without reference points against which we could locate our experience. In other words, we
could extend the kind of argument presented by Kant in the 'Refutation of
Idealism' to make the case that Kant's own 'constructionist' project would
not get off the ground unless there were something outside the world of the

finite limited being to stem the possibility of our spatio-temporal world spinning out of sense.

It is possible to claim, moreover, that the argument being offered here is
different from claims about the noumenal. The argument being proposed here
is that unless there were some kind of reality – something or some process at
least relatively permanent – existing outside our spatio-temporal world, then
that very world would make no sense. This is an argument, like Bhaskar's,
that is Kantian in form but that is not one proposed by Kant himself. We
might put such an argument in terms that could constitute more of a challenge
to Kant by claiming that Kant, on his own premises, is unable to account for
the coming into being of the temporal – if this view can be made sensible.
Again, using Kantian-inspired arguments, one might claim either that time
has always existed in which case it would be difficult to account for change,
or that time came into being, in which case, time could not be the form of
inner sense of beings like us.

However, this argument has its limits. It would not tell us anything at all
about the kind of reality that exists independently of the self – what qualities
it has and whether it comprises 'real things and their powers' as Bhaskar suggests, or something else.

Meillassoux, developing his critique of 'correlationism', makes a similar
realist point to this one, but offers a different argument for it. For him, it is
difficult for a Kantian to explain the known scientific fact that fossil evidence
suggests that there was a world that existed before any human came into
being to experience it. But Kant might reply simply that we do not truly know
these things in the sense he requires when describing the conditions under
which we know something to be the case. So a Kantian might simply use the
following steps, as summarised by Gardner: (1) it must be explained how
objects are possible for us; (2) transcendental realism cannot explain how
objects are possible for us; (3) the possibility of objects for us is explained
by supposing that we have a priori representations that constitute objects;
and (4) the possibility of objects for us requires that they be conceived as
transcendentally ideal.[35] For Kantian reasons, then, any realist proposal will
be speculative. If we assume it to be about 'things' and 'powers', this will
remain a speculative hypothesis. So, to take another example, the German
Absolute Idealists each made some sort of assumption about Being as a
whole that Kant would claim they cannot prove to be the case. As he showed,
claims about a reality that lies beyond possible experience are necessarily
impossible to prove.

The realist, then, cannot provide a conclusive argument that would be as
strong as Kant's own argument for her position. It is intrinsic to Kant's position that this cannot be the case, since we cannot step outside of ourselves
and find conclusive proof that the 'outside' takes on a certain character. Yet

it seems undeniable that, for example, contrary to Kant, there must have been a time that is independent of 'our' framework principles, in which beings like us came about. Finite beings like us surely could not have created the temporal conditions that allowed for our coming into being.

Žižek, making a parallel point, reads Kant as unable to resolve the dualisms between the phenomenal and the noumenal, or between freedom and determinism. Yet he does not see this as a failure; rather he argues that Kant has brought to our attention the inevitability of paradox. Our understanding the world and our acting in it are impossible outside the production of antinomies that are incapable of conceptual resolution.[36] As Steven Shakespeare puts it: 'These antinomies are not the unfortunate result of a deficiency in thinking – the encounter with an impassable limit – but the productive force that engenders the very possibilities of conceptual thought, moral action and aesthetic judgment'.[37] Conceptual thought is impossible without a recognition that there are limits to this thought, and moral action is, in Shakespeare's account of Kant, inseparable from the paradox that freedom occurs within a mechanical, causally determined world. For Kant, then, it is important to recognise that there is always something that is outside a certain form of conceptual thought.

This seems to me to be an appropriate concluding comment to this section of the chapter. The critical realist wants some clear conception of the nature of the 'outside' that is independent of ourselves as finite beings. But, for Kantian reasons, this is a demand that cannot be met. This is not to say that there is no such reality, but this reality cannot be conceptualised in the way some realists appear to require. There is almost certainly a 'reality' of some kind 'out there', but any characterisation of its nature will necessarily be speculative. Indeed, thinking about the nature of the 'real' may generate paradoxes. I will suggest, later on in the book, that this reality takes the form of an Absolute but this will be closer to a Schellingian 'ungrund' – a 'yearning' to 'give birth' to the whole, as he puts it.[38] There are some good reasons, I will suggest later on, for accepting such a view.

In this section of the chapter, I have defended an ontological realist theory, although I have cautioned that speculation about its nature, by definition, cannot be proven. I would like to make one final caveat here. Although the claim is that it cannot be conclusively proven, this will not necessarily matter. As will be shown in the next section of the chapter, the early positivist demand for conclusive proof of a claim is itself an impossible demand, and the only proof that can be provided of anything at all is arguments or evidence in its support. This does mean, though, that claims about how reality 'must' be should be treated with caution. So, while claims about ultimate reality remain speculative, this does not mean that they should not be taken seriously. To the contrary, there is evidence and there are reasons that can be provided in support of the claim that there is such a reality.

REALISM IN THE THEORY OF
MEANING AND EPISTEMOLOGY

One form of relatively recent interest in realism was partly in reaction to the claim of the early positivists to the effect that metaphysical claims constituted literal nonsense. Realists reacted against the impossibly strong view, held by the early positivists, of what constituted evidence for any claim about reality. The early positivists wanted such claims to be either certainly true or to be derived, by means of logically valid steps, from claims that were known with certainty. In this respect, their programme was in accord with that of Descartes who also set out to attempt to find a belief that could be known with certainty. It is important, therefore, to note that neither the positivists nor Descartes believed that they were outlining actual experience or reality as it is. Insofar as, for example, Merleau-Ponty gives a radically different account of embodied experience from him he is not critiquing Descartes, but doing something different. Both Descartes and the positivists were abstracting from experience, in all its vitality and ontological depth, and were setting out to uncover a bare claim that could be known with as much certainty as possible.

According to the perspective of the positivists, any assertion about the nature of ultimate reality or about the ultimate constituents of the universe or indeed about the diversity and richness of actual experience will be literally meaningless since any such claim is very unlikely to be capable of verification in the manner prescribed by them. Indeed, the critical literature on early positivism suggested that it is well-nigh impossible to verify anything at all in the manner they stipulated. This fact, however, has not stopped theorists in many disciplines, from sociology through to international relations, using some assumptions connected to the positivist tradition.

Realism, in accounts of meaning, is said to be a theory that separates out the conditions for the verification of a theory or a proposition from the conditions for its truth. The early positivists or the 'logical empiricists' as they were sometimes known – the members of the Vienna Circle, around Moritz Schlick, Rudolph Carnap and others – held an opposing view of meaning. For them, a statement was only cognitively meaningful if it was either analytic or it could be shown, by conclusive verification, to be either true or false or entailed by one of the latter types of statement. For example, if 'this is red' is conclusively verifiable then so is any statement 'this is red' entails.

This debate uses premises that I would want to contest. The view that it is possible to isolate a sentence or a statement in this fashion implicitly assumes a static spatialised view of the relation between a subject and the rest of the world. In fact, I want to suggest, in this book, that matters are very different from this. As a commentator on Bergson puts it: '"Life", "Materiality", "the self", "duration", and many more on Bergson's pages convey meanings they never had before. It is the nature of philosophical and scientific progress to keep their concepts in a flux'.[39] Bergson himself wrote: 'In order to generalize we have to abstract similarity but, in order to disengage similarity usefully we must already know how to generalize'.[40] Nature itself is probably infinitely complex. As Akeley has put it: science may be more like music and art but it sometimes presents itself as though it comprised a finished product.[41]

There are many provisos, therefore, to what follows. However, it is important, I believe, to engage within existing debates as well as challenging them from the outside, and, in my view, although the premises of the debate below are open to challenge, this does not mean that there is nothing of value within the discussion. So with this introductory proviso, I enter the debate itself.

For some, the epitome of logical positivism was the text by A.J. Ayer, published in 1936, *Language Truth and Logic*.[42] According to Ayer, 'one way of attacking a metaphysician who claimed to have knowledge of a reality which transcended the phenomenal world would be to inquire from what premises his propositions were deduced. Must he not begin, as other men do, (sic) with the evidence of his senses? And if so, what valid process of reasoning can possibly lead him to the conception of a transcendent reality?'[43] Or, as Hempel puts it: 'The defining characteristic of an empirical statement is its capability of being tested by a confrontation with experiential findings i.e. with the results of suitable experiments or focussed observations.'[44]

In contrast to these views, realists about meaning assert, as Koethe puts it: that we might be 'brains in a vat' and so the theory that is 'ideal' from the point of view of operational utility, inner beauty and elegance, 'plausibility', 'simplicity', 'conservatism' and so on 'might be false'.[45] Verified does not imply true. The concept of truth is transcendent of anyone's knowledge. The world and a true description of this world might be different from the best possible verified theory.

How do realists argue for these claims? How might we adjudicate between the two theoretical approaches? I will now present some arguments against the positivist view of meaning.

One argument against the positivist view is the following: in their search for the 'foundational statements' on which other claims to know something rest, positivists were led to sense experience. The view was that sentences like 'I seem to see red' were more likely to receive a high degree of verification than a sentence like 'there is a table over there'. The former simply described experience and therefore could not be falsified. However, one objection to this was that these sentences describing private experience could not be used to verify law-like statements about the world. Second, it was argued that they are not verifiable in the manner outlined by the verificationists. As Sellars argued: the apparent veracity of a claim like 'I have a pain' derives from the fact that nobody dares to question it rather than from its certainty.[46] Moreover, as Wittgenstein showed, a 'private' language is no language at all. In order to understand the meaning of the word 'red' a public language is required. So Sellars, Wittgenstein and others therefore questioned what became known as the 'Myth of the Given'.

Furthermore, Hempel himself provided some objections to the strict interpretation of the principle of verifiability. He made the following points: the principle was formulated as follows: take the law 'A entails B'. This is confirmed by an instance of an A which is B and disconfirmed by something that is 'A but not B'. However, (i) this principle does not help with propositions of the form 'There exists life on the stars'; and (ii) take the two claims: (a) 'A entails B' and (b) 'For all A's that are not B's, they are not A's'. The first of these two claims is confirmed by the proposition 'X is an A and a B' but the latter is not. However, (a) and (b) are logically equivalent.[47]

Although the following claim has been disputed, by and large, the positivists, like Descartes, were foundationalists. That is, they believed that there is a core of 'foundational' beliefs which can be justified with certainty. Other justified beliefs flow, by entailment, from these core beliefs. In this way, the sceptic about knowledge could be defeated. However, Kant provided an objection to Descartes's formulation of foundationalism, and Kant's argument form was taken up by others much later. Descartes's famous foundational belief was 'Cogito ergo sum' or 'I think, therefore I am'. However, Kant argued that my existence does not follow from the mere fact of my thinking. This objection indeed was generalised by Laurence Bonjour, who argued as follows: 'According to the foundationalist, we must have direct access to the fact that the feature in question is relevant to the truth of the claim. So we must have direct access to a belief X that has the characteristic P'. But we are not justified merely from knowing that P in inferring anything about X. The person would also need to know that X has P and that beliefs of this sort are likely to be true. The latter though would not be known by direct access.

RORTY ON BOTH FOUNDATIONALISM AND REALISM

Richard Rorty, who was a significant figure in these debates, actually challenged both foundationalism and realism.[48] So while he was not a materialist realist, he also questioned a key claim of both the positivists and of Descartes. His view was that realism is the view that 'the mind' represents the world and it is possible to have infallible knowledge of the contents of the mind. So realism and foundationalism, according to him, are linked and traditional philosophy is 'held captive' by the idea of the mind mirroring the world. Instead, philosophy, for Rorty, ought to be understood as a 'cultural genre' a 'voice in the conversation of mankind'.[49] These kinds of phrases have led some to associate him with postmodernism, an association which he would have rejected.

I'd like to concentrate, in the next section, on Rorty's criticisms of a realist – Hilary Putnam.[50] Rorty considers, in this context, questions about theory change in science. He argues that questions like 'Do the Neuer refer to the soul as quoth?' are not usually answered by 'matching one word expressions in one culture' by 'one word expressions in another'. However a question like, 'Was Aristotle wrong about motion being divided into natural and forced?' or 'Was he talking about something different from what we mean by motion?' do seem important.

He suggests that one possible answer – namely that people are really talking about the essence of a thing characterised by analytic expressions explaining the meaning of the word for that thing or process, has been undermined by Quine. Quine, in his essay *Two Dogmas of Empiricism*,[51] had challenged – successfully many believe – the distinction between 'analytic' statements and 'synthetic' ones.

Therefore, instead of looking to definitions of essence in response to the question posed– about whether Aristotle was using the word 'motion' the same way as later thinkers – people began looking to theories of reference. There are two arguments of Putnam that Rorty accepts. One is that quoted earlier by Koethe – namely that a true theory may be different from the best possible verified theory. Rorty accepts this point but suggests that since we cannot ever know the true one in these circumstances, the claim does not establish realism. Second, Rorty considers, and accepts, Putnam's point that scientific theories tend to converge. But the former argues that this does not establish realism since they might converge for other reasons than that realism is true.

Putnam, however, has another argument. He suggests that we should not accept any theory that leads us to conclude that electrons are just like phlogiston. While the word 'electron' refers to a real entity or potentiality, the word 'phlogiston' never did. The former word refers to a real 'entity' while the latter does not. In other words we must make a distinction between words that really refer to some entity and those that do not.

I would like to remind the reader at this point that some materialist realists have doubted that we can use expressions such as 'words' and 'entities'.

Instead we ought to use expressions like, for example, 'discursive practices' that interact dynamically with material practices. However, as noted before, if we are only able to do this, while I am sympathetic to the point, we will not be able to engage with the above debates, since we would simply be operating in incommensurable frameworks. So while I will ultimately suggest that it may be preferable to use different expressions from 'words' and 'entities', it is also important to operate from the outlook of the consciousness of a human self: an epistemic perspective. What seems to me to be wrong is not that it is impossible to operate on the assumption that there are 'subject' and 'objects' separate from one another, but rather the ontological assumption that this is the picture of reality as it must be. In fact, in my view, humans are part of the material processual reality. However, it is possible to abstract from this and enter the Rorty/Putnam debate on its own terms. When we do this, it is possible, I will suggest, to arrive at conclusions that are perfectly compatible with a metaphysic that ultimately rejects the language of 'words' and 'entities'.

Returning to Rorty: he rejects the concept of reference. He argues that it is a 'confused expression' that runs together two distinct ideas – on the one hand it has been used to mean 'X picks out a really existent entity Y'. On the other hand it has been used to mean 'X picks out a non-existent entity in cases where what makes someone's beliefs about X true happens to be a non-existent entity'. The theory of reference, Rorty argues, represents a confusion between the epistemological quest for foundations and the generic quest to find out what people are 'really talking about'.[52]

However, it is important to point out that there are versions of realism, including that of Bhaskar, that are non-foundational and that rely on some notion of reference. Rorty therefore is wrong to suggest that those who wish, rightly, to distinguish words like 'phlogiston' or 'unicorn' from words like 'electron' are confused foundationalists. It is possible to accept the need for these distinctions while wholly rejecting foundationalism. Bhaskar, for one, was highly critical of foundationalism and also of mind/body dualism. So Rorty's argument does not apply to this version of realism. It is possible to believe in reference in the simple sense that a word picks out something really existing in the world, at one moment of time, without accepting any of the foundational trappings. Bhaskar wrote of Rorty that he seems to believe that any epistemology must be foundational.

To quote from Bhaskar:

> The crucial questions in philosophy are not whether to be a realist or a anti-realist but what sort of realist to be (an empirical, conceptual, transcendental realist). ... Rorty unwittingly imbibes and inherits Hume's and Kant's chosen descriptions of the reality known by the sciences.[53]

In other words, Rorty implicitly conflates 'reality' and 'empiricist reality'. The form of realism I want to defend, to reiterate, is a Darwinian-inspired one that upholds the view that there is a world independent of humans and humans emerged from such a world.

Moreover, in support of a realist theory of meaning, one might claim that the phenomenon of incommensurability, where the same expression in two different theories has radically different senses, could not be described unless there were something over which the two theories disagreed. It is not possible to say of two theories that they clash unless there is something or some process over which they disagree.

Finally, the sentence 'All x's are Y' is said to range over a denumerable infinity of individuals. The verification condition for such a sentence would be a denumerable infinity. But it is impossible for anyone ever to establish that such a condition obtains. We must therefore distinguish the conditions for the truth of such a theory from its verification conditions.

So far, I have defended a form of realism. I have not described what sort of realism I believe to be correct. I have not, so far, defended the form of realism-vitalist materialism – that I will move to defend in the rest of the book. Rather I have tried to defend realism against some common objections.

I have been operating here, to reiterate this point, within the terms of reference of a debate that uses expressions, such as 'subject' and 'object' that I will ultimately reject. But I have arrived at a conclusion, using these words, that there is a 'reality of some kind that is independent of the human'. So far, nothing has been said about the nature of this 'reality'.

In the rest of the book, I will challenge the taken-for-granted assumption that is made in much of the foregoing literature, to the effect that our 'ontology' must be 'objects' of knowledge that are separate from the observing subject and that these 'objects' take the form of 'things'. To quote Karen Barad once more:

> Physicist Niels Bohr won the Nobel Prize for his quantum model of the atom, which marks the beginning of his seminal contributions to the development of the quantum theory. Bohr's philosophy-physics (the two were inseparable for him) poses a radical challenge not only to Newtonian physics but also to Cartesian epistemology and its representationalist triadic structure of words, knowers, and things. Crucially, in a stunning reversal of his intellectual forefather's schema, Bohr rejects the atomistic metaphysics that takes 'things' as ontologically basic entities.[54]

I will suggest, in what follows, an ontology of becomings – one where human subjects emerge from a reality that pre-exists them but where, once they have emerged, they become part of this dynamic reality. Humans are not merely causal effects of other processes nor are they wholly causally responsible for the rest of the material world. No material thing is purely that – 'matter' is neither a blank slate nor a passive receptacle ready to receive meaning; rather it forms part of systems of meaning that are in continuous interaction with other systems. I will also suggest, in the rest of the book, some reasons why we ought to accept such a perspective.

CONCLUSION

In this chapter, I have defended a version of Bhaskar's transcendental materialist realism but in a different way from that used by Bhaskar himself. I have argued first that Kant's argument form is used by Bhaskar but in a less strong way than in its original form, as given by Kant himself. Rather than this leading me to reject transcendental realism, however, I have argued that there are arguments that can be found in Kant's own work that require a strong version of realism akin to that of Bhaskar. Although, I have suggested, any realist claim will be speculative, nonetheless good reasons can be provided for upholding such a position.

I then moved to suggest that realism in the theory of meaning and in epistemology makes more sense than the main alternative – positivism. I have presented various arguments against the positivist position and some in favour of realism. Chapter 2 will move to articulate my own form of vitalist materialism.

NOTES

1. See for example the work of Jane Bennet, Elizabeth Grosz and Diana Coole, among others.

2. Rick Dolphijn and Iris van der Tuin, *New Materialisms: Interviews and Cortographies* (Ann Arbor, MI: Open Humanities Press, An imprint of Publishing, University of Michigan Library, 2012).

3. Jane Bennett, "A Vitalist Stop over on the Way to a New Materialism," in *New Materialisms*, eds. Diana Coole and Samantha Frost (Durham, NC: Duke University Press, 2010), 48.

4. Alison Assiter, *Kierkegaard, Eve and Metaphors of Birth* (London: Rowman and Littlefield, 2015).

5. Diana Coole, "The Inertia of Matter and the Generativity of Flesh," in *New Materialisms*, op.cit., 93.

6. Ibid.

7. Rosi Braidotti, *The Politics of 'Life Itself'*, eds. Diana Coole and Samantha Frost, op.cit.

8. See Roy Bhaskar, *A Realist Theory of Science* (London: Verso, [1975] 1998).

9. Ibid., 12.

10. Barad, "Post-Humanist Performativity," 803.

11. Rosemary Hennessey, *Materialist Feminism and the Politics of Discourse* (New York, NY: Routledge, 1993), 46.

12. Quentin Meillassoux, *After Finitude: An Essay on the Necessity of Contingency*, trans. Ray Brassier (London: Continuum, 2007).

13. James Lovelock, *Novacene: The Coming of Age of Hyperintelligence* (Harmondsworth: Penguin, 2019), 3.

14. It is important, given how commonplace this view of Descartes is, to correct it a little. It is undoubtedly true that Descartes was a dualist and that he argued, from his assumption that he as doubting, that he was therefore thinking and that he existed as a "thing" that thinks. He also argued for a mechanical notion of material things. But there are two significant qualificatory remarks that ought to be made. First, Descartes was mostly emphasising the regularity and predictability of the behaviour of many "mechanical" things when he referred to "mechanical behaviour." Secondly, he believed that machines were better at performing many actions than humans and that they were "objects of wonder and awe" (see Baker and Morris 1996).

15. Bergson himself dispensed with the word "thing" since the believed that, by using this word, we remain caught up in a misleading debate between "idealists" and "realists". See Henri Bergson, *Matter and Memory*, trans. Nancy Margaret Paul and W. Scott Palmer (New York, NY: Dover Publications, 2004), Chapter 1.

16. Fiona Ellis, *God, Value and Nature* (Oxford: OUP, 2016). In this important book Ellis argues that reductive materialism actually presupposes something much stronger than it would like to accept.

17. Barad, op. cit., 802.

18. Meillassoux, *After Finitude*.

19. See Bergson, *Matter and Memory*, Chapter 3.

20. Ibid., 170.

21. See Henri Bergson, *Time and Free Will* (Mineola, NY: Dover Publications, 2012), 122.

22. Henri Bergson, *Creative Evolution* (New York, NY: Dover, 1998), 202–3. CE.

23. Meillassoux, *After Finitude*, 6.

24. Ibid., 7.

25. Ibid., 5.

26. See Bhaskar, *A Realist Theory of Science*.

27. I believe that it would also include Berkleyan idealism, although there are those who argue that Berkeley wanted to defend a form of realism. This point was made to me by Fiona Ellis.

28. I am using the word 'thing' here in inverted commas since that is the word used by Kant and Hegel. However, the point applies whether or not this word is replaced by process or system of powers. In later sections I add the rider "or some process" to show that this is my position although I am quoting from philosophers who refer to things. However, to reiterate the point, it is important for me, contrary to some other recent materialists, that humans emerge from a reality outside them. This is why I am considering the arguments of Bhaskar and Kant here.

29. Immanuel Kant, *Critique of Pure Reason*, trans. Norman Kemp Smith (London: Macmillan, 1970), A20/B34.

30. Ibid., B276.

31. Ibid., A239/B298.

32. See Solomon Maimon, *Essay on Transcendental Philosophy*, trans. and eds. Alistair Welchman, Henry Somers-Hall, Merten Reglitz, and Nick Midgley (London: Continuum, 2010) and see also Fredrick C. Beiser, *The Fate of Reason: German Philosophy from Kant to Fichte* (Cambridge, MA: Harvard University Press, 1987), 285–323. For a useful collection including work on Maimon, see also Jeremy Dunham and Paulien Pheister, *Mondadologies* (London: Routledge, particularly the article by Richard Mark Fincham. 2019).

33. Dustin McWherter, *The Problem of Critical Ontology: Bhaskar Contra Kant* (London: Palgrave, 2013).

34. Bhaskar, op.cit., 22.

35. Sebastian Gardner, *Routledge Philosophy Guidebook to Kant and the Critique of Pure Reason* (London: Routledge, 1999), 105.

36. Slavoj Žižek, *The Parallax View* (Cambridge: MIT Press, 2009), 22.

37. Steven Shakespeare, *Kierkegaard and the Refusal of Transcendence* (Basingstoke: Macmillan, 2015), 169.

38. Friedrich W.J. Shelling, *Philosophical Investigations into the Essence of Human Freedom*, (trans. Jeff Love and Johannes Schmidt) (New York, State University of New York Press, 2006), 350.

39. Bergson and Science Author(s): Lewis Ellsworth Akeley. Source: *The Philosophical Review* 24, no. 3 (May 1915): 270–87, 271.

40. Bergson, *Matter and Memory*, 208.

41. Akeley, 274.

42. A. J. Ayer, *Language, Truth and Logic* (Garden City, NY: Dover Books, 1952).

43. Ibid., 4.

44. C. G. Hempel, *Aspects of Scientific Explanation and other Essays in the Philosophy of Science* (New York, NY: The Free Press, 1964), 3.

45. J. Koethe, "Quoting Putnam, Putnam's Argument against Realism," *Philosophical Review* lxxxviii, no. 1 (June 1979): 92.

46. Wilfred Sellars, "Empiticism and the Philosophy of Mind," in *Minnesota Studies in the Philosophy of Science*, vol. I, eds. H. Feigl and M. Scriven (Minneapolis, MN: University of Minnesota Press, 1956), 253–329.

47. Hempel, op.cit., 11–12.

48. R. Rorty, *Philosophy and the Mirror of Nature* (Oxford: Blackwell, 1983).

49. Ibid., 264.

50. Hilary Putnam, "Meaning and Reference," *Journal of Philosophy* 70, no. 19 (1973): 699–711.

51. W. V. O. Quine, "Two Dogmas of Empiricism," *The Philosophical Review* 60, no. 1 (1951): 20–43.

52. Rorty, *Philosophy and the Mirror of Nature*.

53. R. Bhaskar, *Reclaiming Reality: A Critical Introduction to Contemporary Philosophy* (London: Routledge, 2010), 205.

54. Barad, "Post-Humanist Performativity," 813.

Chapter 2

A New Form of New Materialism

Chapter 1 has defended a very strong version of materialist realism. I have argued that it makes sense to suppose that there is a reality that is external to the human domain. I have suggested that there are good reasons for believing that there is a world of some kind or a process of some kind that pre-exists in a temporal sense and also exists in a spatial manner, outside the world of the human.

If this position is accepted then a possible implication is that humans emerged from a reality that pre-existed them. I would like, in this chapter, to suggest a model of humanity, as a whole, that fits with such a suggestion. It will be a picture derived from Schelling, Bergson, Kierkegaard and supported by Darwin as well as by contemporary biologists. On the view, humanity is continuous with the rest of animal nature, and emerges from that nature. Thus I propose to defend a position, as already noted, similar to that of some of those who have been described as 'new materialists'. But it will be my own version of such a position. Furthermore, the notion of a human right will be re-conceptualised in accordance with this model, so that instead of deriving from humanity as autonomous beings, separate from the rest of the animal and natural world, these rights will derive from powers of human beings, powers they share with the rest of the animal world, but that they exhibit in somewhat differentiated form. So humans will be viewed as embodied beings continuous with the rest of the natural world but simply 'more differentiated', to use an expression of Schelling's, than members of other animal species. This view would therefore lend itself less to a positivist reading of the concept of a human right and more to a view that sees rights as expressions of the needs of humans, expressed as powers, some of which are shared with other animals.

Much of the philosophical tradition, from the ancient Greeks, through Kant and Hegel, Levinas and Lacan, to give just a few illustrative examples, by contrast to the above view, has divided the animal from the human and has placed the human on a pedestal, viewed as radically distinct from the animal. This perspective is no doubt derived partly from a Christian tradition which saw humans created in the image of God and therefore as radically distinct from all other creatures. Descartes and Kant are two of the most obvious 'modern' exponents of the latter view. For Descartes, the separation of the human from the animal flows from his philosophical starting point, a point that is radically distinct from the realist perspective outlined in chapter 1 and in the above paragraph. Instead of seeing the human as emerging from a reality that pre-exists it, he began his thinking from the point of view of himself. He asked the questions: 'What can I know?' 'What can I be certain of?' I can be certain that I am thinking and therefore that I exist. From such a starting point, he derived the existence of God and the existence of the external world. His starting point, in other words, is what he himself can know to be the case. He does not ask the questions: 'Why do I begin here?' 'Where do my thoughts come from?'

Moreover, although Kant developed a form of thought that is different in many respects from that of Descartes, he shares the Cartesian starting point. He too starts from himself and from the question: 'How is knowledge possible?' 'How is Newtonian science possible?' He did move, as argued in chapter 1, however, further than Descartes in a realist direction. Indeed the fact that he accepts that what we 'sense' through the faculty of sensibility comes from somewhere suggests that he has realist antennae.

I would like, in this chapter, to suggest a radically different starting point for a philosophical system from that of Descartes and Kant, or any of the other philosophers mentioned in the tradition of Descartes.

VITAL MATERIALISM

As noted previously, there is a recent body of work – the new materialism – that strongly challenges the aforementioned way of thinking, from what Jane Bennett calls a 'vital materialist' perspective.[1] This body of work, which includes the new materialists but is not restricted to them, comprises the following thinkers, some of whose works I will engage with – Bruno Latour, Diana Coole, Elizabeth Grosz, Andrew Collier, Karen Barad, John Dewey (or particular works of his) and Bergson. Many of these thinkers draw, for primary inspiration, on the work of Spinoza. For example, in a late chapter of her book *Vibrant Matter: a Political Ecology of Things*, Jane Bennett names Spinoza as the originator of a pair of concepts – *natura naturata* and *natura naturans* –that are central to her outlook. Collier,[2] too, in defending his version of a moral theory that both recognises the worth of all beings and removes the dualism of reason and emotion, draws on Spinoza. It seems to me, however, that a more significant figure for the position I would like to outline in this book, that has some strong affinity with vital materialism, is Schelling.

BERGSON

I'd like to begin, however, with a brief outline of an approach which is analogous in some respects to that of Schelling and which describes a possible starting point for this alternative approach to philosophical thinking. This starting point is lucidly outlined by Bergson, in his *Introduction to Metaphysics*.[3] He describes two approaches to knowing a thing: 'The first implies that we move around the object: the second that we enter into it.'[4] The first is the approach of Descartes and Kant, outlined above, and it has an affinity with that of many other philosophers in the tradition many readers will probably inhabit. But the second approximates to the view I would like to attempt to outline in this book. The second implies that there is a reality outside the human that exists independently of it and that the philosopher will make an attempt to understand and even 'enter into', in the fashion of a therapist attempting to understand a client. The first is the approach to knowledge taken by some of the sciences and it is a vantage point which they sometimes need to take in order to produce data that can be understood and explained. But the second is important as well, and it recognises that no science or approach that focuses on what humans are able to know, understood in the first of the two ways, can fully comprehend a reality that has its own existence, its own 'being'. An analogy used by Bergson to outline this latter way of thinking is that of myself making a movement of my arm. When I raise my arm, 'I accomplish a movement of which (I) have from within, a simple perception'.[5] But for a person watching, from the outside, 'my arm passes through one point and then another and between these two there are many other points'.[6] If I think of 'objects' in the world independent of myself by analogy with the former then I imagine or 'intuit' them as having an internal world as well.

According to Jane Bennett,[7] there was, just before the First World War, in the United States, a sense of the world as infused with life – an outbreak of vitalism, drawing on the work of Bergson.[8] Bergson's creative works critiqued a view of matter as lifeless and as subject to deterministic forces. Bergson, according to Bennett, was a hero of this period because he developed a view of life as containing some notion of freedom. Following the Kant of the *Third Critique*, Bergson elaborated an organic view of the material world. As Grosz puts it, Bergson makes 'difference the proliferative engine of life itself'. 'Life' she writes, for Bergson, 'shares characteristics with non-life'[9] Darwin, Grosz argues, has shown how humans emerge from the animal. Bergson adds to this a demonstration of the emergence of the human, also, from the non-human. Moreover, change and movement, rather than stasis, are the characteristics of experience. The present, in Bergson's thought, is infused with the past, with many forms of memory. As he puts it: 'There are not two identical moments in the life of a conscious being.' 'Take the simplest sensation, suppose it constant, absorb in it the entire personality: the consciousness which will accompany this sensation cannot remain identical with itself for two consecutive moments, because the second moment always contains, over and above the first, the memory that the first has bequeathed to it'.[10]

Deleuze offers a useful explanatory paragraph of this notion:

> We have great difficulty in understanding the survival of the past in itself because we believe that the past is no longer, that it has ceased to be. We have thus confused Being with being present. Nevertheless, the present *is not*; rather, it is pure becoming, always outside itself. It *is* not, but acts. Its proper element is not being but the active or useful. The past, on the other hand, has ceased to act or to be useful. But it has not ceased to be. Useless and inactive, impassive, it IS in the full sense of the word: It is identical with being in itself.[11]

We tend to locate life in a spatial frame. Instead, in Bergson's view, space occurs through the movements of matter; assuming a spatial frame reduces matter to the geometric or the mechanical. But he does accept, as already noted, that this tendency is important for humans in order for them to survive in the world. For me, a useful illustration of this point is spelt out in the following law: 'No two things can be in the same place *at the same time*'. The latter clause is necessary in order to understand the principle and yet, if we adopt the view of Bergson and others, such a claim is actually an impossibility given the above description of a moment of time.

A mechanistic view of the universe, according to Bergson, assumes that the whole is given all at once in a mathematically predictable manner. To see the living world in this manner would be to ignore the evolutionary process. Moreover the whole itself is always in transition. Life itself is a process of 'unceasing creation'.[12] 'Pure duration excludes all idea of juxtaposition, reciprocal externality and extension'.[13] The universe that results from the flow of forces is itself engaged in a process of change. Indeed, the forces might produce dissonance as well as harmony. 'Harmony, therefore, does not exist in fact; it exists rather in principle'.[14] There may be arrests or sudden variations in the process of evolution. This factor, indeed, influences the process of evolution from animals to humans – Bergson suggests, in his work *Creative Evolution*, that accidental occurrences might disrupt the process of survival of the fittest.

This very brief outline summarises Bergson's version of some elements of the broad philosophical position I would like to defend in this book. I will now move to give a brief outline of some key ideas of another philosopher in this tradition, whose thought is key for my position.

SCHELLING

Schelling, in his *Freiheitsschrift*, makes a very large claim. He writes: 'The whole of Modern European philosophy since its inception (through Descartes) has this common deficiency that nature does not exist for it and that it lacks a living basis'.[15] The *Freiheitsschrift* presents an active process ontology that, significantly, 'precedes our thinking of it'.[16] In other words, there is Being before thought. Nature, for Schelling is the 'living ground' of philosophy'.[17] He calls the form of philosophy exemplified by Descartes and Kant, 'negative philosophy'. The latter is concerned with experience but not with reality. Human beings ought, according to him, rather, to be concerned with their natural ground and this means considering them as emerging from nature and as parts of a whole rather than as separate beings. 'Negative philosophy' is one sided, as it fails to recognise the ground of the knowledge had by the self.[18] Certain versions of idealism stultify the 'vital power and fullness of reality'[19] Hegel's philosophy, indeed, is included among those expounding 'negative philosophy'.

Schelling argues, against the Newtonians and the Kantians, that matter and force cannot be separated. We cannot understand how matter can generate force – indeed it is generally agreed that Newton found it difficult to explain the force of gravity. However, it makes sense to take force or power as primary – stars, for example, form through gravity pulling molecular clouds and interstellar gas together.

Forces and their effects can be depicted in terms of ground and consequent and this distinction, in turn, underpins Schelling's system. Every organic being is dependent upon forces and in turn on further beings and further forces.

In Schelling's process system, unlike that of Hegel, as he has been read by many, there is an 'indivisible remainder' in nature that can never be resolved into reason.[20] For Schelling, everything participates in a process of becoming. The ground does not reveal itself as a ground until the existent has come into being. The existent is dependent upon its ground for its 'becoming' but not in its being. One obvious example illustrating this is the idea of a mother. A woman does not become a mother until after her child is born.

This depiction of reality, indeed, for Schelling, includes all the elements of consciousness and specifically freedom. As Iain Hamilton Grant puts it, 'Nature itself must furnish the only possible basis for a philosophy of freedom.'[21] Freedom indeed is not separated from nature, as it is in the case of the views of many philosophers, including Kant. For the latter, and for many broadly 'idealistic' philosophers, freedom is a quality of conscious human beings while the rest of nature is causally determined. Kant, for example, saw freedom as the 'self -causation' of a radically distinct kind of self from the self that is subject to the law of causal determination. Schelling, however, critiques the mechanistic view of nature. He suggests, according to Alderwick,[22] that such a perspective cannot explain subjectivity and freedom nor can it account for the interconnections within nature. A bacterium exhibits a rudimentary degree of freedom, for Schelling, as does a virus. Humans possess freedom to a greater degree than the virus, and freedom may, indeed, constitute an emergent property of humans. But this freedom is not distinct in kind from that of a monkey or a bee.

Evil or sin, for Schelling, arises when the self takes itself to be its own ground. As Schelling writes, 'The general possibility of evil consists, as shown, in the fact that man, instead of making his selfhood into the basis, the instrument, can strive to elevate it into the ruling and total will and conversely to make the spiritual within himself into a means'.[23] It is important to note that Kant himself had recognised, although he understood this in a very different way, that evil results from a form of self-love.[24]

Speech, as well, is part of this dynamic nature. As Bernard Freydberg puts it, for Schelling, whoever utters the sentence 'The body is a body' is unifying two thoughts into one. 'The tauto in tautology names the gathering of two non-identical thoughts.'[25] The expression of the thought is an act of gathering two thoughts into a unity. Freydberg further argues that when the philosopher thinks about thinking something different again occurs. Through thinking, for example, about the operation of the law of identity, thought, which occurs in time, directs thought to occur atemporally, and therefore to think outside immediacy, imagining the atemporal ground of the whole. A dynamic thought and a dynamic being are aspects of the process of nature's evolution.

For Schelling, in the *Freiheitsschrift*, things are abstractions from collections of forces or processes. His interpretation of, for example, the sentence 'S is P' differs from that of both Aristotle and Hegel. In Aristotelian logic, the sentence 'S is P' ascribes a property to a subject. 'S' cannot be both 'P' and 'not-P' at the same time. For Hegel, in his *Science of Logic*, by contrast, 'P' is subsumed under some more general concept and, at that more general level, 'P and not-P' are subsumed under some 'R'. So, if the claim is 'The body is blue', both blue and not-blue are subsumed under the concept 'colour'. But for Schelling, the position is different again. For him, the claim would be read as 'The collection of forces that makes up the body is manifesting itself bluely'.

The process system of Schelling culminates in a Being (*Ein Wesen*), that is simultaneously ground and excess of ground.[26] This notion – an ungrund – that precedes all differentiation is 'an absolute identity of light and darkness, good and evil'. He writes: 'There must be being before all ground and before all that exists, thus generally before any duality – how can we call it anything other than the original ground or the non-ground [ungrund]?'[27]

This, then, is a very brief description of a complex philosophical system. It serves, however, to exemplify a philosophical position that contrasts strongly with the approach to the subject given by Descartes and Kant. It is also very different from the positivist system of thought, outlined in chapter 1.

SCHELLING AND SPINOZA

There are certain core features of the above account which are shared with Schelling's significant predecessor, Baruch Spinoza. For the latter, as well, reason, desire and knowledge are 'embodied and dependent'.[28] The reason, for Spinoza, produced by any collective body will always 'bear the marks of that bodies' genesis'.[29] Consciousness, for Spinoza, is a mode of Being. Furthermore, as Moira Gatens has put it, for Spinoza, bodies are 'radically open to their surroundings'.[30] The perceived central difficulty, in his own period, however, with Spinoza's philosophy, was, as Jacobi puts it, its 'fatalism'.[31]

It is this perceived difficulty with Spinoza's thought that is picked up by Schelling in his characterisation of an alternative system of philosophy to that of the Kantians. Schelling writes that 'an opinion' 'has been decisively expressed in the phrase: the only possible system of reason (*as an alternative to the former* – my addition) is pantheism, but this is inevitably fatalism'.[32] 'Absolute causality in One Being brings only unconditional passivity to all the others'.[33] Schelling explains that the association of Spinozism with fatalism does not occur as a result of his pantheism, but rather 'the error of his system lies by no means in his placing things *in God* (Schelling's italics) but in the fact that they are *things* – in the abstract concept of beings in the world, indeed of infinite substance itself, which for him is also a thing'.[34] The arguments, Schelling maintains, against pantheism ought to concern the determinist reading of causation in Spinoza's work, rather than the pantheism itself. Spinoza treats the will as a 'thing' and his system therefore becomes lifeless.[35]A dynamic view of nature, by contrast, he argues, can transform Spinoza's system.

It is important to offer a caveat to this position.[36] Although some versions of 'substance' or 'things' view them as lifeless and inert, it may be an assumption of Schelling's that Spinoza's substances are inert.

NATURE AS A BODY THAT CAN BIRTH

My own position is analogous to this and it derives from a reading of Kierkegaard's multifarious and brilliant works, partly from a Schellingian influence on him.[37] My outlook shares something in common with the 'new materialists' but it also has some specific additional features. One of these is that it offers an account of the emergence of characteristics that are usually seen to be crucial for the attribution of humanity to beings like us – rationality and freedom. In his *Notes on Schelling's Lectures*, Kierkegaard described the emergence of freedom in humans alongside the creation of the universe. The creation, he wrote, was 'built upon moving ground'.[38]

Ironically, there is material in the work of the Kant of the *Third Critique*, which is suggestive of my view. In his third *Critique*, Kant sets out to attempt to reconcile the two domains, those of nature, on the one hand and freedom, on the other – to show how the two realms might interconnect. He aims here to unite: 'The immense gulf between nature and freedom'.[39] The work is partly concerned with teleological judgements or maxims describing how we ought to judge nature. In this regard he describes natural objects that appear, even to him, to exhibit a form of causation that is radically different from that outlined in the *Second Antinomy* of the first *Critique*. For this new Kant, a thing can be viewed as a natural purpose 'if it is both cause and effect of itself'.[40] In the case of natural purposes, the parts depend upon the whole. A tree, for example, is self-organising in three ways: (i) the tree produces itself in relation to its species –'within its species, it is both cause and effect';[41] (ii) the nourishment taken in by the tree enables its development; and (iii) the various components of the tree depend on and link with one another.

However, Kant was unwilling, because of his Newtonianism, to go the whole hog and accept that purposiveness really existed in the non-human natural world. So instead he argued that a judgement that something is purposive is regulative only and does not constitute any object.

For Kant, moreover, in CJ, the ultimate exemplification of purposiveness is not a tree or any other plant but 'man' acting as a moral agent.[42] We rational beings have to suppose, for the understanding of morality, 'man' to be the ultimate purpose. 'Man' acting as a moral agent is the purpose against which we judge the purposiveness of everything else. Kant writes that 'man is the only being on earth that has understanding and hence an ability to set himself limited purposes of his own choice, and in this respect he holds himself lord of nature; and if we regard nature as a teleological system then it is man's vocation to be the ultimate purpose of nature, but always subject to a condition; he must have the understanding and the will to give both nature and himself reference to a purpose that can be independent of nature, self-sufficient and a final purpose'.[43]

Kant's Newtonian view of the natural world, then, led him to believe that the objects constituted by the category of causation were not living and active, like a tree, but rather inert and 'dead', as we might intuitively view a billiard ball. On the one hand, Kant offers a detailed and full account of the nature of teleological causation. On the other hand, he believes that, rather than objects like a tree really being purposive, it is simply that we judge them as though they are purposive. So instead of seeing purposiveness as existing in the natural world, he sees the best exemplification of purposiveness to be the rational will. We might claim, then, that he reverses real purposiveness in nature and projects it into the rational will of 'man' when 'he' acts well as a moral agent. Instead of seeing the processes of birth and growth as the best exemplifications of purposiveness in nature, he sees the rational will as better fulfilling this role. However, coming full circle, this makes it difficult for him to offer an account of how this 'free' self can also do wrong.

One might argue, then, that Kant reverses the process of birth, from a mother or some equally clear-cut exemplification of purposiveness in the natural world, into a 'lord' of nature who becomes the ultimate purpose, so long as this 'lord' uses his understanding and his will effectively.

Elsewhere in the third *Critique*, however, Kant offers a completely different picture. There is a section that, although not often noted in the commentaries, is recognised as, in a significant sense, prefiguring Darwin. Kant talks, here, about genera of animals sharing a common schema; about their having been produced according to a common archetype. He suggests that the species of animals is 'produced by a common original mother'.[44] He writes, as noted, 'He can make mother earth (like a large animal as it were) emerge from her state of chaos, and make her lap promptly give birth initially to creatures of a less purposive form, with these then giving birth to others that became better adapted to their place of origin and to their relations to one another, until in the end this womb itself rigidified, ossified, and confined itself to bearing definite species that would no longer degenerate, so that the diversity remained as it had turned out when that fertile formative force ceased to operate'.[45]

What is wrong with this account, according to Kant? I find two reasons in Kant's work for rejecting this account. First, he writes: 'In giving this account, the archaeologist of nature will have to attribute to this universal mother an organisation that purposively aimed at all these creatures, since otherwise it is quite inconceivable [how] the purposive form is possible that we find in the produce of the animal and plant kingdoms. But if he attributes such an organisation to her then he has only put off the basis for his explanation. This is no explanation at all'.[46]

In other words, Kant is arguing, using his metaphysical account that derives in part from his Newtonianism, coupled with his perspective on morality, that the only way this kind of view of the origins of purposiveness can function is if this 'mother' had a super intelligence and could 'see' her capacity to produce her effects. But this would effectively turn her into the supersensible ground considered earlier. The material and biological processes of birth cannot, for Kant, function as the ground, basically because the ordered nature that we know is itself produced by us and produced by us in a fashion that is shaped by a Newtonian view of causation.

Second, Kant argues, against the view of a 'mother earth', that those who think in terms of the whole think of it in terms of an 'all-encompassing substance'– which is Spinozism, and only therefore a more determinate version of pantheism. So, in this objection to his own account, Kant has removed the process element of the 'mother' and of the evolution of other species and turned it into inert, mechanical matter, which, being inert and mechanical, clearly cannot ground a process system. Putting this differently, then, it is hard for Kant to see the earth as a living system analogous to a 'mother' because the science he so admired and accepted did not allow this. Yet he was, even in proposing this metaphor, and in thinking about the processes by which trees grow, thinking ahead of his time and in process terms.

For Kant, the Newtonian, to reiterate, the categories shape the nature of matter as the sum of appearances. Kant's view of natural science has it deal with substantial bodies dependent upon external forces for change. This, then, is one reason why he cannot accept the metaphor of the earth as a 'mother'.

But another reason has to do, surely, with Kant's view of women and his picture of the nature of inner bodily space. Christine Battersby has pointed out how difficult it is for Kant, in his view of the nature of space and time and of matter, to account even for his own inner bodily space, let alone for that of a body that is capable of giving birth. Knowledge of things in space presupposes 'outer sense' and knowledge of such matters is knowledge of something other than the 'I'. Time is the form of inner sense. So, as Battersby puts it, 'Kant needs a body in order to be a self; but the body he needs is neither self nor not self'.[47] Of course, this 'inner bodily space' includes the 'purposiveness' of the female body in producing another self from within itself. The capacity of a body to 'birth', therefore, is inexplicable because it is literally outside (actually 'inside') his view of space.

Moreover, women, for Kant, are refused the kind of personhood that entails free will and pure rationality. Women are fully animal and human.

However, frequently they are denied the status of 'persons' in the sense of being full moral agents. They are grouped together with 'domestic servants, apprentices, hairdressers and other "passive" citizens'.[48] They therefore cannot have the 'active' thinking capacity that goes along with being a person.

Further Kant's view of purposiveness is itself intuitively odd. It is strange to see the purposiveness of a cat in eating a mouse to quiet its hunger as something imposed by humans on the cat. As Hans Jonas has put it: the picture according to which, by following Occam's razor, we deny purposes to non-humans, and deny that, for example, there is a whole organism in which molecular life inheres, is a fiction. It is a fiction that is useful for certain forms of biological investigation. If you are concerned with cell metabolism you don't need to worry about the whole organism.[49] But this does not mean that the scientist doesn't know that the cells are part of a whole organism. Similarly, this means, as he puts it 'if he does not take refuge in a fantastic dualism',[50] 'he has recognized mind, indeed subjectivity and interests in general, to be an efficacious principle *within* nature – thus implicitly broadening his concept of nature beyond his asserted model'.[51]

There were, in his own period, as we saw in chapter 1, critics of Kant's work who saw a deep limitation of his work. Maimon, for example, in his autobiography and then in his *Essay on Transcendental Philosophy*,[52] developed a particular critique of Kant's system. He challenged Kant's dualism between 'sensibility' and 'understanding' on the ground that there is no need for a 'given' element of cognition. Maimon claims that such a step need not be taken. Instead of characterising finitude in terms of the need for a passive faculty of receptivity, Maimon insists that finitude only implies incompleteness in our cognition. The content of sensibility is simply that which is passive in cognition – namely, that upon which the understanding operates. What we take to be merely given to us in experience can in fact be explained in terms of a productive – and hence active – capacity of the mind, although the procedures of this activity remain unknown to us.

In this respect Maimon revives the Leibnizian notion that there is not a difference in kind, but only in degree, between a finite and an infinite intellect. Indeed, Maimon, in certain key respects, anticipated the work of someone valued by Jane Bennett, and that is the vitalist, Driesch.[53] Driesch values Kant's work in the third *Critique*. Indeed, he goes so far as to accept Kant's view that it is not possible to endow matter with a 'property' – that of life. He accepts, in other words, that there is no 'extra' part of a living thing that consists in life-giving power. He accepts that we – finite beings – cannot 'know' what it is that gives rise to life. For Driesch, this power must be conceived as neither 'psychical' nor 'mechanical' but it is, in some sense, different from both. He labels this 'something' 'entelechy' from Aristotle – a self-moving and self-generating power that animates matter.[54] Driesch does not, however, go quite as far as Maimon.

I believe that this point is important – a power or a capacity is not a 'property' of a thing but it is rather a power of some kind that will have primacy in some sense over 'things'. It will also 'animate' matter.

MY OWN VIEW

Drawing on Kant, but challenging his view that 'purposiveness' is not really in the natural world I will now summarise my own perspective, that develops ideas from Kierkegaard.

Assuming, now, contrary to Kant, that most living entities arise from some 'ground' or notion of purposiveness, for many entities, their ground lies in some power or capacity that is, at least in part, external to them. For example, I was born from a capacity or a power of my mother. An oak tree emerges from a seed. But, as Schelling pointed out, in his *Freiheitsschrift*, only God or Being as a whole has its ground within itself. Schelling also expresses this ground in the following terms: 'The first beginning for the creation is the yearning of the one to give birth to itself or the will of the ground. The second is the will of love whereby the word is spoken out into nature and through which God first makes himself personal'.[55] These metaphors are the expression of the opposing forces that are required for generation. Generation of any kind requires opposing forces analogous to the positive and negative powers of electricity. Just as electric charge is a conserved property comprising positive and negative forces, so too is the universe itself, along with all of its contents, characterised in this way.

Jane Bennett has, as she puts it, 'experimented' with 'narrating events as themselves bona fide agents rather than as instrumentalities, techniques of power, recalcitrant objects, or social constructs'.[56] 'What would happen, she writes, to our thinking about politics if we took more seriously the idea that technological and natural materialities were themselves actors alongside and within us – were vitalities, trajectories, and powers irreducible to the meaning, intentions or symbolic values humans invest in them'.[57]

I would like to go a step further than Bennett and show how there is, deriving from Schelling and Kierkegaard, a plausible theory that explains how, as noted above, the specific type of capacities possessed by humans – freedom and rationality – are both analogous to capacities of the rest of the natural world and emergent from this natural world. The accounts of Schelling and Kierkegaard, while both deploy the concept of God in a mythical way to describe the ground of the whole universe that 'has its ground within itself' can be understood in a fashion that does not presuppose the God of any received religion. Rather it is possible to construe this figure in terms of a complex of powers and capacities analogous to those in matter. Contemporary physicists refer to 'dark matter' that is required to explain the gravitational pull of the galaxy, Schelling uses the expressions 'the will of the ground' and the 'will of love'. Contemporary physicists speak of 'particles' as strands of energy that vibrate in several dimensions.[58] Schelling speaks of 'organics'. He writes 'unrestricted mechanism would destroy itself'.[59] This is directly in contrast to Kant's view, expressed in *Metaphysical Foundations of Natural Science*, where he expresses concerns about 'hylozoism' – the notion of living matter.[60]

In Schelling's system, a system which is expanded upon and developed, I have argued, by Kierkegaard, there is a constant process of production. This process culminates in what he describes as a 'yearning' of 'the one' to give birth to itself.[61] This is a 'yearning' of the whole galaxy to create itself. In his system, the capacity to give birth 'the ground' could be construed as the 'becoming' of which the being that is born is the consequent. As I put it in my *Kierkegaard, Eve and Metaphors of Birth* 'in most cases the capacity to give birth presupposes a being that has this potency. But nature as a whole creates itself and therefore creates the creative force that gives rise to other dependent beings'.[62] Ultimately the series, in order to avoid an infinite regress, must culminate in a being that gives birth to itself – an 'ungrund'.

There are many commentators on Kierkegaard who have noted his focus, like that of Schelling, on process or 'becoming'. Instead of seeing the world as comprising static substances, instead, Kierkegaard views it as being composed of processes or powers that are actualised in objects. Pattison, for one, writes that, for Kierkegaard, the world is 'permeated by temporality or becoming'.[63]

After listening, in 1842, to Schelling's lecture, Kierkegaard famously wrote; 'I am so pleased to have heard Schelling's second lecture ... indescribably ... . The embryonic child of thought leapt for joy within me. As in Elisabeth when he mentioned the word "actuality" in connection with the relation of possibility to actuality. I remember almost every word he said after that'.[64] I suggested in my previous book that Kierkegaard might here be conceptualising the Schellingian creation story – outlined above.

Furthermore, in that previous book, I suggested that Johannes's text *Stages in Life's Way*, which offers a reading of Plato's *Symposium*, implies that for Kierkegaard, woman and the erotic represent finitude. Rather, however, that this being intended to denigrate woman, instead this quality is valorised by Kierkegaard.[65]

Kierkegaard has often been represented as an anti-feminist. He is thought to denigrate women because he, according to the critics, attributes 'essentialist' and 'negative' characteristics to them.[66] Leon notes that, for Kierkegaard, woman represents a 'creature whose existence', assimilated to biology, 'culminates in the act of procreation'. I concur with her reading. However rather than seeing this as a negative characteristic, I see it, rather, as Kierkegaard valorising women's capacity to give birth. 'Man' for Leon's Kierkegaard, is 'an autonomous whole, a complete individual'.[67] However, once again, while I entirely accept these readings of his texts, I believe Kierkegaard intended to valorise the ability to give birth and to downplay the significance of Kantian reason and autonomy. Kierkegaard, I suggested, is critiquing, in many of his works, the deep denigration, in much of the western tradition, ontologically, of qualities that happen to be associated with women.

In *Stages on Life's Way*, Kierkegaard writes 'woman is a power weaker than his own (Johannes) and yet stronger'.[68] As representing the dynamic and creative natural world, woman is stronger than the male. Johannes, in SLW, writes: 'Necessity teaches even the gods to surpass themselves in inventiveness. They searched and pondered and found. The power was woman, the wonder of creation even in the eyes of the gods a greater wonder than man, a discovery on which the gods in their naiveté could not help congratulating themselves. What more can be said to her honor than that she would be able to do something of which even the gods did not think themselves capable, what more can be said than that she was capable of doing it; how wonderful she must be to be capable of it!'[69]

The later feminist philosopher Luce Irigaray also concerns herself with the *Symposium*. Reading Plato, she reclaims Diotima, from the *Symposium*, the wise woman who teaches Socrates about love. In Irigaray's reading, Diotima sets out to recover the traces of the maternal from Plato's Cave metaphor.Luce Irigaray, Speculum of the Other Woman , trans G.C. Gill, (Ithaca, Cornell University Press, 1985).[70] This metaphor can be read as suggesting a transcendent reading of the forms, with the cave as the inert matter containing the deceptive world of the senses from which 'man' has to move into the transcendent realm of the Forms – the world of light and truth.

Irigaray seeks to destabilise this version of the Cave myth by demonstrating a blind spot in this reading of the journey of the prisoner en route to truth. As Rachel Jones puts it, 'the ideal father of visible offspring supplants birth from a mother. In this way, the horizon of metaphysical thought obscures the more primordial horizon that orients human beings in the world, namely our relationship to our material origins'.[71]

DARWIN, OTHER BIOLOGISTS AND NATURE

Something of the philosophical picture outlined above is borne out by Darwinian Theory. Darwinian Theory challenges the familiar philosophical perspective that relegates the animal to the 'other of the human'. This view, indeed, as Elisabeth Grosz has put it, is commonplace and it lies in a : 'More or less continuous tradition (that) is sorely challenged and deeply compromised by the eruption of Darwinism in the second half of the nineteenth century.'[72] She argues that 'philosophy has yet to recompose its concepts of man, reason and consciousness to accommodate the Darwinian explosion'.[73] Darwinian Theory showed that humans are descended from other animals, and, indeed, from other life forms, including protozoa and bacteria. It also suggests that humans remain animals. Humans are simply more developed forms of other animals. To quote Darwin:

> In considering the origin of the species, it is quite conceivable that a naturalist, reflecting on the mutual affinities of organic beings, on their embryological relations, their geographical distribution, geological succession, and other such facts, might come to the conclusion that each species had not been independently created, but had descended, like varieties from other species.[74]

'The structure', he wrote 'of every organic being is related, in the most essential yet often hidden manner, to that of all other organic beings with which it comes into competition for food or residence, or from which it has to escape or on which it preys'.[75] To the point that his critics argued that it is nonsense to ascribe an analogue of volition to plants, he replies, 'It has been said that I speak of natural selection as an active power or Deity; but who objects to an author speaking of the attraction of gravity as ruling the movements of the planets?'[76]

OTHER BIOLOGISTS

There are, moreover, contemporary biologists who adopt a similar view. One of them, Francisco Varela, indeed, has noted a convergence in thinking 'between the re-awakening of philosophical discussion concerning natural purposes (with Hans Jonas as the central figure) and an independent but convergent stream of thought concerning biological individuality and the organism.'[77]

The contemporary biologists H. R. Maturana and F. J. Varela[78] have argued, partly following in Darwin's footsteps, that life extends all the way down to the bacterium. However, it is also important to note that Varela has also argued that Darwin was primarily (against both the scientific and the religious thoughts of his time) concerned with 'external seemingly purposive design', which he conceptualised as the result of contingency and natural selection. Intrinsic teleology, he argued instead, is concerned with the (Aristotelian)_ internal purposes immanent to the living, which was also

Kant's main concern.[79] Varela emphasises the notion of an internal organism, as opposed to 'an array of genetic and physiological processes whose unity is left unaccounted for'.[80]

Life as a whole, in its turn, can be conceptualised along the lines articulated by Kant in his third *Critique*, as noted above, as a 'system' which is cause and effect of itself. Life is described by Maturana and Varela as an 'autopoietic system'.[81] Such systems are self-organising and self-controlling, and they do not require the inputs and outputs that are presupposed by heteronomous systems. They offer 'a naturalised, biological account of Kant's notion of a natural purpose'.[82] Every part of a natural purpose exists for the sake of the other parts, but also reciprocally produces them. Organisms are 'subjects, having purposes according to values encountered in the making of their living'.[83]

A thing, as noted, appears to be a natural purpose, for Kant, if 'it is both cause and effect of itself'.[84] A tree reproduces itself over successive generations. Each generation of trees plays a role in the causal chain – being an effect of the previous one and the cause of future generations. Each individual tree, in its turn, produces and reproduces itself through its own growth and generation. Moreover, each part of the tree is dependent on every other part. This Kantian notion, then, could be viewed as an autopoietic system.[85]

A minimal notion of an autopoietic system, for the above contemporary biologists, is a living cell. In the view of these contemporary biologists, furthermore, cognition is a dynamic phenomenon that ought, in its turn, to be understood as an instance of autopoiesis. So the brain is such a system, with behaviour that is neither random nor ordered and predictable; rather, it is in-between, exhibiting changing and unstable patterns. Cognition, then, is constituted by a relationship between the agent and its environment.[86] The theory, furthermore, allows for emergent processes: processes that arise out of the organisation of the elements of the whole. Part and whole work together.

Extending this conception of system to the whole of nature, the latter can be viewed as a Gaia. James Lovelock[87] hypothesises that the totality of living organisms, the atmosphere, the oceans, the rocks and the soil makes up a single planetary entity that is self-regulating and self-sustaining. Organisms interact with their environment to form a self-regulating system. According to the theory, the 'biota' – for example, the components listed above – evolve together with their environment. So organisms don't merely 'adapt' to a 'dead' world, but rather they 'live with a world that is the breath and bones of their ancestors and that they are now sustaining'.[88] The whole earth is a self-regulating system, made up 'from all of life, including the air, the oceans and the surface rocks, not just organisms alone'.[89] 'Gaia is best thought of as a super-organism'.[90] Lyn Margulis, in a related claim, that concerns autopoiesis but that she also offers as a description of Lovelock's 'Gaia' hypothesis, writes: 'Gaia is not itself an organism directly selected among many. It is an emergent property of interaction among organisms, the spherical planet on which they reside, and an energy source, the sun'.[91]

Lovelock argues that the world evolved from early simple bacterial forms towards the oxygen-enriched atmosphere that supports more complex life forms. Geo-physiology, which is the discipline of Gaia theory, in Lovelock's words 'sees the organisms of the Earth evolving by Darwinian natural selection in an environment that is the product of their ancestors and not simply a consequence of the earth's geological history. Thus the oxygen of the atmosphere is almost wholly the product of photosynthetic organisms and without it there would be no animals or invertebrates, nor would we burn fuels'.[92] Lovelock, as noted, sees Gaia as a super-organism. He notes that, although the sun, as an ageing star, is gradually hotting up, the temperature of the planetary surface of the earth has hardly varied for thousands of years. As he puts it: 'Gaia does this'.[93] Lynn Margulis, describes Gaia as an autopoietic system like a cell: 'The simplest, smallest known autopoietic entity is the single cell. The largest is probably Gaia'.[94]

Lovelock, indeed, deploys a philosophical system analogous to the theories outlined in the early part of this chapter to make sense of his notion. He writes: 'As Newton found long ago, logical thinking does not work with dynamic systems, things that change over the course of time. Quite simply you cannot explain the workings of something alive by cause and effect logic'. He continues (in a polemical vein) 'Most of us, especially women, have known this all along'.[95]

Critics of this notion argue that the Gaia is not a reproducing individual and it should not therefore be accorded the status of a living entity. Richard Dawkins, for example, claimed that if Gaia was an organism why couldn't she reproduce?[96] Evan Thompson's suggestion, however, in response to this, is that the criticism assumes an evolutionary, reproductive process. If the Gaia is construed, rather, 'as a self-producing but non-reproducing individual' then the objection does not apply. Gaia would be a super-organism just like a cell. The latter would be among the smallest such systems and the former among the largest. Both are self-sustaining and self-regulating systems. In a response to his critics who have made this point, Lovelock writes, 'But something that lives a quarter of the age of the universe surely does not need to reproduce, and perhaps Gaia's natural selection takes place internally as organisms and their environment evolve in a tightly coupled union'.[97] Indeed, the earth does not produce (or not as far as we know) further earths that are autonomous from this one. But it does make sense to suggest that the earth is self-reproducing.

Living systems, moreover, must be understood partially in terms of norms. A living cell modifies its behaviour according to internal norms of its activity.[98] A bacterium, according to this conception, partially operates in accordance with the norms that its autonomy brings about. In an interpretation of this process, Hans Jonas[99] has argued that we must attribute a rudimentary notion of freedom to the bacterium. The bacterium has an internal identity and 'needful freedom'. Thompson characterises this by offering an account of the 'motile bacterium' that swims about in a gradient of sugar. The cells make a 'choice' to swim in the direction of increased exposure to sugar.[100]

Varela's system is a living and dynamic one, that is dependent not only on inert and external causal relations but upon norms that govern each autopoietic system as well as relations among systems and between them and the whole. In turn, if biologists were to ask the question about the ground of the whole, then they might be led to something like Schelling's conception of the ground. Overall, the metaphor of ground and consequent, deriving from Schelling, encapsulates this process.

I would like, at this point, to note that there is a further critique both of the notion of autopoiesis and of Gaia from the brilliant theorist Donna Haraway. When I originally read her *Cyborg Manifesto*, many years ago, I believed she was doing something radically other, radically different from my own concerns. Perhaps I read her too literally, in terms of some kind of science fiction. When she wrote: 'A cyborg is a cybernetic organism, a hybrid of machine and organism, a creature of social reality as well as a creature of fiction.'[101] I thought that her concerns moved way beyond those I believed at the time to be important. I can now see she was truly radical at the time, and perhaps more so even than I would like to be now. When she envisaged a world without gender, I baulked at the implied suggestion.

In her Forward to the *Cyborg Handbook*, Haraway described 'Gaia' in the following terms: 'the evocation of a planetary hypothesis called Gaia – "named after the Greek goddess who gave birth (incestuously) to the Titans" – was the brainchild of an atmospheric chemist-cum-cybernetics and freelance NASA and Royal Dutch shell contractor, and "not the intuition of a vegetarian feminist mystic'.[102] For her, at least in her early works, the notion of 'autopoiesis' is too closed, too self-sufficient. For her, the concept is insufficiently relational. As she puts it in an interview: 'The reason I am sceptical about autopoiesis was taught to me by one of my current graduate students, Astrid Schrader, whose first formation was as a physicist. She is upset with autopoiesis because of its closures – because nothing self-organizes – it's relationality all the way down and self-organization repeats the trouble of systems theories, and so she goes to Derrida in ways that really helped me'.[103]

Haraway expanded both the concept of autopoiesis and the notion of Gaia to incorporate her own 'cyborg or 'human-machine' interface'. She imagines a category that, she believes, better enables a genuinely interactive universe of many kinds of being in process with one another.

For Lynn Margulis, however: 'Autopoesis involves continuous self- reproduction. Living systems, from cells to much larger entities, self generate, until they produce the capacity to reproduce. Complex systems comprise collections, in symbiosis with one another, of simpler autopoietic systems'.

Lynn Margulis herself was clear that she was outlining characteristics of living systems rather than machines. Autopoiesis involves continuous self-reproduction. Living systems self-generate until they are able to reproduce. Machines, she believed,[104] (see letter to Lovelock) can comprise parts of auto-poietic entities, but they do not themselves constitute such entities. Machines don't metabolise. Machines can be produced by autopoietic systems but don't themselves constitute such systems. She describes the 'Viking landers' who entered Mars but then disintegrated as 'once autopoietic' but no longer so. Machines are not self-maintaining like cells or organisms or indeed like the atmosphere of the earth. Machines, though, can effect a certain autonomy by existing alongside living systems. In the whole interconnected system, living and non-living matter interconnect. However, as we evolve and come to depend more upon machines, the latter interact more and more with auto-poietic systems.

I would like, therefore, to remain within the Margulis hypothesis to the effect that autopoietic entities might interact with machines and there are, indeed, entities or processes that incorporate interactions between machines and living systems. But it seems to me to be important, at least for the purpose for which I am drawing on these literatures, to maintain the distinction between autopoietic and non-autopoietic or once-autopoietic entities.

In her recent work *Staying with the Trouble*[105] Haraway has extended her analysis of the world of the 'post-anthropocene' in imaginative and innovative ways, drawing on feminist literatures, string theory, contemporary biology, Deleuze and Guattari and many more literatures. In a fashion that is partly science fictional, she imagines a world of genuine processual becoming; of interactions between 'humans' and other species, including bacteria and spiders. In a deeply significant manner, she explores, from von Uexküll, the interaction between a cell that has 'perceptual and receptor signs'[106] and other species. The 'autopoietic' is not only not relational enough but also insufficiently collective and integrative as a category to do the work she imagines. She sets out to develop an imaginary that is genuinely non-anthropocentric. Similarly, Lovelock has recently imagined a new era of the 'Novacene' that will supersede the 'anthropocene'.[107] He argues that it is unlikely that such new creatures will go to war with humans; rather intelligent machines are more likely to regard us somewhat as we now view our animal pets. He suggests, indeed, that the contemporary environmental issues – the necessity for new ways of cooling the earth to maintain 'Gaia' – are likely to be resolved by machine intelligence. It seems then, that it is no longer possible to argue against 'cyborgs' or their equivalent. However, my primary purpose in this book is different.

ETHICS

When we think ethically as humans about other humans, we think in terms of our responsibilities or obligations to others. If nature as a whole is a living entity, then this responsibility is extended so as to incorporate its various constituent parts and processes. The metaphysical model of nature gives rise, as Plato's did for him, to an ethic. It is an ethic that is vital for the contemporary world.

The ethical concern includes a need to care for the nature that, in Quentin Meillassoux's words, 'pre-exists' the human, and, I would like to add, makes the human possible.

A sceptic might continue to ask, however: why should we accept any of this? The sceptic might claim that I have given some arguments in chapter 1 that support a realist position, but these do not extend to providing evidence for the position I am now outlining. I would like, therefore, in chapter 3, to give a summary of an argument I have developed elsewhere (see my *Kierkegaard, Eve and Metaphors of Birth*) that suggests a reason for preferring the work of Schelling over that of Kant. It is a reason which will foreground the subsequent work in this book.[108]

CONCLUSION

This chapter has extended the arguments of chapter 1, to give an account of the human as emerging from a natural world that pre-exists it. This is a realist account insofar as it presupposes a nature outside the human that provides the latter with a ground from which the human emerges.

NOTES

1. Jane Bennett, *Vibrant Matter: A Political Ecology of Things* (Durham, NC, USA: Duke University Press, 2010).
2. Andrew Collier, *Being and Worth* (Abingdon, Oxfordshire: Routledge, 1999).

3. H. Bergson, *Introduction to Metaphysics*, intro. John Mullarkey (London: Palgrave, 2007).

4. Ibid., 1.

5. Ibid., 5.

6. Ibid., 5

7. Bennett, *Vibrant Matter*.

8. Ibid., 63.

9. Elizabeth Grosz, *Becoming Undone: Reflections on Life, Politics and Art* (Durham, NC, USA: Duke University Press, 2011), 26–27.

10. Ibid., 8.

11. Gilles Deleuze, *Bergsonism*, trans. High Thompson and Barbara Haberjam (New York, NY: Zone Books, 1991), 55.

12. Bergson, *Introduction to Metaphysics*, CE, 23.

13. Ibid., IM, 9.

14. Ibid., CE, 51.

15. F. W. J. Schelling, *Philosophical Investigations into the Essence of Human Freedom*, trans. Jeff Love and Johannes Schmidt (New York, NY: State University of New York Press, 2006), VII, 355.

16. Ibid., VII, 421.

17. Ibid., 357–58.

18. See F. W. J. Schelling, *The Grounding of Positive Philosophy: Berlin Lectures* (New York, NY: State University of New York Press, 2008).

19. Schelling, *Philosophical Investigations*, 31, SW, 1/7 356.

20. Ibid., SW, 360.

21. Iain Hamilton Grant, *On an Artificial Earth: Philosophies of Nature after Schelling* (London: Continuum, 2006).

22. Charlotte Alderwick, "Nature's Capacities: Schelling and Contemporary Power," *Angelaki, Journal of the Theoretical Humanities* 21 (2016).

23. Schelling, *Philosophical Investigations*, SW, 474–76, 54.

24. See Immanuel Kant, *Religion within the Limits of Mere Reason Alone*, trans. Theodore M. Green and Hoyd Hudson (New York, NY: Harper and Row, 1960).

25. Bernard Freydberg, *Schelling's Dialogical Freedom Essay* (Albany, NY: State University of New York Press, 2008), 23.

26. Schelling, op.cit., 2006, 28–29, SW, 431–33.

27. Schelling, op.cit., 2006, 404–5.

28. Benedictus Spinoza (Baruch), *The Collected Writings of Spinoza*, 2 vols., trans. Edwin Curley (Princeton, NJ: Princeton University Press, vol. 1: 1985; *The Ethics* is in vol. 1. Ethics), 111.

29. Ibid., 100.

30. Moira Gatens, *Imaginary Bodies: Ethics. Power and Corporeality* (London: Routledge, 2013), 110.

31. See Friedrich Heinrich Jacobi, *The Main Philosophical Writings and the Novel Alwill*, trans. and ed. George di Giovanni (Montreal: Magill Queens University Press, 1994), 187 and see Frederick C. Beiser, *The Fate of Reason: German*

Philosophy from Kant to Fichte (Cambridge, MA: Harvard University Press, 1987), Chapter 2.

32. Schelling, *Philosophical Investigations*, 11.

33. Ibid.

34. Ibid., 20.

35. Spinoza does distinguish natura naturans from natura naturata so this may not be a fair reading of his work.

36. This important point was made to me by Fiona Ellis.

37. This section is a summary of some of the argument of my previous book *Kierkegaard, Eve and Metaphors of Birth* (Assiter 2015).

38. Søren Kierkegaard, "Notes on Schelling's Berlin Lectures," in *The Concept of Irony with Continual Reference to Socrates and the Notes*, ed. and trans. Howard V. Hong and Edna W. Hong (Princeton, NJ: Princeton University Press, 1989), 337.

39. Immanuel Kant, *Critique of Judgment*, trans. Werner S. Pluhar (Indianapolis, IN: Hackett Publishing, 1987), CJ, 175–76.

40. Ibid., 370.

41. Ibid., 371.

42. Ibid., 400.

43. Ibid., CJ, 318.

44. Ibid., CJ, 304.

45. Ibid., 304.

46. Ibid., 305.

47. Christine Battersby, *The Phenomenal Woman: Feminist Metaphysics and the Patterns of Identity* (London: Routledge, 1998), 70.

48. Immanuel Kant, *The Metaphysics of Morals*, ed. and trans. Mary Gregor (Cambridge: CUP, 1996), 92, This quote was drawn to my attention by Battersby, op .cit., 64.

49. Hans Jonas, *The Imperative of Responsibility: In Search of an Ethics for the Technological Age* (Chicago, IL: Chicago University Press, 1984), 70.

50. Ibid.

51. Ibid.

52. S. Maimon, *Essay on Transcendental Philosophy* (London: Bloomsbury, 2010).

53. Hans Driesch, *The Science and Philosophy of the Organism* (Whitefish, MT: Kessinger Publishing, 2006).

54. See Bennett, *Vibrant Matter* on Driesch, *The Science and Philosophy*.

55. Schelling, *Philosophical Investigations*.

56. Bennett, *Vibrant Matter*, 49.

57. Ibid.

58. See, for example Brian Greene, https://www.youtube.com/watch?v=kF4 ju6j6aLE, accessed January 3, 2020.

59. Schelling, *On the World Soul*, 58.

60. Immanuel Kant, *Metaphysical Foundations of Natural Science*, ed. and trans. Michael Friedman (Cambridge: Cambridge University Press, 2004).

61. Schelling, *Freedom Essay*, 431–38, 28.

62. Assiter, *Kierkegaard, Eve and Metaphors of Birth*, 117.

63. George Pattison, *The Philosophy of Kierkegaard* (Chesham: Acumen, 2003), 40.

64. Kierkegaard, "Notes on Schelling's Berlin Lectures," quoted in Ibid., 44.

65. See Assiter, *Kierkegaard, Eve and Metaphors of Birth*, Chapter 6.

66. See, for example, Celine Leon, *Neither/Nor of the Second Sex: Kierkegaard on Women, Sexual Difference and Sexual Relations* (Macon, GA: Mercer University Press, 2008).

67. Ibid., 41.

68. Søren Kierkegaard, *Stages on Life's Way*, ed. and trans. Howard V. Hong and Edna H. Hong (Princeton, NJ: Princeton University Press, 1980), SLW.

69. Ibid., SLW, 75.

70. Luce Irigaray, Speculum of the Other Woman, trans G.C. Gill, (Ithaca, Cornell University Press, 1985).

71. Rachel Jones, *Irigaray* (Cambridge: Polity, 2011), 47.

72. Elisabeth Grosz, *Becoming Undone* (Durham, NC: Duke University Press, 2011), 13.

73. Ibid.

74. C. Darwin, *On the Origin of Species by Means of Transmutation, or Preservation of Favoured Races in the Struggle for Life* (New York, NY: Modern Library, 1998), 4.

75. Ibid., 94.

76. Ibid., 73.

77. See Andreas Weber and Fransisco J. Varela, "Life after Kant: Natural Purposes and the Autopoietic Foundations of Biological Individuality," *Phenomenology and the Cognitive Sciences* 1 (2002): 97–125, 97.

78. See H. R. Maturana and F. J. Varela, *Autopoiesis and Cognition: The Realization of the Living*, eds. Robert S. Cohen and Marx W. Wartofsky (Dordrecht: Springer Netherlands, 1st edition 1973, 2nd 1980).

79. Weber and Varela, op.cit., 100.

80. Ibid., 101.

81. Ibid.

82. Evan Thompson, *Mind in Life: Biology, Phenomenology, and the Sciences of Mind* (Cambridge: Belknap Press, 2007), 140. It is important to note that, in their early work, Maturana and Varela did not see autopoietic systems as teleological. They saw them rather as purposeless and analogous to "autopoietic machines" (see Maturana and Varela, Autopoiesis and Cognition). Yet later, partly in response to the criticisms of, for example, Robert Rosen (Robert Rosen, *Life Itself: A Comprehensive Inquiry into the Nature, Origin and Fabrication of Life* [New York, NY: Columbia University Press, 1991]), Varela came to revise his view (See F. J. Varela, "Organism: A Meshwork of Selfless Selves," in *Organism and the Origin of Self*, ed. A. Tauber [Dortrecht: Kluwer Academic Publishers, 1990], 79–107; and Thompson, *Mind in Life*, Chapter 6).

83. Weber and Varela, op.cit., 102.

84. CJ, 370.

85. It is important to note that Kant began, in his unfinished final work, *Opus Posthumum*, to develop a fuller account of a purposive natural world that itself might give rise to the transcendental subject.

86. See Thompson, *Mind in Life*, 119.

87. James Lovelock, *Gaia: A New Look at Life on Earth* (Oxford: Oxford University Press, 1979).

88. James Lovelock, *A Final Warning: The Vanishing Face of Gaia* (London: Penguin, 2009), 112.

89. James Lovelock, *The Ages of Gaia* (New York, NY: W. W. Norton, 1998), 15.

90. L. Margulis, "Biologists Can't Define Life," in *From Gaia to Selfish Genes: Selected Writings in the Life Sciences*, ed. C. Barlow (Cambridge: MIT Press, 1991), 237.

91. Lynn Margulis, *Symbolic Planet: A New Look at Evolution* (New York, NY: Basic Books, 1999), 119.

92. James Lovelock, A Final Warning, 31.

93. James Lovelock, *Novacene: The Coming Age of Hyper-Intelligence* (Harmonsdswoth: Penguin, 2019), 12.

94. L. Margulis, "Biologists Can't Define Life," in *From Gaia to Selfish Genes: Selected Writings in the Life Sciences*, ed. C. Barlow (Cambridge: MIT Press, 1991), 237.

95. Lovelock, *Novacene*, 18.

96. Richard Dawkins, *The Extended Phenotype* (Oxford: Oxford University Press, 2016).

97. Lovelock, *A Final Warning*, 31. He also writes, in *Novecene*, "no 4-billion year old organism needs to reproduce". Lovelock, *Novacene*, 14.

98. Thompson, *Mind in Life*, 74.

99. Jonas, *The Imperative of Responsibility*.

100. Thompson, *Mind in Life*, 157.

101. Donna Haraway, *A Cyborg Manifesto, Science, Technology and Socialist Feminism in the Late 20th Century, Simians, Cyborgs, and Women: The Reinvention of Nature* (London: Free Association Books, 1991).

102. Donna Haraway, Forward to *The Cyborg Handbook, Cyborgs and Symbionts: Living Together in the New World Order*, ed. Chris Hables Gray (London: Routledge, 1995), xii.

103. Interview with Donna Haraway, "When We Have Never Been Human, What is to be Done?" *Theory, Culture and Society* (London, Thousand Oaks, and New Delhi: Sage) 23, no. 7–8 (2006): 135–58, 141,

104. Lynn Margulis, *Letter to Lovelock*, 1985.

105. Donna Haraway, *Staying with the Trouble. Making Kin with the Chthulucene* (London: Duke University Press, 2016).

106. Jakob von Uexküll, "A Foray into the World of Animals and Humans: A Picture Book of Invisible Worlds," in *Instinctive Behavior: The Development of a Modern Concept*, ed. and trans. Claire H. Schiller (New York, NY: International Universities Press, 1957), 5–80; repr. in *Semiotica* 89, no. 4 (1992): 319–91.

107. James Lovelock with Bryan Appleyard, *Novacene: The Coming Age of Hyper-Intelligence* (Milton Keynes: Pengion, 2019).

108. As noted earlier, some of the last section of this chapter is based on my previous book *Kierkegaard, Eve and Metaphors of Birth*.

Chapter 3

Moving towards the Ethical

Chapter 2 offered a description of a metaphysical position, deriving from Bergson, Schelling and Kierkegaard, of humanity emerging from a reality that pre-existed it. Specifically, I elaborated upon a position I derived from Kierkegaard, namely that the whole natural world could be viewed as analogous to a birthing body that gave birth to itself.

This chapter will begin the move towards the ethical that I will suggest is intertwined with the metaphysical position outlined. Indeed, the chapter will have the further aim of defending some of the theses of the critical realist philosopher, Andrew Collier. I will claim that there is a further reason, deriving from an ethical issue, why the perspective I have been outlining, ought to be accepted. I will begin by, once again, outlining a problem, but this time, a very different problem that arises, in my view, for Kant.

KANT AGAIN

Kant argues that acting well, or doing good, is a matter of following the Categorical Imperative. Acting well entails acting from duty and we act well when we act in such a way that we can universalise the precept from which we act. So the principle 'We ought not to lie' can be universalised, and so it counts as a moral principle. A human being, for him, acts freely and well when he or she follows the moral law.

On his view, then, we are free when we follow the moral law. There is an argument that can be found in the first *Critique* and also in the *Groundwork*, which Henry Allison has labelled the Reciprocity Thesis.[1] According to this, there is a mutual entailment between the following claims:

1. The rational will is free.
2. The moral law is unconditionally valid for the rational will.

In the *Groundwork* much of the argument is about freedom of the will being a presupposition of the practical standpoint of the moral law.[2] A 'free cause' is one that operates in accordance with a special kind of causality – a causality in accordance with a law. If human beings were 'holy wills' then they would necessarily follow the universal and mandatory principle of morality.

It is more difficult, however, for Kant to explain what it means for someone to act badly. It is important for him that a person should be able to be held responsible for acting well or badly, since otherwise we would not be able to praise or blame them. However, the question arises, whether or not it is possible, on Kant's ethical premises, for someone to be responsible for evil.

In the previous book[3] I considered various possible ways that have been suggested, by a number of commentators, on how Kant might circumvent this problem. However, I argued there, it is very difficult for him to do so. Although there could be other ways in which Kant might show how the freedom to do wrong is compatible with his view of the freedom to act well in accordance with the moral law, it is difficult for him to do so, given his view of nature and of human nature. Kant's view of nature is limited by his Newtonianism. For the latter, a position that Kant took up in his early writings as well as in the later, the quantity of matter remains always the same and every change has an external cause. For Newton as well as for Kant, nature is a determined system: a system consisting in a collection of substantial things, externally related to one another, through mechanical causation. Kant's view of mechanical nature shapes his perspective on the free self as a radically different kind of thing. The self, then, becomes a divided entity. It is divided between a phenomenal, desiring, natural thing determined by Newtonian causal principles and a rational and free being, shaped by the moral law. Even if we view these two elements as aspects of one whole, as Allison does,[4] there remains a divide between the sensory and desiring element of the self and the element that strains to be moral. So it seems, then, that it is difficult for Kant to account for the freedom to do wrong, and difficult therefore for him to allow that moral agents can be held responsible for wrong doing. This seems, therefore, to me to be a significant limitation of his moral theory.

It seems to me that these various views of Kant's are connected. The difficulty he has in explaining the possibility of freely doing wrong is linked with his perspective on nature and with the model of causation he takes, expressed in the *Second Analogy*, to be the definitive model. Even if one tries, and a number of commentators have attempted to do this, to detach Kant's view of practical freedom from his metaphysic, it is hard to escape this difficulty.

This, in its turn, I have suggested, gives rise to the difficulty Kant has, of explaining the origin of freedom.

A FURTHER CRITIQUE OF KANT: COLLIER

Moving on from the arguments of my previous book there is a related point about Kant's view of morality that I would like to mention. This is a view I take from Andrew Collier.

In his myriad writings, Andrew Collier[5] sought to defend a view that, at the time, was distinctly unfashionable, and that I myself, among many, both challenged and failed to understand. In a collection of essays on Collier's work, published in 2004, Ted Benton wrote, of Collier's ontological theses: 'I'm not sure whether I disagree with (those) claims or whether I don't understand them.'[6] This was from someone who was very sympathetic to the idea of deep ecology and to taking the notion that non-humans have moral worth seriously, but who nonetheless was sceptical about some of the deeper ontological claims of Collier. So what were these claims? As laid out by Benton, they included the following:

1. All being as being is good.
2. There is a hierarchy of beings; some exist in a greater degree, and have more good, than others.
3. We ought to love beings in proportion to their goodness.[7]

Collier argues, in his book *Being and Worth*,[8] not only that Kant's moral theory, along with the moral theories of many other philosophers, is 'subjectivist and anthropocentric' in that it concerns itself only with the moral worth of humans, but it is also 'moralistic'. What he calls the 'moralistic' paradigm of ethics has dominated ethical thinking and, in fact, it is often identified with 'morality as such'.[9] This paradigm can be reduced to the following set of claims: (i) there is a special set of 'moral' injunctions and (ii) it is our 'duty' to obey these injunctions. Not doing so is to be immoral. Each person, on the Kantian view, must strive to obey the Categorical Imperative. Collier argues, though, that an abstract elucidation of categories cannot provide us with ethical content. Ethics based on universalising strategies depends on a prior selection of ethical principles that are not themselves subject to universalisation and that therefore lead to an empty formalism. 'In order to make the universalizability principle look plausible one has to presuppose that the description under which the act will be universalized is the relevant one'.[10] But universalisation in itself is an empty signifier. Universalisation, he argues, then, is vacuous since it depends on a description in one set of terms and it does not choose which terms these are. So, for example, in order to get a prescription that is universalisable, one has to make certain assumptions – in the case of the liar, the assumption that is made is that it is impossible to universalise lying, for if it were universalised, it would become impossible to tell the difference between truth telling and lying. But, even in this case it is important to note that there is an assumption, that is distinct from the principle of universalisability, that it is important to be able to tell the truth from what is not the truth. This is a normative claim that is different from the purely formal principle.

Indeed, Collier's argument could be extended to the case of Kant's theory of sovereignty. There is arguably a distinction, in Kant's political writings,[11] between the Head of State or the Sovereign, in a moral sense, and that person as a physical person. Insofar as s/he embodies the constitution, rebellion, for Kant, is not allowed. He deploys a *reductio ad absurdum* argument form (as he did in the *Antinomies*) to argue that, if the Sovereign could be coerced, then he would not be the Head of State and the hierarchy of subordination would extend indefinitely. Here Kant seems to be using, once again, a formal argument to suggest that there is a contradiction involved in rebelling against the Head of State, since, by definition, the latter represents the embodiment, in law, of the moral principle. But the problem with this, as a formal principle, is that the Sovereign only embodies the ultimate principle of morality if the content of the sovereignty is spelt out. Indeed, Kant's private support for the French rebels was so adamant that it earned him the nickname 'the old Jacobian' among his circle of friends and colleagues.[12] I mention this point since it will be relevant to the final section of the book.

Collier extends his point beyond Kant's theory to argue that while utilitarianism, for example, sets out to explain the moral in terms of non-moral ends, it still binds in exactly the same way. Each person must strive to place utilitarian ends before any other. This approach to morality might be generalised, perhaps surprisingly, also, then, to those religious forms of morality that, in similar fashion, direct their followers to act in accordance with beliefs that are grounded in one particular interpretation of a religious text.

While the following illustrative cases do not comprise an arbitrary formalism, they do constitute parallel examples of moral systems that depend upon a principle which is simply assumed to be true and that is supposed to be accepted without any challenge. One contemporary example might be the case of Orbàn's Hungary, which purportedly sets out to justify practices seen to be out of accord with basic human rights, in terms of a specific reading of the Christian Bible. A parallel case might be those readings of the Koran which purport to forbid same-sex relationships.

At first sight these look like radically different approaches to morality from that of Kant's. Yet the similarity lies in each of them prescribing a set of principles which they justify in a way that appears not to be open to challenge – the principle of universalisability as a formal presupposition of all moral theories, on the one hand, and the word of God, or of a religious text, in the case of the theories mentioned above. All are assumed not to need independent justification and are simply taken to be obviously true for all moralities. The critique could be generalised, then, to claim that there is no generalisable set of values in the fashion that each of these theories assumes to be the case. There is no fixed set of values. The assumption that there is a fixed set assumes that morality is frozen in time.

In fact, famously, Kant argues in *The Conflict of Faculties*, against theological voluntarist moral theories that God's will ought to be obeyed simply because it is God's will. There he claims if it is our obligation to follow God's will then we must already know that this is the right thing to do in which case we are not simply following God's will. On the other hand, if God commands us to do something that is morally wrong, then we ought not to do it. However, one could make the same points about Kant's own conception of the Sovereign. Either we simply know that the Sovereign represents moral good, in which case we don't need a Sovereign. Or, if the Sovereign commands us to do something that is wrong, then we ought not to do it.

Collier argues that the key problem with Kant's view of ethics is that it causes avoidable evils and prevents moral ends. One such evil is the famous case of the 'murderer at the door'. The example runs that if a murderer is at the door of a house and the person who opens the door knows that the victim is inside then the person who opens the door is committed against lying. While Kant may have a way around this case, it is often quoted as offering a central difficulty with his moral theory.

There are two separate difficulties alluded to in the foregoing, therefore, with Kant's moral theory. I would like, in the next section, to summarise a way in which I believe Kierkegaard – read in the way I suggested in chapter 2 – can overcome these difficulties.

ARGUMENT FOR FREEDOM EMERGING INTO HUMANS

Kierkegaard's account, offered in *The Concept of Anxiety*, drawing on the reading of his work given in chapter 2, can be reconstructed to run as follows: In the biblical story, Eve and Adam, as natural beings, in a world of similarly constituted natural beings, existed. Adam and Eve, in other words, were part of a living and active natural world that pre-existed the domain of the free and thinking being. Adam, at that point, was neither free nor not free. Adam had no awareness of the possibility of choice. Adam, though, had pre-existing drives and desires, some of which he shared with other natural beings. Eve – in some way a derived person – came into being later. She, via the serpent, seduced Adam. At that point, Adam became aware, through sensuality, of good and evil. Through the first sin, sinfulness or the capacity to reflect on our passions and desires and to enact some and not others – in other words, human freedom – came into Adam. Adam may have existed alongside other natural objects. These natural objects possessed powers, capacities, drives and desires that were akin to our human conceptual apparatus, but they were also different. The natural objects existing alongside Adam were not, in other words, purely inert mechanical things. Strictly, freedom emerged first in Eve, rather than Adam. 'The woman was the first to be seduced, and that therefore she in turn seduced the man'.[13] Sin, then, in Eve and Adam, is grounded in nature, the nature of which both were part before they became free. Yet the science that explains the grounding of each individual in its precursor cannot completely account for sin and for freedom.

Adam, as well as each subsequent individual, is responsible for his own sin. The explanation, according to Haufniensis, of Adam's sin must also explain the sin of every other person. Adam and Eve, as the first individuals, represent both themselves and 'the race'. 'With sinfulness, sexuality was posited. In that same moment the history of the race begins'.[14] Adam and Eve, prior to the act of eating the fruit, are in a dreamlike state of innocence. 'Innocence is ignorance. In innocence, man is not qualified as spirit, but is psychically qualified in immediate unity with his natural condition'.[15] Freedom 'enters into' Eve via a 'qualitative leap'.[16] In other words, Eve existed alongside all other natural beings, and she emerged, as they did, from her ground. If Eve and Adam are placed outside history then the story cannot explain anything. Haufniensis writes, 'As soon as Adam is placed fantastically on the outside, everything is confused.'[17] What happens to Eve and Adam is reflected in the emergence of freedom subsequently in each individual who sins. The qualitative leap brings about anxiety and the awareness, in Eve and Adam, of right and wrong, good and bad. Eve and Adam become aware that some of their desires are good and others are bad.

There are two points Kierkegaard is making, then, in response to Kant. First, the free will cannot be wholly outside time because it would be unable to operate if it were so placed. But secondly, although Kierkegaard accepts Kant's point that the notion of freedom of the will cannot be explained in either logical or mechanical causal terms, he does not accept the conclusion that it cannot be explained at all. For Kant, either Adam is wholly outside history or he is wholly inside history. But there is a third alternative: namely that Adam is partly inside and partly outside history – the history of beings like us. He is outside it as an innocent and natural being and inside it as a being that has become rational and free.

In language reminiscent of Schelling, Haufniensis writes: 'The annulment of immediacy is therefore an immanent movement within immediacy, or it is an immanent movement in the opposite reaction within mediacy. Innocence is something that is cancelled by a transcendence'.[18]

There is an important implication here. This is that, once freedom has 'emerged' in Adam, it becomes an ontological condition of the human. Rather than freedom being a characteristic of 'the will', freedom becomes part of what it means to be a being like us. As Sartre would come to claim later, freedom is a condition of being a conscious being. However, unlike Sartre,[19] Kierkegaard, I suggest, is claiming here that if freedom is to emerge in humans from a natural world, then there must be some analogue of that already existent in that natural world. To put it in Sartrean language, 'being-itself' must already include 'not-being' in some form. Sartre begins his philosophising, like Descartes and Kant, with the self, while Kierkegaard, I am suggesting, in Darwinian vein, sees the self as emerging from a world that pre-exists it. There is, however, an intentionality that is shared by all forms of consciousness that enables each form of consciousness to operate in the world and to modify and change it. But this intentionality, that is shared by all beings, in some form or other, is never an inert process, as is assumed by those who see causes as externally determining and mechanical. The world that is external to me, then, when I consider my future intentions and actions, is not mechanically inert but depends on the way in which I interact with it. Moreover, each one of us is never merely a 'for itself' but is also an embodied being, that interacts with other such beings. Each of us is a desiring being that interacts with other such beings who themselves have desires and drives.

Kant's difficulty in explaining the notion of freedom to do wrong stems from his radical separation of the free will from the finite natural phenomenal being. It stems, furthermore, in Kierkegaard's view, from Kant's restriction of nature to that which can be accessed by human phenomenal experience. Nature, for Kierkegaard, then, by contrast, must be understood in two ways: first as human nature – natural intersubjective embodied experience as well as the nature that can be accessed by rational and finite beings. But there is also a second sense of the notion –the living dynamic nature that includes plants, bacteria and other animals and that, according to this reading, included Adam and Eve prior to the emergence of freedom in them. This nature must pre-exist Adam and Eve, must constitute some sort of 'great outdoors', to return to Meillassoux's expression, in order for it to ground the possibility of freedom in beings like us. This does not, I accept, constitute the kind of proof that a sceptical epistemologist might want, that there is such a nature, but it is, nonetheless, a speculative hypothesis that offers an account of something that remains inexplicable for Kant. On Kierkegaard's account, when 'spirit' enters into Eve, since the human is the synthesis of spirit and body, she becomes aware of both good and evil. She becomes 'anxious'. The future, for her, at this point, becomes wide open – she has the possibility of making a range of choices. Since she has become relatively independent of her ground, she is capable of following norms that are 'self' grounded, that could lead her into wrong doing. Morality, for Kierkegaard, as expressed in this text and elsewhere, instead of being about following 'universalisable' formal or socially inscribed imperatives, is about recognising that this radical freedom gives rise to profound and difficult choices about how to behave, where we sometimes have no guidance apart from our own sense of what is right and wrong. Principles may vary dependent upon the situation in which one finds oneself. In his famous text *Fear and Trembling*, Kierkegaard, now though the mouthpiece of de Silentio, presents us with the most difficult possible ethical demand – the demand placed on Abraham that he sacrifice his son. Abraham, however, in the text, is said to 'believe by virtue of the absurd'. He believes 'the paradox'. There is no guidance that anyone can provide about how to behave except that here Abraham is guided by his love – his love of God and his love of his son. He is able, because of these deep and powerful feelings, to act in a way that he believes will preserve both of two seemingly incompatible matters – that Isaac will be sacrificed and that he will survive. Freedom, then, for Kierkegaard, is not just an absolute condition of following universalisable principles, but it rather requires each of us to think carefully about how to act and what is right and wrong. In his later text, *Two Ages*, he rails against those who simply mouth the Hegelian version of Kant's morality, without any thought about why they are following it or taking it seriously. Although Abraham, in *Fear and Trembling* is guided by God and he appears to follow God's command, his actions are primarily guided by a strong sense of his own freedom and his own belief that he will be able to do the right thing. Abraham is free and he makes a choice that he believes will be fulfilled. I do not propose, in this book, to defend the actions of Abraham, nor do I wish to go quite as far as Kierkegaard here.

I would now like to move to develop further some ethical implications of the foregoing. One point I would like to note at the outset is that if humans, in the form known, can come into being, then they can also go out of existence.

HANS JONAS

In his significant book *The Imperative of Responsibility, In Search of an Ethics for the Technological*,[20] Hans Jonas has suggested that the key issue facing moral thinking in the present epoch is the very survival of humankind. He points out that most previous ethical theories have been both anthropo-centric and, more significantly, they have been theories that assume that the agent and the 'other' of his actions 'are sharers of a common present'.[21] For example, the maxim 'Love thy neighbour as thyself' assumes that the agent and the 'other' are alive now and bear some relationship to me. In other words, Jonas suggests, in parallel with the argument of chapter 2, that ethical theorists, along with the rest of us and many scientists, implicitly spatialise the moral universe and assume that we need only concern ourselves with imaginary beings who share, if not our present concerns, at least a view that we are all located, if not quite in a static state but in a relatively limited period of time.

Knowledge of ethical matters, on the perspective of most moral theorists, he points out, as Kant believed, has been available to all human beings and doesn't require any special thought or reasoning powers, since each person is in possession of sufficient moral acumen to understand that their family, friends and neighbours deserve to be treated well. Jonas suggests that until the present era with its huge strides in technological power, it didn't matter so much that morality did not concern itself with future generations and therefore with the natural world that grounds the possibility of their existence.

Jonas further argues that it is the *threats* to the future existence of humans that helps us to protect the normative view of humanity that needs to be preserved. This notion is precisely parallel to the view that we don't understand the value of life unless we know about killing, and the commandment 'thou shalt not kill' brings the sanctity of life into focus.[22] Knowledge comes from knowing what to avoid. Just as the responsibility for preventing avoidable death comes from the awareness of killing, so too does responsibility for future generations and the future of the natural world arise from a fear of the evil alternative. Since it is unlikely that we are ever going to be able to bring about a future utopia, rather than a responsibility for good being our primary concern, avoiding possible evil – in the form of the non-existence of our species – ought to be at the forefront of our moral concerns.

The steps in Jonas's argument are complex, but I will summarise them here and then develop some components of the argument that I believe to be particularly important, in what will follow. So the first step is to consider the possible non-existence of our species. Although such an eventuality would be horrific for us, we can imagine the destruction of our sons, daughters and our grandchildren and to desire a world fit for them to inhabit. It is harder for us to imagine generations way into the future. But we can imagine the destruction of the whole species. We can want this not to happen.

The question then arises: why should we want this? Why should we desire that the human race continue? Why should we desire that the natural world in its entirety continue? This can be generalised into the fundamental philosophical question 'Why is there something rather than nothing?' This is, of course, a huge question but it can also be considered very simply and clearly: relative to non-existence pure and simple, something surely is better. Something of some kind or other has more value than nothing. In a particular case, if we imagine the destruction of the whole world, as many novelists have done, it is better that one fragment of a tree survives rather than nothing survives. It is better, partly because, from that one tree, one can imagine something else emerging – maybe another tree, and then maybe further species of a creature or a plant.

This does not of course mean that it is better that I exist than I don't but rather that something in general should exist rather than nothing.[23] It is simply better that something exists than nothing does. But this then leads into a discussion of what it means to be 'better' than something else. In order for one tree to be better than another, we need to have a sense of what is valuable and what is not valuable. In other words, we need to have a concept of more or less good. Therefore we need, in the extreme, to know what counts as good and what counts as bad. We need to be able to choose between good and bad and to have some idea of how to make this choice.

I have suggested, in the early section of this chapter, that what humans have, over the rest of the natural world is a greater degree of freedom and therefore of responsibility. This gives humans the power to feel a care and concern for those elements of the natural world that possess these characteristics to a lesser degree. So humans, therefore ought to be concerned about the rest of the natural world, not only because the continuation of this world is crucial for the continuity of our species but also, and importantly, because, if the perspective has anything to recommend it, humans have emerged from this world. This does not give us an algorithm for choosing the good over the bad, but it gives us a sense of our great responsibility, as humans, a responsibility that we all share, for the rest of the natural world. This does not, of course, give us a reason for defending the interests of a tree over that of a human, or for suggesting that the tree has as much right to continue in existence as a human. As Peter Singer has put it, we don't have a way of assessing the relative value of different types of living thing 'Is a two-thousand-year-old Huon pine more worthy of preservation than a tussock of grass?'[24] This, however, raises questions about moral choices that I don't want to enter into here. The point, at the moment, is to accept that the concept of moral value is not restricted to humans, even though most humans have a type of consciousness that is not possessed by most types of other animals. There is a body of work, including that of Tom Regan,[25] on animal rights, and that of a number of people, on ecological ethics[26] that offers suggested arguments about how humans ought to behave and act, given these assumptions, but my purpose in this book, is different.

As I have suggested, humans 'emerge' from the rest of the animal world. Emergent properties cannot be radically and completely distinct from that from which they emerge and it follows therefore that the human and the animal and the rest of the natural world share something in common.

Therefore, it seems most plausible to claim that 'good' or value lies in 'being' as a whole, as Collier suggested, although I have justified this view in a very different way from him. Nature, by virtue of having ends of aims, or purposes, has value. Since ends are in nature then they are effectively facts. Again to quote Jonas, 'In purposiveness as such, we can see a fundamental self-affirmation of being, which posits it absolutely as the better over and against non-being. In every purpose being declares itself for itself and against nothingness.'[27] Even saying 'no' to beings, he continues, betrays an interest and purpose. 'The mere fact that being is not indifferent towards itself makes its difference from non being the basic value of all values.'[28] Living becomes a positive concern through its constant confrontation with the possibility of not being. Humans, as the most differentiated purposive being on earth (to use Schelling's expression) have a greater degree of freedom than any other animal and, concomitantly more responsibility for themselves and for the natural world around them. They have, therefore, responsibilities and rights. These are expressed as aspects of their purposive nature.

Responsibilities and rights presuppose (i) causal power – acting affects the world; (ii) action is under the agents control and (iii) that the agent has some ability to foresee the consequences of their acts. In this sense a person is both accountable for their actions and responsible for the 'object' of their responsibility, which may be another agent. In this sense, then, responsibility and rights stem from the purposiveness of human agents, from their causal powers, which they share, but in a more differentiated form, with the rest of the natural world and of which they form a part. To draw once more on Jonas: 'Every living thing is its own end which needs no further justification. In this man has nothing over other living beings, except that he alone can have responsibility also for them, that is for hoarding their self- purpose.'[29] The paragraph below, from Jonas, is very important for the argument that will follow in this book, so I will quote it at length:

'But the ends of his fellow sharers in the human condition (my addition – humans towards other humans), whether he shares these ends himself or merely recognizes them in others, and the ulterior self-purpose ("end-in-itself") of their being as such, can in a unique manner be included within his own end; responsibility is first and foremost of men for men and this is the archetype of all responsibility. This subject object kinship in the relation of responsibility, implies that the relation, although unilateral in itself and in every single case, is yet, on principle reversible and includes possible reciprocity. Generically indeed, the reciprocity is always there, insofar as I, who am responsible for someone, am always, by living among men, also someone's responsibility. This follows for the non-autarky of man; and in any case, at least the primary responsibility of parental care *everybody* has first experienced on himself. ... Man's distinction that he alone can *have* responsibility means also that he *must* have it for others of his like – that is for such and that, in one or another respect he in fact, always has it. Here the mere capacity is a sufficient condition for the actuality'.[30]

So humans, then, share a core set of powers with the rest of the natural world, although in more differentiated form. Humans therefore have an obligation to attempt to preserve these powers, both in other humans and in the rest of the natural world. Would it not be wonderful if humans were able to inhabit a world where the general emotions of anthropoids approximated more closely to a world-preserving set of feelings and beliefs?

In the rest of the book, rather than being concerned with discussing what sort of ethical system makes sense of the overall perspective outlined here, I shall return to the human side of the equation. If humans are fragmented into different groups, as they are in many theoretical perspectives taken in cultural studies, postcolonial theory and other areas, then it is difficult even for humans to concern themselves about other humans, let alone the rest of the natural world. I would like, therefore, to move to defend a view of universal humanity and a theory of human rights that, I suggest, might derive from a perspective like that outlined here. I shall concern myself more with the correlate of responsibility – that is rights as derived from needs. I shall focus, in addition to the usual concern with the rights of others in the here and now, also on future rights and responsibilities. In chapter 4, I will argue for a position that is a prerequisite of the moral outlook outlined here, and that is an assumption of a universal humanity. I will also argue for a notion of a universal woman.

NOTES

1. Henry Allison, *Kant's Transcendental Idealism: An Interpretation and Defence* (Yale, MI: Yale University Press, 1983).

2. See GM, 4: 446–47.

3. Assiter, *Kierkegaard, Eve and Metaphors of Birth.*

4. Henry Allison, *Kant's Theory of Freedom* (Cambridge: CUP, 1990).

5. See Andrew Collier, *Being and Worth* (London: Routledge, 1999) as well as other writings.

6. Ted Benton, "Realism about the Value of Nature? Andrew Collier's Environmental Philosophy," in *Defending Objectivity: Essays in Honour of Andrew Collier*, eds. Margaret Archer and William Outhwaite (London: Routledge, 2004), 239.

7. Ibid., 243.

8. Collier, *Being and Worth.*

9. Ibid., 9.

10. Ibid., 697.

11. See Immanuel Kant, "Towards Perpetual Peace," in *Practical Philosophy*, trans. Mary Gregor (Cambridge: CUP, 1996).

12. See Christine Korsgaard, "Kant on the Right of Revolution," in *Reclaiming the History of Ethics: Essays for John Rawls* (Cambridge: Cambridge University Press, 1997), 300.

13. CA, 47.

14. Ibid., 52.

15. Ibid., 41.

16. Haufniensis distinguishes his own understanding of this 'leap' from Hegelian logical understanding.

17. CA, 28.

18. Ibid., 37.

19. Jean Paul Sartre, *Being and Nothingness*, trans. Hazel E. Barnes (London: Routledge Classics, 2003).

20. Hans Jonas, *The Imperative of Responsibility – In Search of an Ethics for the Technological Age* (Chicago, IL: Chicago University Press, 1984).

21. Ibid., 5.

22. Ibid., 26–27.

23. See Ibid. Chapter 2 for a discussion of this topic.

24. Peter Singer, *Practical Ethics* (Cambridge: CUP, 2007), 277.

25. Tom Regan, *The Case for Animal Rights* (Berkeley, CA: University of California Press, 1983).

26. Patrick Curry, *Ecological Ethics, An Introduction* (Cambridge: Polity Press, 2006).

27. Jonas, *The Imperative of Responsibility*, 81.

28. Ibid.

29. Ibid., 98.

30. Ibid., 98–99.

Chapter 4

A Defence of Essentialism and Universalism

In chapter 3, I have argued that value inheres in all beings and that humans emerge from the rest of the natural world. I have also suggested that humans have a special degree of responsibility for themselves and for the natural world, because of their higher degree of 'purposiveness' than the rest of the animal and plant world.

Just as understanding what is good requires that one also knows what it means to be bad, so too understanding responsibility requires that humans also have corresponding rights. So if I am responsible for your welfare then I have the correlative right to believe that someone will be reciprocally responsible for mine and therefore that I have certain rights that correlate with these responsibilities. This means, also, that these rights and responsibilities are possessed by all humans, wherever and whenever they live. So it seems, on the face of things, therefore that it is obvious that there are universal characteristics of all humans. As Marx argued in his 1844 *Manuscripts*,[1] 'man' [*sic*] is a *Gattungswesen*, or a 'species-being'. *Wesen* means 'essence' or 'being'. Humans constitute, for him, a species of being with some kind of essence. A core part of our essence, for Marx, is our needs. His view contrasts with that of Kant, for whom motivation by needs is heteronomy 'and the free will determines itself in abstraction from all such motivation'.[2]

It is also very important, in light of the arguments of previous chapters, to note that the very 'purposiveness' which humans share with other animals and with plants, indicates that any characteristics of humans include not only present needs, desires and responsibilities but also their potential – their potential capacities and powers and their responsibilities towards future generations and towards matters that might take place in the future. It follows that humans have responsibilities towards other humans – present and future members of the human race. Correlatively, it also follows that humans – all humans including future humans – have rights as well.

Before moving to look in more detail at the concept of a right I will need to defend the concept of universal humanity as well as universal womanhood. What is seen by some to be obvious is not at all that way for many others. So I will now move to suggest that if one adopts the perspective outlined in the first three chapters then one must revive what is a distinctly unfashionable view and that is a 'universalist' or 'essentialist' perspective of humanity and also of 'woman'. Some of what follows will focus on women but the points are generalisable to the whole of humanity. I focus on the category of women in particular not in order to exclude the category black, or any other potentially universal category of an oppressed grouping, but because many of the arguments against universalism in general have been made by feminists against generalising about all women.

It is important to note at the outset that some might argue that there is an incompatibility between considering the rights of all humans and arguing also for the category 'woman'. Mary Wollstonecraft, for example, demanded that women be included in the entitlements claimed by the 'rights of man', so there is no need for a separate category of 'woman'. However, I believe that there are circumstances where it is important to refer to universal humanity but it is also necessary, at times, to refer to universal 'woman'. As Kate Soper[3] once wrote,

> Feminism should be both "humanist" and "feminist" – for the paradox of post-structuralising collapse of the feminine and the move to 'in-difference' is that it reintroduces – though in the disguised form of an aspiration to no-gender – something not entirely dissimilar from the old humanistic goal of sexual parity and reconciliation.

This is to get ahead of myself, but one can be committed to the universality of humanity and also recognise that there are circumstances that require universal womanhood as well. Where there remain substantial inequalities between men and women, as feminists have argued is the case, there continues to be a need for the universal category 'woman'. The same point applies to the notion 'black' in 'black lives matter' as well as to other groups of people who have been discriminated against. There may are also 'intersections' between the various groups but that does not obviate the need for universal categories.

The arguments below, therefore, involve a response to those who decry reference to universality per se.

Feminist academics writing about 'essentialist' feminism have assumed that, in the words of Alison Stone,[4] it is a 'hopeless non-starter'. In an earlier era, according to Midgley and Hughes, 'the suggestion of natural sex differences' was seen to be 'not only mistaken but wicked'.[5] This negative view of 'essentialism', indeed, is generalisable to all forms of universalism. Diana Fuss[6] has argued that the essentialism/ constructionism binary blocks innovative thinking. Gayatri Spivak[7] defended 'strategic essentialism' but also criticised her own category as theoretically unviable. Moreover, as Ian Hacking[8] puts it, 'most people who use (essentialism) use it as a slur word, intending to put down the opposition'.

Basically, then, essentialism and universalism have been seen to be not only simply false as descriptions of social reality but also as rather wicked views. Sexed bodies and bodies in general are said to be not external but internal to the gendered character of social practices and meanings. The meaning of bodies is thought to vary indefinitely with cultural context. The reason for this deep concern about essentialism is that (a) it has led, in its early form as biological essentialism, to discrimination against women as well against those in the BAME category; and (b) it is necessarily thought, in the case of the category 'woman' to exclude some women . As an example of (a), in the nineteenth century, the science of 'craniology' which proclaimed that women had smaller brains than men, was used to justify differential treatment. In relation to (b), it is argued that biological essentialism will exclude trans women.[9] There are also painful issues for some people, in relation to the category 'black' as to who counts as falling within its remit. I will return in the last part of the chapter to some of these important points.

On the one hand, then, essentialist thinking has been assumed to be obviously wrong. On the other hand, and in contradiction to the above, it is argued by others (see Phillips[10] and Hacking) that 'essentialising thinking' is trivial insofar as it is built into our conceptual systems. Whenever we make generalisations about anything or anyone, we are assuming that the matters in question have essential attributes of some kind. Somehow, however, essentialising feminisms and universalising theorists about humanity as a whole are assumed to go much further than this and, usually, are believed to commit a political fault.

The critiques have continued despite a recognition that, at least in the case of feminism, if it is to warrant calling itself by its name, there needs to be something or some quality or process that is shared by all women or at the very least some function shared by all women. Indeed, if humanity is to act as a group in co-ordinated fashion, to save the environment on which it depends, then there needs to be something[11] shared by the whole of humanity. Moreover, to put the point differently, if our freedom is intersubjective and interpersonal, as we have argued in earlier chapters, then each of us is, at least indirectly, responsible for the emancipation, in the case of women, from their oppression. As far as all humans are concerned, there are reciprocal obligations among all of us, for each other.

In recognition of the above conundrum, feminists critical of all essentialising forms of the subject have sought to find a way around the problem. I will begin the chapter by considering three such attempts and I will argue that each either fails or it presupposes exactly what they deny and that is a stronger form of essentialism. The following two theoretical approaches were developed in relation to feminism but the points made can be generalised to the whole of humanity.

It is worth mentioning at the outset, because it is such an influential approach, the view of Judith Butler[12] to the effect that the view that there is an 'essence' of woman is a quasi-'ideological' construction. Indeed, her criticism is a special application of the theory of gender as performativity to the subject of feminism. Feminism, according to the view, normatively brings into being the subject (under the category of women), which it subsequently claims to represent. For Butler, as we have seen, there is no such thing as a pre-discursive, natural body, and she derides the view that there is as 'reductive' and 'essentialist'. The implication of her view is that the feminist discourse does not represent subjects that are already there; it only represents what it has produced in the first place. If this is really the case, feminism cannot emancipate an already existing oppressed subject; rather feminism becomes in part an exercise of power that brings a certain category of subject into being and makes it intelligible. I will respond to this point in the final section of the chapter.

STRATEGIC ESSENTIALISM

In recognition of what, according to her, was an impossibility – the idea of finding characteristics or experiences that are shared by all women, but appreciating also the need for something shared for political reasons, Gayatri Spivak[13] introduced a new notion – 'strategic essentialism'. This conception did not describe any characteristics possessed by all women, but it was said to be an 'imagined' identity, deployed for the purposes of unifying the group of women when they found it necessary to do so.

On the 'strategic' essentialist view, instead of women sharing some experiences or attributes, they were supposed to act on the basis of an 'imagined' set of beliefs or attributes and this 'imaginary' would enable them to act together as feminists. In theory, then, for Spivak, while there is no actual set of shared characteristics of women, they might, on certain occasions, act as though there were such an identity, in order to bring about certain goals. Irigaray used a similar expression – mimesis – where women would imitate supposed shared characteristics, in order to undermine them.[14] However, Irigaray is doing something different from Spivak with her expression 'sexuate' – which refers to the bodily, psychic and cultural dimensions of femininity – and, according to Irigaray it does not exist within the current patriarchal and phallocentric culture. It is 'morphological' – bodily in its widest sense – perceptual and relational. Indeed it is a dynamic mode of becoming.

This is certainly a radically different conception of 'essence' from the one held by those who applied it to describe a fixed set of characteristics of a woman. Irigaray's notion, indeed, is important for developing an ontological category and for exposing the hidden phallocentric assumptions underlying much of western metaphysics. But her goals are not explicitly 'feminist'[15] in the sense of characterising something on the basis of which women might act together politically.

Returning to Spivak, if the 'imagined' set of attributes were sufficient to create a sense of shared purpose on the part of women then would it not therefore become essential in some stronger sense? Perhaps, if the set of imagined characteristics were merely a one-off, then it would be simply a fluke that the group had a shared purpose. However, if the purpose remained over time, then would not these 'imagined' characteristics turn into something stronger than that?

Alternatively, as Alison Stone[16] has claimed, an 'imagined' set of shared goals or identities would not be sufficient to create a sense of shared purpose in political contexts. Stone suggests that in fact what is required is a shared set of goals deriving from shared experience or characteristics and if these are absent, then the collective goals will be difficult to achieve.

Either, then, it appears that strategic essentialism reduces to a 'real' essentialism in which case it encounters all the problems it was designed to resist or it is unlikely to do the work it set out to do.

One other possibility is that the 'imagined' reality functions somewhat like an ideology – so, for example, if women in general believe that they are all inferior in some way, then, despite the fact that this is not true, they might act in accordance with that belief. But of course, this would undermine the theory in a different way. If the beliefs were ideological then that would imply that they were false and so women would therefore be acting on the basis of false beliefs.

However, it is surely not wrong to claim that, once again, this view either reduces to an actual essentialism (based on this set of beliefs that they are all supposed to hold) or the beliefs are not strong enough to amount to a basis for a political position.

A GENEALOGICAL APPROACH

Another approach to essentialism I would like to discuss is the account of Alison Stone.[17] She defends a form of 'genealogy' among women that allows, according to her, women to act together as women but forgoes any commitment to an unacceptable form of essentialism. According to this account, women are connected to one another over a period of time, not through the possession of common properties or experiences but rather by means of a 'genealogy'. Stone draws, for this concept, on Nietzsche and on Butler's reading of Foucault. She argues that the concept 'woman' and the group itself both have a genealogy; this genealogy constructs groups of women historically in multiple, shifting, ways, their fluctuations in meaning registering changes in social relations of power. The history of women is constructed in overlapping but not necessarily consistent ways.

Nietzsche had argued, in *The Genealogy of Morals*,[18] that historically shifting concepts such as 'guilt' and 'duty' have shaped social realities and social experience and the latter, in turn, has influenced the concepts. Stone suggests that something similar occurs with the concept and the lived reality of women's lives. Nietzsche denies that there are any common concepts shared by the various approaches to morality over historical time. Stone suggests that the same may be true of women's lives. The character of the object of study – women's lives – may be fluctuating and heterogeneous. Groups of women, throughout history, will accommodate, or refine or alter, conceptions of womanhood in accordance with their own desires and needs. It is possible, she argues, though, that there is nothing in common between historical periods, thus the notion of genealogy is radically distinct from a conception of essence.

A difficulty with this notion, however, is this: if reference to any shared characteristics or shared beliefs among groups of women disappears over an extended period of historical time then it is difficult to see what the notion of 'genealogy' means. If the notion is interpreted in terms of a quasi-causal series where the original cause may give rise to further causes and so on, there would be interconnections between the groupings and a shared causal story. But this shared story would then effectively become the 'essence' of women, so the approach would not escape the 'essentialist' label. If, on the other hand, there were no such causal chain, but rather a series of disconnected and contingent 'links' then it is difficult to see how this could constitute a 'genealogy' of one group at all rather than a series of groupings with some vague interconnections but these would not be sufficiently strong to warrant the label of a shared grouping. If there were radical 'incommensurabilites' between the various groupings over a period of historical time, then it would be difficult even for those from one grouping to understand the perspective from another, so they would not in fact share anything in common.

So it is difficult to see how this 'new' genealogical notion of women can escape either having an essentialising character on the one hand or not being a genuine grouping at all on the other.

There is one other view I would like to mention and that is Charlotte Witt's 'uniessentialism', which she set out to distinguish from both 'realism' and 'nominalism'. She wants to guard against the 'essentialist' assumption that she believes to be mistaken and that is that there are shared characteristics of all women. She rejects 'kind' essentialism. Instead, she defends a version of essentialism, one she calls 'individual' essentialism which itself divides into 'uniessentialism' and 'identity essentialism'. The version that interests her is the former. Essence, she suggests, in this sense, is 'the cause of the being of the individual'.[19] 'Essence' then becomes a functional property that answers the question 'what is this individual?' Summarising her argument, she claims that while biology plays a role in this notion, 'gender' is the primary social role that unifies all other roles. Gender is the organising principle that shapes all the roles – mother, labourer, etc. – that the individual occupies. Gender produces an ontological category of 'social individual' but significantly, for her, it allows that the social individual can change gender and, moreover, it allows for multiple genders.

This theory is unique in offering a form of essentialism but allowing for flexibility on the question of which gender an individual takes on. However, it is possible to challenge the account in a number of ways. First, why is this notion of an overriding social function necessary? Why should it be 'gender'? Why is gender, if it is not a set of shared characteristics, on the theory, an 'essentialising' overriding category?[20] But more importantly for the argument I have developed earlier in the book, it seems to me to be important to distinguish biological sex from gender because it is as biological and sexed beings that we lie in a continuum with the rest of the natural world. Witt argues both that there are more than two biological sexes and that the division into two sexes is a cultural and not a biological matter. However, I have argued that biology is a deeper natural reality than this viewpoint assumes to be the case. I will not enter into the argument here as to whether or not the existence of hermaphrodites shows that there are more than two sexes. However, I have argued that biology is important and cannot be reduced to a social or a cultural construction. Given the dynamic and powers based ontology I have argued for, what counts as a biological male or a biological female may change, but it continues to be important that there are biological sexes and therefore sex based rights of women. This does not exclude other rights including intersectional rights of black women or trans women. However, sex-based rights remain important.

A CRITIQUE OF COMMON CRITIQUES OF ESSENTIALISM

Now I would like to do what may be regarded as the impossible, and that is to defend essentialism. First, I would like to respond to some of the most common critiques of essentialism. Cressida Hayes[21] suggests four potential ways of characterising the notion: (1) metaphysical essentialism, the belief in real essences (of the sexes) which exist independently of social construction; (2) biological essentialism, the belief in real essences which are biological in character; (3) linguistic essentialism, the belief that the term 'woman' has a fixed and invariant meaning; and (4) methodological essentialism, which encompasses approaches to studying women's (or men's) lives which presuppose some essential properties. I would like to defend (2) above but by means of re-thinking (1). In fact a combination of (1) as it stands above and (2) has often been described as 'biological reductionism' and has simply been assumed to be false. I would like to distinguish my own position from this.

In my view many critiques as well as defences of essentialism have taken for granted a metaphysical assumption, exemplified in the characterisation of the first form of essentialism – metaphysical essentialism – that is questionable. Challenging this metaphysical position, along the lines of the earlier chapters of this book, I will suggest, removes some of the opposition to essentialism. Before moving to that, however, I would like to respond to some of the common critiques of essentialism.

RESPONSES TO CRITIQUES OF ESSENTIALISM

The most common critique of essentialism is that it is simply false. It is false because it involves a generalisation about the group that fails to apply to all members of the group and it therefore leads to some form of discrimination against the excluded members of the grouping. One form of such a critique appears in a paper written by Anne Philips, in 2012.[22] She writes:

> The problem (of essentialism) here is one of over- generalisation, stereotyping, and a resulting inability even to 'see' characteristics that do not fit your preconceptions. In practice, this leads to discrimination: 'I would never employ, marry, believe an X, because they are all unreliable.' As regards gender differences, it is widely thought that girls have better communication skills than boys and that boys are better at maths.

This belief, which Phillips demonstrates to be false, can then be used in a discriminatory fashion against one or the other group.

To reiterate, then, the critique of essentialism is that a generalisation about X is assumed and this leads to discriminatory behaviour towards some members of X.

This critique is actually a form of the famous one given by Paul Gilroy in his book *Black Atlantic*. He argued for a cross-diasporic conception of 'black identity' against an Enlightenment ideal that was partially constructed on a premise of slavery. Paul Gilroy[23] wrote: 'Incredulous voices have drawn attention to the bold, universalist claims of occidental modernity and its hubristic confidence in its own infallibility'. Gilroy's work, alongside that of others, has demonstrated the exclusionary nature of certain Enlightenment concepts. Gilroy's famous thesis is that some Enlightenment concepts of 'the human' were built on the exclusion of others, and indeed, they were built on the assumption and the practice of slavery. Some Enlightenment thinkers excluded women and certain races from the scope of the notion of a right. Human universality, then, has been seen as an Enlightenment conceit. Feminist universality or feminist essentialism has been viewed as inevitably presupposing the imposition of purportedly and falsely 'universal' values on those falling outside the invariably European and white norm.

These critiques of versions of universalising and essentialising thinking are important – indeed Gilroy's work was groundbreaking in its characterisation of the way in which certain concepts which had been taken for granted were in fact false and racist.

This point has also been expressed in a slightly different form by those who have argued that the very idea of a civic public which is implicit in universalising thinking excludes groups defined as different.[24] The notion of a republic or of citizenship, it has been argued, is always implicitly racialised or sexed.

Phillips's examples also indicate that there are occasions, and perhaps many more occasions than many of us would like to believe, when stereotypes of groupings are used to exclude people or to act in racist or sexist ways towards some people. The step that is taken by many who are critical of essentialism in general, though, is a different one. Phillips could have argued that the false 'stereotyping' is the problem. But in fact she argues that the problem is not the stereotyping but rather that 'over generalisation' instead is the problem. She goes on to admit that generalisations are often necessary. But she is still critical of 'generalisation' in many contexts.

A significant case of potential exclusion of a grouping that is thought to be a direct result of forms of biological essentialist thinking is that biological essentialism is thought to refer to properties that are innate and fixed and this excludes those who transition from one sex to the other. It has also been argued to have been characterised in a fashion that is biased towards heterosexual women. However, later in the chapter, I will challenge the assumption here, namely that biological qualities are fixed and innate.

We use generalisations all the time and it is not trivial to do so. To draw a crude and simple analogy – when we are explaining the meaning of the word 'aeroplane' we look for necessary and sufficient conditions for being an aeroplane. This may not in fact be the best way of describing the meaning of the word and we may get these necessary and sufficient conditions wrong. But the response would not be that it is always wrong to try to describe these necessary and sufficient conditions. It may be that we believe that a causal theory of meaning offers a better approach to the question but that is a matter in theory of meaning and is not a question of never being able to describe necessary and sufficient conditions for being an aeroplane.

That is, of course, a non-political example because it doesn't really make sense to say that it is possible to discriminate against aeroplanes whereas it is not only possible but factually the case that generalisations about women have led to racism, homophobia, anti-trans positions and many more forms of discrimination. It is therefore a highly charged and politically sensitive matter how we go about characterising women.

Bearing that in mind, it is possible to respond to Phillips's and Gilroy's critiques by saying that neither Gilroy's famous case nor Phillips's less well-known ones involved proper universalising. So instead of the qualities that Enlightenment theorists ascribed to all humans or to all women, we should look for other, more acceptable qualities, such as biological characteristics – chromosomes, gonads and secondary sexual organs. Maybe it is even possible to describe the capacity to give birth as essential to a woman. In line with the arguments of chapter 3, though, none of these will describe fixed characteristics. At the core of each one of us will be powers or capacities that can be actualised in a range of ways.

The critics of essentialism will argue, however, that there will be exceptions to each quality assigned to the kind and certainly to the above list. If it is possible, the critics may argue, for a trans man to give birth, then it is possible for a man to give birth and this quality is no longer the prerogative of women. Some women, indeed, are unable to give birth. Moreover, and equally important, the critics of essentialism have also argued that biology is socially inflected and so we cannot make generalisations about biological characteristics because we cannot separate them from social and cultural influences.

There is one point I would like to make, here, in favour of a form of essentialism but using the same form of argument that the critics of essentialism deploy. There are criticisms, from a 'progressive' point of view, about generalisations that are intended to be supportive of a particular group. The response, in some cases, however, has not been to forgo generalisation but rather to opt for a greater degree of generalisation. For example, Chetan Bhatt[25] has critiqued the ready association of non-western with 'victim' and 'other'. He suggests an association of this with the simultaneous denial both of full subject-hood to the 'subaltern' or the 'non-western' and of the possibility that some such 'victims' might themselves also be attacking, for example, the secular spaces of Asian peoples. The alternative, he suggests, is not to forgo generalisation about anyone but rather to accept that the 'sub-altern' is a full member of humanity. Here we have a case that makes the opposite point from that made by the critics of essentialism. Instead of critiquing generalisation, the political point being made is to opt for a greater degree of generalisation.

In another illustration of this, Neil Lazarus and Rashmi Varma,[26] make the following point: 'From the Haitian Revolution of the late eighteenth century to the Indian freedom struggle of the mid-twentieth, from Toussaint L'Ouverture's challenge to French ideas of citizenship to Gandhi's strategic ironisation of 'Western civilisation' as a 'good idea' (his tongue-in-cheek suggestion, of course, was that it would be a good idea if the west were to become civilised!), the history of anti-colonial struggle is replete with instances not of 'alternative modernity' but of claims made to civic rights, freedom and citizenship on the ground of modernity.[27]

In other words, rather than 'particularising' anti-colonial peoples, the suggestion is that postcolonials ought to be seen to be part of a common humanity, in this case, all sharing rights, freedom and citizenship.

A MATERIAL AND NON-REDUCTIVE ESSENTIALIST FEMINISM

Many who are critics as well as some who are defenders of essentialism, as noted, have assumed the metaphysical assumption made in (i) above – namely that 'essentialism' involves ascribing necessary qualities to a 'thing'.

Instead, I would like to view the concepts 'human' or 'woman' or 'black' or 'minority ethnic' as creative ones, in a process of constant construction. This is a similar, in some respects, to the 'genealogy' developed by Alison Stone and others but with one important difference.

Many of those who articulate a developmental notion of 'woman' claim that it is not possible to distinguish the 'biological' body from the social and cultural one. Some go further still and argue, as we saw, with Judith Butler, that the concept of 'woman' is a construction of the very people who set out to emancipate 'it'. However, I would like to argue, by contrast, that the concept of woman begins rather in her material body, so that an ontological conception of the woman is at least partially biologically formed, that is, constituted by a vital matter which proceeds as an 'autopoietic system'. The materiality here is neither a rigid or determinist biologicism nor is it an empty form of hylomorphism. By contrast, it forms the self-organising and self-controlling dynamism of an active and creative energy, and derives from the perspective developed in earlier chapters – vital materialism. This body of work, as articulated, views reality as comprising processes in constant evolution rather than things with properties. Darwinian theory showed that humans are descended from other animals, and, indeed, from other life forms, including protozoa, bacteria and viruses. It also suggests that humans remain animals. Humans are simply more developed forms of other animals. To quote Darwin: 'Each species had not been independently created, but had descended, like varieties from other species.'[28] So, Darwin argued that differences between living species are differences of degree rather than of kind, so that the whole world of life comprises a continuity.

Darwinian theory has received a renewed impetus from some thinkers of ontological difference, who consider radical difference as the motor of the evolutionary process. As we have seen, for authors like Bergson, Deleuze or Elisabeth Grosz, 'difference' is the motor of life. Evolutionary theory, along with an ontology of radical differing, allows a concept of living matter in infinitely processual terms. All matter fundamentally comprises living forces, and it makes sense to claim that there is a rudimentary notion of freedom in all such processes.

As we have seen, inspired by evolutionary theories, the new vital materialisms assert the continuity of the human and the non-human, organic and inorganic forms of life throughout the immanent deployment of a living materiality. Nature and culture, organisms and environment, conscious and unconscious life are intertwined and new characteristics constantly emerge. Biologically speaking, humans in general as well as women in particular, lie in continuity with the rest of the mammals. The female sexed body is constituted by chromosomes and genes, cells, neural networks, hormones, gonads and phenotypes. It constitutes an assemblage of particles, energies and movements intra-acting one into another. Luciana Parisi describes woman's body as a complex entanglement of 'microfeminine particle-forces'[29] in permanent movement. Each woman is a unique and unrepeatable matrix of multiple and heterogeneous particle-forces, sexed from within her vital materiality.

Rather than being a static 'kind' therefore with similarly static 'essential' properties, these properties will be undergoing a constant process of evolution and change. Indeed, the 'kind' itself comprises living forces in dynamic interaction with one another and with other forces. But this does not mean that we cannot offer a broad characterisation of what it means, at any one time, to be a woman. What counts as a woman can change and evolve, but it does not follow that it is not possible to categorise her. Darwinian theory proposed the evolution of species but he could not have characterised his thesis unless he held on to the notion of species. At any one time, it will be important to ascribe necessary and sufficient conditions for being a biological woman, and this will include a chromosomal make up, gonads, cells, neural networks and so on. This claim will not be a trivial one – it is not only a matter, as with the aeroplane, of being able to tell what is an aeroplane and what is not, so it is not only a trivial matter of how to categorise. It is important, for the normative reasons outlined earlier. Women need to know who counts as a woman in order to act to promote justice for all women. There may be very good reasons for continuing to believe in sexual reproduction and in some kind of distinction between male and female that will be partially biologically based and these reasons may be quite distinct from biological essentialism – in the sense of being inert and 'given' or depending, as Parisi argues is the case, on a 'traditional western model of representation'.[30] There is a biological link between female identity and sexual reproduction, but such a link does not exhaust the meaning of the female. The reduction of female sexual identity purely to reproductive functions is mistaken for it suggests that the biological domain is a 'given' or inert or reified nature. Biology, like all aspects of living beings, can change and develop and therefore what counts as a woman or a man can change. Biology, as noted, is socially inflected. Essence is not based on the substantialist framework of properties and things, but rather on the self-reflective paradigm of potencies and powers. There are groups of people who may not fit the category of woman, as it is characterised at any one time, such as those who are inter-sexed. There are those, such as cross-dressers, who choose to present themselves as members of the opposite group. Indeed, in the case of race, it is even more difficult to categorise a person on the basis of biology. Gary Younge has referred to a pair of identical twins who were black by racial heritage, but one of whom presented themselves as white and the other as black.[31]

It is important, though, not to deny the significance of biology in general and biological reproduction in particular. Some post-humanist authors like Luciana Parisi seem to suggest that sexual identity involving sexual reproduction is 'embedded in the western tradition of (bad) essentialism'.[32] However, I reject her claim as well as her reading of Bergson as contradicting Darwin. Biological reproduction is important, as long as it is required for the reproduction of the species.

In chapter 1, I argued that a processual metaphysic does not prevent us, at times, from seeing the world as though it were static, in order to categorise and order it. Likewise, we can imagine a static moment when we can categorise humans in general. We can also, at any one time, characterise necessary and sufficient conditions for being a woman. On the basis of these necessary and sufficient conditions, women as a group will be able to act together to ensure that no woman, whether she is trans, lesbian, black or poor, is discriminated against. It is also politically important to ascertain that no woman suffers discrimination because she is a woman. Importantly, however, and this distinguishes the position I am outlining from that of some of the earlier 'essentialist' thinkers, the fact that 'woman' is in process, is evolving and changing, allows for alterations in how we categorise her; it allows that, for example, if a trans person who has undergone painful and serious surgery suffers further if 'woman' is defined as 'being categorised that way at birth' or as possessing a particular set of secondary sex organs, then those characteristics, which were, at one time, deemed essential for womanhood might have to be changed. This is exactly what happens as all of us learn about forms of discrimination that are invisible to some of us and that we have to learn to take serious note of. Sometimes, as many are well aware, deciding these issues will be painful and difficult for many, as is the case, for example, with battles over who counts as a woman and who counts as black. But it is important, for all of us, that we remember our biological bodies, since it is in virtue of these that we share a concern for the rest of the natural world on which we all depend and from which we have all emerged.

It is true that biological characteristics interact with social and cultural ones. It is even the case, according to contemporary biologists, that genes can evolve, with cultural change. But just as my eyes interact with my brain, but it doesn't follow that I cannot distinguish my eyes from my brain, so too is it possible to distinguish biological characteristics of woman from social and cultural ones. The vast majority of women are born with XX chromosomes in their cells and men with XY, and the XX chromosomal combination may, indeed, give women an immunological advantage.[33]

It is wrong to develop universal or essential characteristics of a woman that exclude some women. But it is equally wrong to throw out the metaphorical baby with the metaphorical bath water. If we deny that there are ever any essential characteristics of any controversial grouping, then not only do we prevent ourselves from identifying who is a member of that category but we also prevent ourselves from noticing shared characteristics of our 'kind' and acting to prevent discrimination against anyone in the kind. One consequence of the refusal to countenance essential characteristics of humanity as a whole as well as of women as a group has been the multiplication of categories and groupings each of which has legitimacy as a group – African American women differ, for example, from American African women. But there are also commonalities between the two groups. The experience of racism or sexism will be different for every individual. But, as Simone de Beauvoir puts it: 'Wanting to talk about myself, I became aware that to do so I should first have to describe the condition of woman in general.'[34] And as Direk has put it:

> The lived experience of her sexed body as girl, teenager, young woman, old woman – signify as they do, in virtue of the historical effectiveness of the cultural, and social practices. Patriarchy begins to form woman's corporeality as soon as she comes in the world.[35]

According to Darwin, sexual difference is a product of evolution. Natural selection and sexual selection (individuals who have sexually attractive features have easier time mating to perpetuate their kind) are the two principles of the evolution that intertwine but which must be considered separately. Sometimes the two principles fail to work together. Sexual selection may give a creature features that increase the chances of its being the object of predators. The processes of sexual selection and natural selection work in tandem to make life more differentiated and diversified.[36]

Woman's body then is a *continuum* of biology and culture, because the living matter that constitutes her does not form a fixed essence nor does it take on a substantial form. By contrast, her vital materiality is a self-differentiated subject mediated by multiple dynamisms, among which cultural, political or discursive practices are also reflexive autopoiesis of natural forms. Therefore, from the female body there results a 'second nature'[37] 'more than natural', a sort of 'supra-naturalism'[38] reciprocally intra by natural and cultural particle-forces. We could also speak of a 'trans-corporeality' intermeshed with natural and more-than-natural elements[39]without being either wholly 'constructed' by powerful discursive or cultural practices, or immediately given as a simple nature, but always mediated.

Discursive or cultural practices do not 'construct' or 'produce' or 'create' vital matter as if it was a passive and receptive substrate of extrinsic configurations. Rather the two interact in a dynamic process of evolution. However, as noted, this does not prevent us from categorising women at any one moment of time.

These last paragraphs have constituted a response to the criticisms of biological 'essentialism' made on page 3 of this chapter. Essentialism need not be 'inert' and unchanging especially since this criticism assumes a metaphysic of static substances with properties that has been rejected throughout this book. But it also need not exclude anyone, for the basis of categorisation is not fixed and immutable.

CONCLUSION

In this chapter, I have critiqued some of the alternatives to 'essential' woman and also critiqued some of the critiques of essentialism. I have then, in the concluding section of the paper, defended an alternative form of biological essentialism – a processual essentialism that begins from a radically different form of metaphysical starting point from that assumed by many critics of essentialism. Instead of assuming that the world primarily comprises 'things' with 'properties', rather these things are the result of processes or powers that comprise the fundamental constituents of the world.

In a number of places elsewhere I have defended a universalising perspective about humanity, a view that suggests that there are political and moral imperatives deriving from the fact of our universal humanity.

Universalism is important because it is also a normative perspective – a view that there are principles of justice that require that each person, whoever and wherever they are, is treated fairly and equally. Human beings have, as Martha Nussbaum has put it[40] 'a dignity that deserves respect from laws and social institutions'. Respecting human dignity might entail drawing up a set of human needs or rights deriving from these and respecting these. Included among those needs or rights that are either basic or very important would be the right to life, the right to decent food and shelter and the right to freedom from persecution. The satisfaction of basic needs is necessary to ensure human flourishing. This point might be made in terms of needs or in terms of capabilities but, with appropriate qualifications, to be adumbrated in the chapters following, it can be conceptualised in terms of some notion of a right.

Sometimes it will be necessary, in order to ensure the rights of all, to focus on those of a particular group, as has been the case with the movement 'Black Lives Matter'. If a black life is treated less well than a white one then universalism requires a focus on the group that is discriminated against. If all lives ought to matter, then the fact that one group is treated as though it does not matter means that we need to focus on that group.

Underlying the notion of a right is the view that all individuals are entitled to respect as moral agents capable of making choices. Moreover, while the notion of a right is in fact associated with liberal citizenship, it is possible to re-think the notion in a fashion that may be more in accord with a genuine conception of universal humanity.

Having available to us, in our contemporary globalised world, a notion of universal rights will not mean that we ignore the cultural, religious, sexed and racialised aspects of our identities as humans. If the notion of a right, therefore, were genuinely founded upon a conception of universal humanity, or on the needs and the flourishing, appropriately construed, of such a universal humanity, then it would not fall foul of these objections.

When postmodernists and others critique what has passed as universalism, they have derided it as an '"Enlightenment" conceit'. Unfortunately the perceived problems with some aspects of the 'Enlightenment' model of the self have led to misguided and unfortunate challenges to the very notion of universalism about humanity.

Our universal humanity rests partly on biological realities but these need not, as has been illustrated here, be read in a reductive manner. Nor are they, as some have suggested, trivial qualities. Indeed, to the contrary, our shared basic biological needs are the bedrock set of needs that must be satisfied, as I have argued before, if humans are to be able to do anything at all. The natural – biological and environmental – realities affecting all of us will, in deed INDEED, ultimately shape whether or not the human race as a whole continues to reproduce itself. Similar points can be made, as noted in the chapter, about universal woman. If we are to act as women to ameliorate domestic violence against women, to fight against the rape of women, then we need the universal category of woman. All women have rights as women to be treated fairly and well. This is true wherever there is discrimination on the grounds of race, class, sexual orientation and sexual identity. Each group will need to self-identify as a group as well as self-identify as human. The rights of any minority are important not because they constitute a minority but rather because discrimination has denied the group rights that others have.

In chapter 5, I will move to examine the topic of human rights and to offer an alternative account of the concept from that which derives from the European Enlightenment.[41]

NOTES

1. Karl Marx, "Economic and Philosophical Manuscripts," in *Early Writings*, ed. L. Colletti (Harmondsworth: Penguin, 1975).

2. See Andrew Chitty, "The Early Marx on Needs," *Radical Philosophy* 64 (Summer 1993): 26. Chitty argues here that needs are intrinsically social but that they take on a contradictory form in capitalism. In a real socialist society properly human needs would take on the form of the need to satisfy the needs of others. I think this is an important point.

3. Kate Soper, "Feminism, Humanism and Post Modernism," *Radical Philosophy* 55 (Summer 1990).

4. Alison Stone, "Essentialism and Anti-Essentialism in Feminist Philosophy," Journal of Moral Philosophy 1, no. 2 (2004): 135–53.

5. Mary Midgley and Judith Hughes, *Women's Choices: Philosophical Problems facing Feminism* (London: Weidenfield and Nicholson, 1983), 185.

6. Diana Fuss, *Essentially Speaking: Feminism, Nature and Difference* (London: Routledge, 1989).

7. Gayatri Spivak, "Can the Subaltern Speak?" *Die Philosophin* 14, no. 27 (1988): 42–58.

8. Ian Hacking, *The Social Construction of What?* (Harvard, MA: Harvard University Press, 1999).

9. I would like note at this point that there are others who have defended a form of essentialism that is different from the most obvious forms. One interesting and significant example of such a theorist is Charlotte Wiit, *The Metaphysics of Gender. Studies in Feminist Philosophy*, ed. Cheshire Calhoun (Oxford: Oxford University Press, 2011). She defends a theory based on the social and relational character of social individuals, that she labels 'uniessentialism'. I think how theory is very interesting and she draws as I will later on, on Aristotle, but in rather a different way from mine so I will not consider her theory in detail here.

10. Anne Phillips, "What's Wrong with Essentialism?" *Distinktion: Journal of Social Theory* 11, no. 1 (2010): 7.

11. When I use the word 'thing' here I am using it in a loose sense to include properties and powers.

12. J. Butler, *Gender Trouble: Feminism and the Subversion of Identity* (New York, NY and London: Routledge, 1990).

13. Gayatri Spivak, "Feminism, Criticism and the Institution," *Thesis Eleven* 10, no. 11 (1984/5): 175–87. And see also op.cit.

14. Luce Irigaray, *An Ethics of Sexual Difference*, trans. Carolyn Burke and Gillian C. Gill (Ithaca, NY: Cornell University Press, 1993).

15. She explicitly disavows the use of this expression in Luce Irigaray, *Dialogues. Special Issue of Paragraph* (Edinburgh: Edinburgh University Press, 2002), 67.

16. Alison Stone, "Essentialism and Anti-Essentialism in Feminist Philosophy," *Journal of Moral Philosophy* 1, no. 2 (2004): 135–53.

17. See Ibid.

18. F. Nietszche, *On the Genealogy of Morality*, trans. Carol Diethe and ed. Keith Ansell-Pearson (Cambridge: Cambridge University Press, 1994).

19. Charlotte Witt, *The Metaphysics of Gender* (Oxford: OUP, 2011), 10.

20. See Ann Cudd, Comments on Charlotte Witt, the Metaphysics of Gender, vol. 8, *Symposia on Gender, Race, and Philosophy* (Massachusetts Institute of Technology, 2012), 1.

21. Cressida Hayes and Cressida Heyes, *Line Drawings: Defining Women Through Feminist Practice* (Ithaca, NY: Cornell University Press, 2000) and see also "Anti-Essentialism in Practice: Carol Gilligan and Feminist Philosophy," *Hypatia* 12, no. 3 (1997): 142–63.

22. Phillips, "What's Wrong with Essentialism?," 7.

23. P. Gilroy, *The Black Atlantic: Modernity and Double Consciousness* (London: Verso, 1993), 43.

24. Iris Marion Young, "Polity and Group Difference: A Critique of the Ideal of Universal Citizenship," *Ethics* 99, no. 2 (1989): 250–74.

25. C. Bhatt, "The Fetish of the Margin: Religious Absolutism, Anti-Racism and Postcolonial Silence," *New Formations*, Special Issue – Postcolonial Studies After Iraq, 59 (2006): 98–115.

26. N. Lazarus and R. Varma, "Marxism and Postcolonial Studies," in *Critical Companion to Contemporary Marxism*, eds. Jacques Bidet and Stathis Kouvelakis (Leiden: Historical Materialism Series, Brill Academic Publishers, 2008), 309–31.

27. Ibid., 326.

28. Darwin, *On the Origin of the Species*, 4.

29. Parisi Luciana, *Abstract Sex. Philosophy, Biotechnology and the Mutations of Desire* (London and New York, NY: Continuum, 2004), 32.

30. Ibid., 9.

31. https://www.bbc.co.uk/programmes/m000kgnp.

32. Parisi, *Abstract Sex*, 8. 'Bad' is my addition.

33. See for example https://www.nature.com/articles/nri2815?proof=true, accessed April 13, 2020 (although there are some people who are born with XY chromosomes in their cells, who have all the secondary sexual characteristics of females).

34. Simone de Beauvoir, *Force of Circumstance, 1968* (Harmondsworth: Penguin, 1976), 195.

35. Zeynep Direk, …, 69.

36. Grocz 2012, 87.

37. Bennett, *Vibrant Matter*, 115.

38. Johnston 2014, 139.

39. Stacy Alaimo, *Bodily Natures, Sciences, Environment, and Material Self* (Bloomington, IN and Indianapolis, IN: Indiana University Press, 2010), 2–3.

40. Nussbaum 1994, 5.

41. The final section of this chapter is partly based on work I have done with Maria Binetti.

Chapter 5

A New Defence of Human Rights

The book so far has developed a materialist theory of humanity alongside a related account of the relationship of humanity to the rest of the natural world. In chapter 4, I moved to defend an 'essentialist' and 'universalist' view of humanity and of womanhood that drew on the vital materialism of earlier chapters. This perspective, I believe, can be developed further to defend the notion of a human right.

My view of human rights will consist in a broad defence of an analogue of a natural law theory of rights, although it will clearly differ in its expression from a standard classical natural law theory.

Many sympathisers of the concept of a right as well as its critics assume that the high point of the development of the notion is the European Enlightenment. Carole Pateman,[1] for example, one of the foremost feminist political theorists critical of the concept of a right as masculinist, in her book *The Sexual Contract*, assumed that the rights and freedoms of all derive from the concept of the social contract produced by Locke, Hobbes and Rousseau. In turn, there are passages from the texts of these thinkers in the document produced by the Founding Fathers of the United States.[2] Although there are some references to Aristotle's virtues in the Founding Fathers' document, the main contributors come from the European Enlightenment. As Leo Bauch puts it: 'Locke can be said to be the spokesperson for liberalism. He can be called the philosopher of England's glorious revolution.'[3]

It may be that some critics of the concept of a right took the document of the Founding Fathers as the locus of their critique. If that were to have been the case, then the correct label for their criticism ought not to have been that it was Eurocentric but rather that it was Americo-centric. Recent critics though, such as Saba Mahmood whose work I will be examining later in the book, assume rights to be 'Eurocentric' for various other reasons.

But it is important to note that there is a possible different story about the origins of the notion of a right and about the interpretation of the concept. Indeed, the possibility of such a story might reveal that it is the critics themselves who are exhibiting some form of Eurocentrism in their assumptions about the nature and the origin of the concept. Just as, as Jon Stewart[4] has noted, most readings of Hegel on religion ignore the section of his writings on religion that deal with non-western religions, so too is one possible alternative story about the origins of the concept of a right, also, largely ignored or simply assumed to be wrong. I am not suggesting that what follows should be taken as true. Rather I am simply suggesting that it is an account that ought to be given some consideration and not simply ignored.

THE ORIGIN OF RIGHTS

The commonly accepted story, then, is that 'rights' originated in the seventeenth and eighteenth centuries, through the work of such philosophers as Hobbes and Locke. Kant further developed the notion of a right. This context, broadly, was a capitalist one, with its assumption of the significance of liberal individualism, although both Locke and Hobbes articulated, in their different ways, the notion of a 'state of nature'. Individuals, in this state, had 'rights' to such qualities as life and liberty. Locke is said to have formulated the idea, assumed to be a 'natural' condition, that 'men' were assumed to be equal and to possess a number of rights. Hobbes had articulated what later came to be known as the 'positivist' view of rights, that whatever rights a person has are given to him/her/them by the state or the sovereign. It is the prerogative of the state to grant these rights. Locke, by contrast, set out to limit the power of the state and he argued that the rights bestowed on 'men' in the state of nature constituted a 'moral order', which, he argued, ought to be respected. In turn, it is the duty of a sovereign to enforce these rights and to punish infringements of them. 'Reason', for Locke, is the 'common bond whereby humankind is united into one fellowship and society'[5] and the state of nature, whether or not it actually existed, is assumed by him to be simply a more 'primitive' version of his contemporary world. This same 'reason' gave rise to the scientific developments of the Enlightenment against which all other forms of thought were said to be 'primitive' and backwards.

There are significant criticisms of Locke's notion. First, it is important to point out that the common bond of 'reason' allows the 'sovereign' representing the 'moral order' to protect the 'rights' of property owners to keep their property, however it had been acquired. Moreover, women were not given the same 'natural' capacities as men, in the state of nature.

The social contract was also itself, as Pateman famously pointed out, intrinsically patriarchal, for there was an implicit association of consent – the consent of the people to the power of the sovereign – with patriarchalism. This patriarchalism derived from earlier practice in the seventeenth century where it was assumed that 'fathers entered into the social contract on behalf of their families'.[6] But since men could not continue to act as fathers in the new social contract (the role of father became restricted to the family), the men who metaphorically 'defeat' the father and claim their natural liberty, act effectively as brothers. Pateman notes that the revolution in France quoted three clauses of the new liberal doctrine: liberty, equality, fraternity'. The original contract, she argues, is a fraternal pact.

In this period, then, there was a new separation of civil and political society – the 'new public world constituted by the universal bonds of contract between formally free and equal individuals'[7] – from the private familial world constituted by a natural order of subordination. But this separation deprived women of an economic basis for independence.

I will discuss these issues further in a later section of this chapter.

Something along these lines is the story commonly told, of the origin of the concept of a right, both by supporters and by critics of the notion. The only variation is whether or not there is assumed to be some notion of 'natural law' which gives rise to a moral order, or whether, by contrast, the rights are simply whatever 'the sovereign' takes to be the case.

In its contemporary 'positivist' Hobbesian variant, in the version of Kelsen,[8] as Habermas puts it, the '"ultimate source of norms" . . . is nothing other than "the will of the legislator" viz. his "original decision to establish and enforce them" . . . (so) . . . the ultimate source for the binding power of norms would appear to be nothing more than a "threat of sanctions".'[9] This positivist approach, which Habermas is critiquing, while Kant could not be described as a positivist, has some affinity with Kant's view of the sovereign, outlined in chapter 3. Habermas, by contrast, defends a legal theory according to which a 'subject' of the law should be able to find good reasons why she or he should voluntarily submit to the law.

ANOTHER VIEW

But there is an alternative possible account both of the origin of the concept of a right and of what it means. One alternative account of the origin of the concept is that it came about with the ancient Greeks, and particularly with Aristotle, who is said to have developed a version of natural law. Aristotle, indeed, as noted, is quoted in the documents of the US Founding Fathers. In

Book E of the *Nicomachean Ethics*,[10] Aristotle is concerned with a discussion of justice as a virtue, after the fashion of the virtues of courage, temperance or friendliness, for example. In his *Politics*, he argues that 'man' is dependent on community and that the state is 'prior' to individual 'men' and the home. All these claims are based on deductions from natural law.

Aristotle also, though, offers a view of 'life' and living things that is comparable to the view of Jane Bennett, and myself. In chapter 1 of this book I quoted Jane Bennett: 'Seeds, embryos, personalities are all organic wholes'.[11] Aristotle, in *De Anima*,[12] offers a view of living things that is comparable in many respects to this. He argues that plants and animals, living things, have 'souls'. What makes something 'living' is that it has 'what we call self-nourishment itself, growth and decay'.[13] Living things, similarly in some respects, to the 'autopoetic' entities discussed in chapter 2, are self-sustaining, although he adds the rider that they can self-destruct as well. Furthermore, on his view, it is the 'soul' that explains the presence of those features. The soul is the form or the 'essence' of a living thing 'it is not that which has cast off its soul that is potentially such as to be alive, but that which has its soul'.[14] The soul is the 'form' of a natural body that is potentially alive. The soul is the 'actuality' of any body that is alive. The soul is an 'actuality' (entelecheia) which, in the form of a 'first actuality' is a potentiality or a capacity to engage in activity – the 'second actuality'. So the capacity or the potentiality to engage in the activities of growing, moving and so on constitutes the soul. The activities increase in complexity, as we move up the various types of living thing, with intellect or thought as one of the highest categories of activity. Different types of soul correspond to these various levels of activity. The soul, indeed, is not separable from the body – each soul requires a body in order to exist. It is not, in other words, a thing that might exist in its own right. Rather, in analogous fashion to some of the writings of the new materialists considered earlier, it is a power or a capacity.

While Aristotle does not include personalities among his examples of living things with souls, these views of his are similar in some key respects to the views outlined in early chapters of the book.

Animals, for Aristotle, don't possess reason although they can 'perceive'. He writes: 'Next there would be a life of perception, but it also seems to be shared even by the horse, the ox, and every animal. There remains, then, an active life of the element that has reason; of this, one part has it in the sense of being obedient to reason, the other in the sense of possessing reason and exercising thought'.[15] Animals cannot hold beliefs.

It doesn't follow from any of this, therefore, that it will be a requirement to uphold the view that animals or plants must have rights as well as humans. In fact Aristotle allows that animals can be killed for human consumption. It is also important to note that Aristotle held a view of animals and also of women that I would not wish to recommend. Famously, he argued that 'woman is, at it were, an impotent male, for it is through a certain incapacity that the female is female'.[16] He also wrote:

> The male is larger and longer-lived than the female. ... Again the female is less muscular and less compactly jointed, and more thin and delicate in the hair... And the female is more flaccid in texture of flesh, and more knock-kneed, and the shinbones are thinner. ...[17] Woman is more compassionate than man, more easily moved to tears, at the same time is more jealous, more querulous, more apt to scold and to strike. . . ., the male is more courageous than the female, and more sympathetic in the way of standing by to help.[18]

In other words, women were, according to Aristotle, naturally inferior. I am not defending everything he wrote. However, these natural differences occurred within an overall perspective that saw all animal species as 'ensouled'.[19]

Aristotle's is a very different view of 'soul' from that given by the key thinkers of the Enlightenment on whom many people rely for their account of human rights. Descartes, for example, as a central figure in the latter tradition, famously saw 'soul' and 'body' as distinct substances and anything machine-like, that included animals, was purely body, that, in its turn operated according to mechanical causal laws. Machines were material systems unfolding according to the laws of blind physical causation. Indeed, Descartes saw biology, as Michael Wheeler puts it 'as merely a branch of physics'.[20] Machines for him were, indeed 'objects of wonder and awe' but they were nonetheless machines.

In the early seventeenth century there was a groundswell of opinion against Aristotle. As Tom Sorrel puts it: 'In August 1642, over a thousand people gathered in a great Paris hall to hear a public disputation of fourteen theses against Aristotle. But the debate was prevented by official edict.'[21] 'Scholasticism', then, as it was known, was strongly criticised in the seventeenth century, and to some extent, that critique is embedded in contemporary western common sense about science, but also about rights and the social contract.

Aristotelianism is one body of work which offers a different metaphysic underlying the notion of a right, and which challenges the assumption that the concept of a right is derived from the European Enlightenment. The 'rights' of humans defended by Aristotle were rights of living embodied beings, interconnected with the rest of the animal and natural world. These humans were not disembodied minds, as some critics of the notion of the 'rights of man' have argued is the case with some Enlightenment thinkers. They are rather rights to treat and to be treated, for example, with friendliness, to be treated in a temperate way and to demonstrate courage in defending others. There is also an expectation to treat the non-human living world well.

One might note, also, that the conceptualisation of freedom, to take one value-laden concept that is expressed as a right, and is therefore often associated solely with the Enlightenment, is core also to ancient Greek thinking. Hannah Arendt, for example, in her magnum opus, *The Human Condition*,[22] drawing on the ancient Greeks, emphasises how true action of human beings – for example, political activity that recognises and depends upon the activity of others – requires some notion of freedom. In fact, for her, the modern world is characterised by the denial of this form of action, action that ought to exemplify humanity as distinct from animality.[23]

A RADICALLY DIFFERENT ACCOUNT
OF THE ORIGIN OF A RIGHT

There is another source for a radically different view of the concept of a right. This is a much earlier source, in ancient Persia.

There is a case that can be made to the effect that, contrary to the multiple accusations of the Eurocentrism of the origins of the discourse of human rights, it is rather the case that a device known as the Cyrus Cylinder outlines the world's first charter of human rights. Rather than this cylinder being an Enlightenment or western document, it was in fact Persian (or at least it was inscribed in the lands covered by the ancient Persian Empire). It was inscribed in 539BCE and was found in the ruins of Babylon in modern Iraq in 1879 during a British Museum excavation. Rather than any texts of John Locke, or Kant or Rousseau or indeed Aristotle, the Cyrus Cylinder is often proclaimed as the world's first charter of human rights.

The cylinder was written in Babylonian cuneiform on the orders of the Persian king Cyrus the Great (559–530 BCE) after he captured Babylon. 'After his conquest of Babylon in 539 BC, the king issued the Cyrus cylinder, discovered in 1879 and seen by some today as the first human rights document. The cylinder has been linked by some commentators to the decrees of Cyrus recorded in the Books of Chronicles, Nehemiah, and Ezra, which state that Cyrus allowed (at least some of) the Jews to return to their homeland from their "Babylonian Captivity'.[24]

There are disputes as to whether or not the cylinder is actually the first statement of human rights; whether it is a statement of human rights at all and whether Cyrus was actually an inspired and tolerant leader. For example, one critic, Josef Wiesehöfer, derides the claim that the cylinder is a human rights document.[25] But Tom Holland, by contrast, drawing on a number of sources, including Herodotus, in his book *Persian Fire*, both offers an account of Cyrus's military acumen and also acknowledges his sense of 'righteousness and justice'.[26] Isabelle Broyer writes: 'It is considered the first human declaration of human rights, guaranteeing the rights and welfare of the Babyl (Zartoonians) after the Persians captured the city'.[27]

A further debate among scholars of the subject[28] is whether or not Cyrus was influenced by Zoroastrianism. This is related to the question as to when Zoroaster (تشزرز) lived. . According to one scholar, Williams Jackson (in an article on the influences of Zoroastrianism on Christianity), 'The dates assigned by direct tradition to Zoroaster's life are 660–585 BC as given in the Pahlavi books, but some western scholars and the modern Zoroastrians of Bombay are inclined to place the prophet's date at a period considerably earlier than this.'[29] Indeed it is debated, in the literature, whether or not he existed at all. In her inaugural lecture, Almut Hinze argues that there is a debate among scholars as to whether or not Zoroaster was a human being who lived and died or whether he was rather a creation of the religious tradition itself.[30] What is not open to debate, however, is that the religion existed, and still does, and that there was a figure called Cyrus who lived and died.

A couple of arguments in favour of Cyrus being influenced by Zoroastrianism are that he is said by some to have named his children after Zoroastrian characters. He also, although it is said that he was known to be religiously tolerant, probably sent missionaries to convert people to Zoroastrianism. Some argue, also, that the reason why some Medes peoples (who were, unlike Cyrus, not Persian) fought with him was because of Cyrus's faith.[31] Tom Holland's view is that Cyrus's empire 'was never really Zoroastrian at all'. The Persians, he argues, including Cyrus, continued to worship their ancient gods. However, Cyrus's court, he writes: 'Was not entirely removed from Zoroaster's teaching'.[32] So Cyrus probably was influenced by Zoroastrian teachings.

It seems to me that there are similarities between my interpretation of Kierkegaard's *Concept of Anxiety*,[33] given in chapter 3 and a possible reading of the *Avesta*, the 'Holy Gathas', or 'Psalms of Zoroaster', which is the collection of writings of Zoroastrianism, originally conceived in Avestan or Zend (an ancient Iranian language) but retrieved in Farsi and in an English translation, by D. J. Irani and with a Forward by Rabindranath Tagore.[34] I have acquired an English translation, from the anonymous source, by Arthur Henry Bleeke.[35]

In this body of thought, there are two elements, two opposing forces that are in the world as a whole and also in each one of us.[36] These forces are, on the one hand, the Spirit of Goodness and, on the other hand, the Spirit of Evil. These are akin, in some respects, to the opposing forces in the work of Schelling. The world is created, according to the myth, by the operation of these two opposing forces – Ahura Mazda, the force for good, created 'good' lands but this was countered by an opposing power, Aura Mainyu, the force that was evil. As Hinze puts it: 'At the apex of the good camp is the god Ahura Mazdā. By 'birth', as the Gathas put it, he brings forth out of himself spiritual qualities such as 'creative force'.[37]

Just as fire is accompanied by black smoke, so there are two forces in the world. The 'evil' force 'counter-created' various 'sins' which include the burning of corpses. These two forces continue a process of creation by creating good lands and then counter-creating according to forces of evil. In the Bleeke translation, *Avesta Fargard* 1.1 reads, 'Ahura-Mazda spoke to the Holy Zarathustra'. 1.2 follows: 'I created a place ... a Creation of delight ....' But then, in 1.8, 'Aura mainyus ... who is full of death, created an opposition to the same.'[38]

Humans became free, according to some interpretations of *Avesta Yashna* 29, in an allegory that has resonances of the Eve and Adam story described in chapter 3. The cow – a sacred animal in Zoroastrianism – is given an option to choose between a thrifty husbandman who looks after the cattle and a non-husbandman. The cow eventually chooses the former. 'Towards you complained the soul of the Bull: for whom have ye created me/has created me? He continues to ask his creator to teach him the good things. Then in stanza 29.2 'Then asks the fashioner of the Cow of Asha: where hast thou a lord for the Cow? That he may make mighty those who apply themselves to the breeding of cattle ... where has thou made for a Lord who smites back the wicked...'.[39]

The cow, which is sometimes used to mean 'all cattle' also appears to represent humanity at large, the 'Wise Lord's' great flock of humans. The cow's plight is humans plight and the provider she seeks is the virtuous man who can lead them to prosperity. Zarathustra opens the hymn with the cow plaintively asking her Fashioner why He created for her such a sorrowful existence and imploring him to wrest her from its estate. In verse two, the Fashioner asks Truth to respond to the cow'.[40] Eventually the cow is led to choose the way 'of the truth'.

Human beings, then, as the beings capable of freedom of choice, ought to use their freedom, according to the teachings, to attempt to bring about the dominance of the forces for good over those of evil, in the world. One of the ways in which they ought to go about doing this is to care for the natural world – which is itself made up of these forces. Zoroastrians care for the earth not merely so that humans can seek spiritual salvation but because humans and the earth are in a symbiotic relationship where each requires the other. The sky, water, earth, plant, animal, human and fire are the seven original creations but are also in continual interaction with one another. Zoroastrians never enter a river, for that would be to pollute it.

This set of beliefs, then, encompasses a view to the effect that all humans are free and equal. It also encompasses a respect for the natural world, from which humans emerged and with which humans stand in a symbiotic relationship. Although Cyrus no doubt held his own beliefs, shaped by Zoroastrianism, he argued for religious tolerance. So he believed in the right to choose one's own faith. Other rights, inscribed in the Cyrus Cylinder, include the right to racial equality.

DEFENCE OF THE CONCEPT

I would like, therefore, to defend an approach to human rights that draws on these traditions, in contrast to the Enlightenment. My account will have some affinity with natural law theory, but instead of being grounded in God's will, it will be rather grounded in a moral commitment akin to Collier's view out-lined in chapter 3. Collier defended the view that all being as being is good. This is obviously, baldly put like that, not true. However, there is an obliga-tion on all of us, in line with the arguments of chapter 3, to ensure that the basic needs of all humans, wherever they are, are satisfied. Insofar as I believe that core human rights express needs then there is also an obligation on us to uphold this system of rights. This will apply also, in line with previous argu-ments, to future human beings. It may also apply to animals, but, as I have said earlier, I will not be dealing with that issue in this book.

Clearly, where a law fails to uphold this basic principle then it is not justified. As Aquinas puts the point: 'Every human law has just so much of the nature of law as is derived from the law of nature. But if in any point it deflects from the law of nature, it is no longer a law but a perversion of law.'[41] Unjust laws then would not be laws at all.

To quote another theorist, Blackstone:

> This law of nature, being co-eval with mankind and dictated by God himself, is of course superior in obligation to any other. It is binding over all the globe, in all countries, and at all times: no human laws are of any validity, if, contrary to this; and such of them as are valid derive all their force, and all their authority, mediately or immediately, from this original.[42]

So, according to natural law theory, there cannot be legally valid standards that conflict with natural law; and any valid law derives its authority from this natural law. It seems to me that this principle is a vital one and the only disagreement I have with it, is that the source of its binding quality ought not to be God, but rather the nature of human beings, as articulated throughout this book. If God is the source of the values then there is a risk that bad laws could be given justification, as based on the will of God. Locke,[43] of course, also, argued that there was a moral order against which legal matters ought to be judged.

A natural law writer whose view is closer to mine, Finnis,[44] outlines what he calls basic goods: life, health, knowledge, play, friendship, religion and aesthetic experience. For him, each of these goods is universal. The point of moral principles, on this view, is to enable the satisfaction of basic needs, connected with these core goods. I would challenge the inclusion of some of these but I concur with the basic principle.

While the specific content of laws developed will be based on a conception of the core needs of humans as they stand at the point of development, we must always bear in mind that these laws might need to change as the core materiality of humanity changes and develops. The laws ought also to reflect the need to care for the natural world on which each of us depends for our survival but which is also important in its own right. There will obviously be a great deal of discussion, which, as noted, is not my topic here, on what exactly the 'right to life' means and when it is justifiable to allow killing or at least letting a person or an animal to die. I would like to make the point, though, that, although the biological core of humans is vital, in considering rights, so too is the capacity of humans for self-consciousness and self-awareness. This gives most humans both a special place, in my view, in the consideration of what counts as a right to life, and special responsibilities towards one another and towards other species and the environment. Engaging therefore with debates about how the rights of a new-born baby or of a foetus differ or fail to differ from those of other species of being, although very important topics, will not be my primary task here. Rather I will be concerned with the implication of the metaphysical perspective for humans in general.

The distinction between the 'natural law' and the 'positivist view' of a right is a debate within human rights thinking about the meaning of a right. But there are those who wish to challenge the concept altogether. These critics tend, rather than engaging in the above debate about rights, to align the concept of a right with sexism, racism and, in particular, in the contemporary context, with imperialism and colonialism. There is an assumption, in this literature, as noted above, that rights derive from the European Enlightenment and from philosophical dualism, foundationalism and individualism. As would be expected, instead of the dualism, the foundationalism and the individualism of the Enlightenment view, I have so far provided a distinct metaphysical outlook that offers a radically different perspective on universal humanity. This notion can now be developed to defend at least some aspects of the conception of a human right. Some of the literature on rights, derived as it is from the foundationalism and the individualism critiqued in previous chapters, will be different from the notion of a right that I wish to defend in this book.

So long as it continues to be the case that all humans need food, shelter, clothing and the ability to express the form of freedom outlined in previous chapters then they all have rights to these matters. Of course there will be disagreements about the form in which these rights ought to be expressed and disagreements also about what counts as a right and how rights ought to be ensured. We will see, in the following chapters, how the concept has been adapted and modified to suit particular contexts. However, in my view, a view that I will defend in what follows, the UN declaration, while it is partial and imperfect in its scope and in what it means, nonetheless remains a vital tool to protect people from severe forms of abuse. Moreover, I would like to argue in the following chapters, that some of the deep criticisms made by postcolonial theorists of the concept of a right can be answered.

While I would like to defend a revised notion of a right, I am sympathetic to some of the central criticisms of the existing notion and I will document some of these in what follows.

I have argued, in earlier chapters, in favour of the view that there are natural, biological differences between the sexes. It might be suggested that this view is incompatible with treating the sexes as having equal rights. There have been arguments, as previously noted, to the effect that if men and women are different, then they ought to be treated differently in any legal system. Such arguments were used, for example, to justify denying the vote to women in the UK until 1928. Indeed the possibility of making such claims is one reason for the rush to call the natural difference thesis wicked' or a 'non-starter'. In the United States, the idea that women inhabit a 'separate sphere' (being in the home) was used to justify different legal decisions in the 1960s.[45] However, it is important to make a general point in response to this. Equality does not mean sameness. The fact of universal characteristics of humans does not entail that any two humans are identical. It entails only that there are sufficient qualities or powers held in common by all humans to justify the claim of universal humanity. Equality requires that, despite our differences from one another, we all have rights to equal treatment. To quote Littleton:

> The function of equality is to make gender differences, perceived or actual, costless relative to each other, so that anyone may follow a male, female, or androgynous lifestyle according to their natural inclination or choice without being punished for following a female lifestyle or rewarded for following a male one.[46]

To take one example, discussed by her, men and women share the right to procreative choice and therefore employers ought to provide leave appropriate to the effects of pregnancy. These points are made in relation to men and women, but they are generalisable to any group that has been treated unfairly on the ground of some difference from what is perceived to be the norm.

SOME CRITICS OF THE CONCEPT OF A RIGHT

Early critics of the notion of a right, as noted above, claimed that it explicitly excluded women from the public sphere and relegated them to the domain of the family.[47] The public domain of citizenship was constructed as masculine. Carol Pateman, again as noted above, extended this point to claim that early constructions of the 'rights of man' were produced with male heads of household in view.[48] Locke had given as an illustration of one right – a man's right to give away his daughter in marriage.[49] The daughter herself is non-existent in this way of thinking, except as an object of the man's right. The heads of the family, then, emerged without ever having had to be conceived, born and nurtured.

The private domain, in the writing of J.S. Mill, also, was exempt from government interference. The individual, in the private sphere is 'free'. Individual male heads of household were supposed to protect the rest of the household.

In this model, it is clear that the woman and the children in the household have no rights at all and the model lends itself to the abuse of women and children. These early models, have, however, to some extent been superseded and the concept, as deployed in many contemporary expressions of the concept, has been extended to cover the rights of women and children as well as any other group (like those who did not possess property in Locke's sense).

But there are other aspects of this early thinking that re-appear in the thought of some recent defenders of the concept of a right. In the early view, as we have seen, rights were possessed by individual males who 'had' families. The family members did not stand in relations of care with one another.

While no recent defender of the concept of a right would explicitly exclude women and children from its scope, there remain aspects of the model of the self upheld by the early writers that continue in the works of some influential contemporary liberals. If not explicitly Lockean, there are Cartesian assumptions, for example, in some of the works of John Rawls. I will set out, in the next section, to respond to some of these criticisms.

In his famous 'Original Position' – the device Rawls[50] deploys to illustrate the way in which agreement on principles of justice can be developed – individuals are free and autonomous. As many critics noted[51] Rawls abstracts away, from individuals in this set-up, all religious, moral and political concerns. Individuals in the 'Original Position' merely possess two 'moral powers' – the capacity to develop a sense of justice and the ability to form a notion of the good. Individuals, in the 'Original Position', are, like Cartesian selves, 'rational beings'. They might actually be embodied and caring, but these characteristics are 'abstracted' away from their activity in this hypothetical scenario. Human beings act, in Rawls's famous scenario, purely as 'rational beings' who choose from among the many available reasonable positions, to develop a view of justice that purportedly will work for all.

Critics have argued, though, that, given that some contingent and emotional interactions with others affect the values of all, it is difficult to see how such a model would work in practice. Sandel, in his book *Liberalism and the Limits of Justice* argued (a) that Rawls's theory of justice requires that the moral agent be an abstract rational individual, separate from her ends, personal attributes, community or history. Sandel then claims that (b) it is only by adopting this theory of the person that Rawls's theory makes sense. Finally, he argues (c) that Rawls's therefore has a 'philosophical anthropology' which is inadequate and false and therefore that his form of liberalism fails.

Rawls's reasoning is beings are rational, autonomous and self-interested. An ideal model of society, then, will have individuals tolerating a variety of moral positions. Rawls, along with other liberal thinkers, believed that it is important to recognise that there will be, in any society, a plurality of views about human flourishing. There is a limit, however, on this: each one of the views that are to be tolerated, ought to be 'reasonable'. There is, then, a point of view, for him, which all liberal-minded individuals share, and where they are able to discuss, in a reasonable and tolerant manner, their varied moral standpoints. This domain is governed by what Rawls labels the 'principle of reciprocity'. 'Our exercise of political power is proper only when we sincerely believe that the reasons we offer for our political action may reasonably be accepted by other citizens as reasons for their actions'.[52]

I believe that something analogous to this principle is very important in our troubled times, governed as they are globally by the rise of intolerance and by forms of populism that fail to treat those with whom they disagree with respect and with any kind of care. Indeed, as I have noted above, it was a principle very like this that, it appears, was upheld by Cyrus, when he advocated tolerating those whose religious beliefs differed from his own. However, it seems to me that the foundation of this belief needs to be rethought. In the next section I will outline what I believe to be a limitation of this outlook.

Rawls's principle of tolerance is not unlimited in scope. There are certain beliefs, for him, that lie outside its domain of operation. One Rawlsian[53] thinker, de Weitz, frames the limits of reason in the following manner: there are, implicitly in Rawls's work, two conceptions of rationality. On the one hand, there is the normative conception, according to which individuals are self-defining autonomous agents, who recognise the moral law and determine their own moral beliefs in accordance with this law. On the other hand, there is a more instrumental picture of reason, which encourages individuals to be consistent in the pursuit of their ends.

On the basis of these two principles of reason, de Weitz argues that there are two categories of belief and behaviour that lie outside the scope of the 'principle of reciprocity'. There are beliefs that are 'bizarre', such as belief in the flat earth theory or the view that the moon is made of yellow dresses.

There are, also, beliefs that lie outside the spectrum of tolerance for very different reasons. This second group comprises beliefs that are 'evil'.

However, the scope of what is 'mad' or 'evil' is not defined, and there are numerous views current in the world at the moment that would count, perhaps for some, as 'mad' or 'evil'. Indeed, there is a classic historical example outlined by Foucault in *Madness and Civilisation*,[54] where he describes how, in the seventeenth century, just at the time Descartes was writing, people regarded as insane or mad came to be detained in 'houses of confinement' or hospitals. Whole swathes of the population came to be confined: 'Young men who disturbed their families peace or who squandered their goods, people without profession and the insane.'[55]

Foucault develops this into an argument against Descartes's view in his *Meditations*. Foucault suggests that when Descartes is dealing with scepticism about the senses or when he responds to the hypothesis that he might be dreaming of, he offers a rational refutation of the alternative view. However, when he hypothesises that he might me crazy, he simply rules the idea out of account. He writes: 'If then I should be mad.'[56] Foucault writes that the mad person represents the 'other' of bourgeois rationality. Descartes's argument, according to Foucault, necessarily excludes a whole segment of the population. Whole groupings lie outside the scope of the autonomous person who is deserving of respect.

Writing in 1993, Rawls required us all, as rational autonomous beings, who tolerate others, to recognise that we might be wrong in our strongly held beliefs.[57]

However, this discussion of the 'mad' and the 'evil' suggests a limitation of the operation of the Rawlsian principle of tolerance. There are many in our contemporary world who want to 'no-platform' those with beliefs they regard as crazy or evil.

Woe be it for liberals, though, if we rule out, in today's world, from those deserving of tolerance of some kind, those who are fanatical in their beliefs. Woe be it, indeed, if we rule out of account and rule out of consideration, those who would count, on de Weitz's criterion, as 'evil' or 'mad'. There are many in the contemporary world who want to deny citizenship to those who hold contrary moral beliefs to their own. There are some from all sides of the political spectrum, who wish to close down the voices of those who oppose them. One example of a case, as I write this, is a proposal, in contemporary India: the government has just passed a law offering fast-track citizenship to peoples from nearby states, but not if they are Muslim. In the UK, the recently elected prime minister wants to prevent his compatriots from speaking on the BBC flagship programme: the *Today* programme. But there are also similar cases from those on the 'left' of the political spectrum: according to a report for the *Independent* newspaper, in 2017, nine in ten of UK universities restricted the freedom of speech of someone in that year.[58]

I am not suggesting that we ought to tolerate all views. I uphold, with Rawls, a principle that we ought to reject views that are outside what J.S. Mill would have regarded as the limits of liberal tolerance.

However, it is important for me, that we allow, where it is safe to do so, the expression of diverse views. It is also, and this is the nub of my disagreement with Rawls's perspective, important that we respect the humanity of the person upholding a view, however abhorrent we find the person's beliefs. We need to recognise that all human beings have needs that ought to be satisfied. All humans are interconnected, one with another, whether we all behave rationally or not. As one would-be Labour MP, in Britain, said to me on the eve of our general election that brought Boris Johnson into power with a huge majority: 'I am Jewish (this is in the context of labour being accused of being Anti Semitic) and I believe that Jews are entitled to labour values as much as anyone else'. Jews and non-Jews alike need water, food, a home, the ability to express their views and tolerance. Once we accept that humans are not purely rational beings, but rather they are embodied, natural beings, who interact with other humans and with the rest of the natural world, we can offer recognition and core rights to all of humanity, whether each one returns that recognition or not. It is this extension of the principle of the right to life and recognition of their personhood that I regard as one of the key differentiating features of the account I am proposing from that of the alternative Enlightenment-inspired tradition. This does not mean that we should 'tolerate' evil or mad views. It means, rather, that we should take the person expressing the views into the scope of the discussion. No one ought to be incarcerated or interned for expressing a view, however abhorrent the view in question is. Indeed, if we respond to 'evil' with more evil, then we ourselves have, according to Rawlsian principle, entered the domain of 'evil' or 'madness'. Mill's limitation of the operation of the principle of 'freedom of speech' is important. But a person should not be prevented from speaking if they simply uphold a view that others believe is abhorrent.

From this alternative perspective, we can respond to some further critiques of the notion of a right. Feminists and others have argued that there are conflicts between individuals and groups over what counts as a right. There are, as many postmodern-inspired feminists have noted, differences among groups of women and, one might add, between groups of people in general. Iris Marion Young, for example, has argued that there are many 'faces' of oppression – there is exploitation, marginalisation, powerlessness, violence and cultural imperialism – and therefore many forms of oppression and injustice. Sometimes these will conflict but one needs, she suggests, to develop a conception of justice that contextualises the political subject. Groups, as well as individuals, need representation as citizens. If a group is denied esteem because of its culture then it is important to attempt to rectify this.

I concur with Young that there are times when group rights are very important – it was this recognition that led, in certain countries, to the notion of 'multiculturalism' that has been so important for respecting the rights of 'minority' groupings. However, it is also important, to recognise the rights of individuals within groups. I would like to note the work of Southall Black Sisters,[59] as one significant group in the UK who has defended the rights of individual women within an oppressed cultural grouping who were discriminated against or subjected to violence within the group. The right to be free from undeserved violence is a right that is ubiquitous. Therefore, although it is important, at times, to recognise group rights, it is also vital to work for the rights of individuals to be safe in their homes. Sometimes, in other words, the rights of a group will conflict with the rights of individuals within it. It is also important to work towards equality of all individuals and to recognise and appreciate that sometimes a focus on cultural groupings may obscure this appreciation.

Nancy Fraser,[60] another important theorist in this tradition, proposes a spectrum of injustices ranging from injustices of distribution to those of recognition. Recognition of one's cultural identity or one's sexual orientation, to take two important cases of failure of recognition, in a context where these matters may be hidden or even wholly denied, is vitally important. It is important, that, for example, a trans person's identity is recognised and appreciated in all societies. It is vital, also, that hidden cultural assumptions about all, such as an assumed Christian identity in certain societies, are not imposed unwillingly or unwittingly upon all. It is also important, to take some more extreme cases, that equality of all religions is appreciated. No one should be denied citizenship simply because of their religious beliefs, or, for that matter, for their race or their sexual orientation.

It is said, as we saw in relation to the work of Rawls, that rights presuppose an abstract, isolated self that is cut off from the natural world and from others. It will be obvious by now, however, that this critique does not apply to the concept of a right I am developing here. O'Neill has developed the critique, however, to suggest that 'rights talk' is guided by the question: 'What are we entitled to?' It therefore focuses on recipience rather than on action. It focuses on what we want rather than on what we all ought to do.

However, as will be apparent, I reject this accusation. The rights frame-work is limited, in its application. It cannot by itself remedy all forms of injustice. Indeed, as I mentioned in the Introduction, it may actually be a prelude to making deeper changes in society in the direction of a more just world. However, in a world where, to reiterate once more, the right to speak out, the right to life and the right to equality, to take three fundamental rights, are under threat, it is vital that those of us who recognise their importance seek to defend them. Defending them does not mean defending them only for ourselves or our families or our dear ones, but rather defending them for all humans at all times. In other words, the existence of rights implies duties.

In this chapter, I have considered a couple of possible stories giving accounts of the origin of a human right that, I suggested, ought not to be ruled out of account, as they are in much of the literature on the concept of a right. Those who, in other words, take it as read that rights originated with the European Enlightenment should consider whether or not they are making an assumption that this is the case. This point applies both to those who support the 'Eurocentrism' of the concept and to those who subject its Eurocentrism to critique.

I have then moved to suggest that the Zoroastrian tradition that is probably linked with Cyrus, a leader in ancient Persia, who proposed a concept of a right, offers a theoretical perspective that is similar in some respects to that proposed in the earlier chapters of the book. Finally, in the last section of the chapter, I moved to consider some critical discussion of the concept of a right. In the final three chapters of the book I will consider some further criticism of the concept of a right. Much of this criticism probably applies to the concept in its 'Eurocentric' sense, but some of it might apply more generally to the concept of a right, so I believe it is important to attempt to respond to it.

NOTES

1. Carole Pateman, *The Sexual Contract* (Cambridge: Polity Press, 1988).
2. See https://billofrightsinstitute.org/founding-documents/founders-quotes/.
3. Leo Bauch, *The Political Animal: Studies in Political Philosophy from Machiavelli to Marx* (Amherst, MA: University of Massachusetts Press, 1981), 56.
4. Jon Stewart, *Hegel's interpretations of the Religions of the World: The Logic of the Gods* (Oxford: OUP, 2018).
5. John Locke, *Two Treatises of Government*, ed. P. Lascet (Cambridge: CUP, 1960), 6, 172.
6. Pateman, *The Sexual Contract*, 77.
7. Ibid., 91.

8. H. Kelsen, "Foundations of Democracy," *Ethics* 66, no. 1, Part 23 (1955): 1–101; H. Kelsen, *General Theory of Law and State*, trans. H. Wedberg (Cambridge, MA: Harvard, 1946).

9. J. Habermas, *Between Facts and Norms: Contributions to a Discourse Theory of Law and Democracy*, trans. W. Rehg (Cambridge: MIT Press, 1996). Abbreviated BFN, 101.

10. Aristotle, *The Nicomachean Ethics*, trans. David Ross (New York, NY: Oxford University Press, 2009).

11. Chapter One. This book.

12. Aristotle, *De Anima* (London: Penguin, 1986).

13. Ibid., 412, a 14.

14. Ibid., 412, b 12.

15. Aristotle, *The Nicomachean Ethics*, 3.

16. Aristotle, *Generation of Animals*, TRANS A. L. Peck, Book 1, ch.20 727 a15. Boston, Harvard University Press. Sinclair, T. A. (Harmondsworth: Penguin, 1981). It is interesting that there is a difference of view in the literature as to whether or not Aristotle's views on the various hierarchies among slaves, women and men influences his overall theories. Lynda Lange, for example, in Woman is not a rational animal, argue that Aristotle's views of the sexes influence all aspects of his philosophy. However, I believe that it is possible that this argument stems partly from separating 'matter' and 'form', and associating the former with the female and the latter with the male, in a way that I have just argued one ought not to do.

17. Aristotle, "The History of Animals," in *The Complete Works of Aristotle*, Vol 1, ed. Jonathan Barnes (Princeton: Princeton University Press), p. 851.

18. Aristotle, "History of Animals," in *The Complete Works of Aristotle: The Revised Oxford Translation* (Princeton, NJ: Princeton University Press, 1992), 538a 22 – 38b 10.

19. Ibid., 608b 8.

The primary subject matter of this book is that of developing a metaphysic that views humans as continuous with the rest of the natural world, in contrast to the Enlightenment view. It is also, to defend the notion of an ethic that values all living beings and the earth as a whole. It seems to me that extending the concept of a right to non-human animals does not necessarily do the job of valuing the whole of the natural world. However, dealing with the detailed and difficult questions of what this means in practice would be the subject of another book. I have referred, elsewhere in the book, to literature that considers which ethical theory is the best one to adopt to further these kinds of end and which considers the question of whether or not the concept of a right ought to be applied to animals.

20. P. Michael Wheeler Husbands, O. Holland, and M. Wheeler, eds., *The Mechanical Mind in History* (Cambridge, MA: MIT Press, 2008), 307–30.

21. Tom Sorell, *Descartes* (Oxford: OUP, 1987), 27, 23.

22. Hannah Arendt, *The Human Condition* (Chicago: Chicago University Press, 1998).

23. It is important, indeed, in recognition of another very significant aspect of the work of Hannah Arendt, to appreciate, what she noted in a prescient appreciation of a phenomenon that is a bigger problem now than it was in her day, that the notion of a

natural right ought to be universal in scope. However, as she was all too well aware, the notion was actually interpreted in her contemporary world, as it is now, in terms of the citizenship of a nation state, and that renders vast numbers of people stateless and, in the words of one of her followers, Agamben (Giorgio Agamben, *Homo Sacer: Sovereign Power and Bare Life* [Stanford, CA: Stanford University Press, 1998]) to the vast number of people lingering in refugee camps in the present day and that applied, indeed, to those of Arendt's fellow human beings treated in such an extreme and incomprehensible way, who were victims of the Nazis. The concept of a right, then, if it is to be genuinely universal, must be broader than applying only to citizens who are recognized by some state. In this sense, I am referring partly to an ideal, but I am also recognising and appreciating how significant even the legal concept is, in the contemporary world in which even this concept is under attack.

24. "The Evaluation of Human Rights: An Overview in Historical Perspective," *American Journal of Service Science and Management* 3, no. 2 (2016): 5–12. Md. Kamruzzaman 1, 2, 4, *, Shashi Kanto Das 3.

25. Josef Wiesehöfer, *Ancient Persia: From 550 BC to 650 AD* (London: I.B. Tauris, 2001), ISBN:978-1-86064-675-1.

26. Tom Holland, *Persian Fire* (London: Abacus, 2005), 19.

27. Isabelle Broyer, UN Headquarters.

28. I have tried to read the Avesta in Persian (with some help from a native speaker of contemporary Farsi) and I have also read an English translation.

29. Zoroastrianism and the Resemblances between It and Christianity. A. V. Williams Jackson, *The Biblical World* 27, no. 5 (May 1906): 335–43 (9 pages), Footnote 3, 335.

30. Almut Hinze, "Change and Continuity in the Zoroastrian Tradition," *Inaugural Lecture*, February 22, 2012, Podcast viewed December 31, 2019.

31. See F. Spiegel, *Érânische Alterthumskunde I*, Leipzig, 1871, 700 n. 2; Justi, Namenbuch, s.v.; H. S. Nyberg, MO, 1929, 345; H. Lommel, *Die Religion Zarathustras*, Tübingen, 1930, 16. For later works see M. Mayrhofer, *Zum Namengut des Avesta*, Vienna, 1977, 10, n. 20.

32. Holland, *Persian Fire*, 35.

33. Roe Fremstedal, "In Two Places Mentions a Possible Link between Kierkegaard and Zoroastrianism: Eiriksson's Critique of Kierkegaard and Kierkegaard's (Drafted) Response: Religious Faith, Absurdity, and Rationality," in *Magnus Eiriksson: A Forgotten Contemporary of Kierkegaard*, eds. Gerhard Schreiber and Jon Stewart (Copenhagen: Museum Tusculanum Press, 2017), 145–66 and in "Kierkegaard's Double Movement of Faith and Kant's Moral Faith," *Religious Studies* 48, no. 2 (June 2012): 199–220.

34. Rabindranath Tagore and D. J. Irani, *The Gathas: The Hymns of Zarathustra*, file://localhost/Users/alisonassiter/Desktop/Entire%20text%20of%20Gathas%20 in%20HTML%20format%20(DJI).html.

35. Arthur Henry Bleeke (translator) from the anonymous Avesta (Hertford, printed for the Muncherjee Hormusjee C. M. by Stephen Austin, 1864). Bleeke gives a very useful and interesting history in his introduction to this version of the Avesta, of how the document came to be found, by a European and then re-translated from the original language, that he claims is akin to cotemporary Sanskrit and Persian.

36. For a useful summary of the Zoroastrian community worldwide today and a summary of its influences, see Almut Hinze, "Who are the Zoroastrians?," *British Academy Review* 28 (Summer 2016).

37. Change and Continuity in the Zoroastrianin Tradition, Almut Hintze Inaugural Lecture delivered in SOAS, February 22, 2012, 20.

38. Anonymous, Bleeke translation, *Avesta*, Arthur Henry Bleeke (Hertford, 1864).

39. Ibid.

40. https://lrc.la.utexas.edu/eieol/aveol/10, Lesson 1: Old Avestan Scott L. Harvey, Winfred P. Lehmann, and Jonathan Slocum.

41. Aquinas, *Summa Theologica*, Part I-I, Question 95, Article 1 (Fathers of the English Dominican Province, trans., Christian Classics, 1981), ST I-II, Q.95, A.II.

42. William Blackstone, *Commentaries on the Laws of England*, ed. Josepho Chitty, in 4 vols, 1979, 41.

43. J. Locke, *An Essay Concerning Toleration and Other Writings on Law and Politics, 1667–1675*, eds. J. R. Milton and Philip Milton (Oxford: Oxford University Press, 2006).

44. John Finnis, *Natural Law and Natural Rights* (Oxford: Clarendon Press, 1980).

45. See for example, Christine Littleton, "Reconstructing Sexual Equality," *California Law Review* 75, no. 4 (1290).

46. Ibid., 1291.

47. See Nira Yuval Davies and Pnina Werbner, eds., *Women, Citizenship and Difference* (London: Zed Books, 1999) and R. Lister, *Citizenship: Feminist Perspectives* (Basingstoke: Macmillan, 1997).

48. Pateman, *The Sexual Contract*, 1989.

49. Locke, *Two Treatises of Government*, 1970.

50. John Rawls, *A Theory of Justice* (Cambridge, MA: Harvard University Press, 1971).

51. See M. Sandel, *Liberalism and the Limits of Justice* (Cambridge: CUP, 1982) and, for a useful summary of the many criticisms of Rawls, see M. Sandel, *Liberalism and its Critics* (New York, NY: New York University Press, 1982).

52. John Rawls, "Introduction to the Paperback Edition," in *Political Liberalism* (Columbia, SA: Columbia University Press, 1993), xv1–xv11.

53. S. De Weitz, *Reasonableness, Pluralism and Justice: A Pragmatie Approach, Conference Volume, The Liberal Order: the Future for Social Justice* (Olomouc: Palacky University, 1999).

54. Michel Foucault, *Madness and Civilisation* (London and New York, NY: Routledge, 1965).

55. Ibid., 41.

56. Descartes, *Meditations*.

57. John Rawls, *Political Liberalism* (New York, NY: Columbia University Press, 1993).

58. Independent, Rachel Pells, t Correspondent@rachaelpells, Monday February 13, 2017, 12:19, accessed December 17, 2019.

59. See the work of ….

60. Nancy Fraser, *Unruly Discourse, Power, Discourse and Gender in Contemporary Social Theory* (Cambridge: Polity Press, 1989).

Chapter 6

Human Rights

Eurocentric and Westocentric?

I should like, in the rest of the book, to examine some very recent critiques of the concept of a right. The earlier critiques have been around for some time and have been widely discussed. Recent critics of the concept deride it as Eurocentric or Westocentric.[1] In this chapter, I will offer a response to a few of the key arguments through focussing mainly on one text, although I will consider related work en route. While I am responding primarily to some of the arguments of this one text, the points I will make are generic in form. The book on which I will focus here is called *What's Wrong with Rights?*[2] and its author is an academic, an ex-barrister and human rights activist. I believe that its author, D'Souza, helpfully challenges the notion of a right in a fashion that expresses many of the critical points that are commonly held among these recent critics of the notion.

In the following two chapters, I will concentrate on the work of one theorist in particular – Saba Mahmood. I focus on her work because she is a central figure in these debates. To quote Ratna Kapur on Mahmood:[3] 'Saba Mahmood's work marks a turning point in critical thought and has become part of the canon across a range of disciplines including Islamic studies, postcolonial and feminist theory as well as cultural anthropology. In opening space for thinking beyond the limits of the liberal imaginary, Saba's scholarship encouraged a radical reframing of intellectual thought'.[4]

Although her work has had a substantial following, perhaps partly because of her early and tragic death, there is little that specifically defends human rights against her trenchant critiques.[5]

I begin this chapter by considering some of the central arguments of D'Souza. Alongside an extensive knowledge of the system of human rights as practised over an extended period of time, D'Souza challenges the discourse and practice of human rights in a number of different ways. D'Souza makes many claims in her book, but I would like to distil the book down to what seem to me to be her central arguments and offer some challenges to these. I should state at the outset that I fully concur with D'Souza's stringent closing chapter and with her concluding claim that the huge questions posed, in the contemporary world, particularly for the world's poorer nations and peoples, 'invite considerations of the big questions in philosophy, such as ontology, epistemology, philosophical dualism and non-dualism, the philosophical and sociological foundations of modern science and technology and modern law and institutions'.[6] I hope I have gone some small way, in this book, towards developing such a philosophical underpinning for an alternative framework for universal thinking.

The first claim of D'Souza's on which I would like to focus is that the discourse of rights and the capitalist system are intrinsically connected. D'Souza doesn't put it quite so clearly but she certainly implies, throughout the book, a very strong connection between the two. 'The edifice of capitalism' she claims, 'rests on the tripod of Economy, State and Civil Society as distinct types of institutions'.[7] The relationships between these distinct domains are mediated, she argues, by law. The legal order that replaced feudal systems is 'understood within the rubric of the European Enlightenment'.[8] Rights, she claims, 'have always been an essential precondition for capitalism and colonialism'.[9] Capitalism, however, changes in character over history, and the system of 'human rights' is understood, she argues, very differently in the contemporary post-imperial and postcolonial context, from the way it was viewed at its onset.

I'd like first to focus on the claim that the system of rights goes hand in hand with the beginnings of capitalism. As D'Souza points out, the right of political freedom enshrined in early liberal rights thinking was supposed to 'unlock' economic freedoms.[10] Political freedoms were important in order to transform feudal constraints on property.

I agree that there are facets of human rights thinking that in fact helped promote the development of capitalism. However, it is also important to point out that there were other significant aspects even of European Enlightenment thinking[11] that concerned deeper issues than economic development. Enlightenment thinkers encouraged a belief in the significance of the individual – any individual – as a rational agent. As we have seen in earlier chapters of the book, this notion has its limitations. However the conception of Enlightenment rationality also went hand in hand with developments in medicine and inventions of machinery that had significant uses for people, from the compound microscope to the telescope. It challenged reliance on prejudice, external authority and simple adherence for its own sake, to tradition. Descartes, as the arch individualist thinker, was, in many respects, egalitarian in his outlook. He wrote in the vernacular, rather than

Latin, so that more people could read and understand his works and he argued that 'even women' were capable of engaging with his ideas.[12] Other Enlightenment thinkers, including Locke, Voltaire and Rousseau, focussed on the interests and the rights of individuals. Although Locke, for one, has been widely criticised for failing to universalise his notion of a human rights to women, slaves and non-property owners, to take three very significant groups of people, he did, nonetheless, as we have seen, attempt to ground the notion of a right in a moral order. Moreover, those who criticise Locke's concept of a right on the basis of its limited application –rejecting the whole concept because of Locke's view that 'Indians were unable to raise themselves to the level of the civilised part of mankind'[13] – are choosing to throw out the baby with the bathwater. Just to take two recent exemplifications of the notion of a right, the right to safety as well as to life[14] the former right is particularly significant in the present world, for those who are asylum seekers or refugees.

Moreover, it is also important to make a radically different kind of point that stems from the argument of the previous chapters. There is an element of each of us – the biological dimension – that is not exclusively shaped by social processes. There is always scope, then, to subvert these social processes. Bodies diverge and differentiate. As Elizabeth Grosz puts it, (the) 'body is the site of multiple struggles'.[15] Each individual is the result of many processes and powers and is never wholly shaped by just one set of powers. Individuals and groups always have the power to resist any form of social conditioning.

Moreover, and this second point applies also to another of D'Souza's criticisms of the concept of a right, as expressing certain needs, and in its quasi-legal expression, which is that it expresses the view of the European Enlightenment. As noted, though, the concept is not exclusive to European contexts and to the power of Europe. D'Souza argues that the concept of a right is absent in many non-European traditions. I would like to mention two further cases that challenge this view. Gita Sahgal,[16] for one, has forcefully challenged the view that a secular Universalist human rights perspective stems exclusively from European Enlightenment values and a European context. Indeed, she has argued that the movement in India that challenged the twin ills of colonialism and fundamentalist Hinduism was, and still is, the universalising discourse of human rights. Moreover, and relatedly, and as mentioned previously, Chetan Bhatt[17] has critiqued the ready connection of non-western with 'victim' and 'other'. He suggests an association of this with the simultaneous denial both of full subject-hood to the 'subaltern' or the 'non-western' and of the possibility that some such 'victims' might themselves also be attacking, for example, the secular spaces of Asian peoples. In a later chapter, I will refer to the work of Afia Zia[18] who challenges the ready critique of universalizing human rights discourse as western, by focusing on the use of the concept in the Pakistani context.

In a further response both to the point that the discourse of human rights goes hand in hand with capitalism and that it is a broadly 'westocentric' and imperial project, it is important to remember both the context and the composition of the drafting committee of the UN Declaration of Human Rights. The immediate reason for the Declaration, on the part of the signatories, was not to defend capitalism, but to provide a clear means for offering a legal and statutory condemnation of the atrocities committed by the Nazis prior to the Second World War.[19] Indeed one of the areas of disagreement among the signatories to the document was over whether or not the concept of a right ought to be understood in individualist or in collectivist terms. Those representing the 'communist' regimes of Eastern Europe favoured a more collectivist view while others preferred more of an individualist focus.[20]

Moreover the Convention Declaration was drafted not only by representatives of 'western' nations but also included Hansa Mehta from India, PC Chang of the Republic of China, Charles Malik from Lebanon, Hernàn Santa Cruz from Chile and Alexander Bogomolov from the Soviet Union.

The first three Articles concern broad and basic rights of the individual such as the right to life and the prohibition of slavery. It is surely difficult for anyone to challenge such rights and they clearly fit with the notion of a universal need or right. The whole declaration, which includes more controversial social and cultural rights, was adopted by the UN on 10 December 1948 with a vote of 48 to 0 (with eight abstentions that included the Kingdom of Saudi Arabia, the Ukrainian Soviet Socialist Republic and the Union of South Africa).

A further controversy at the time was whether or not the document constituted a legal framework or whether it rather had purely moral status. In fact it had no legal teeth until 1976 when the International Covenant on Civil and Political Rights came into force.[21]

Article 1, which lays down the philosophy on which the Declaration is based, reads: 'All human beings are born free and equal in dignity and rights. They are endowed with reason and conscience and should act towards one another in a spirit of brotherhood'. The article thus defines the basic assumptions of the Declaration: that the right to liberty and equality is 'man's' birthright and cannot be alienated: and that, because man is a rational and moral being, he is different from other creatures'.[22] This first Article then, offers a broad formulation of the nature of 'man'. The claim that 'man' is 'different from other creatures' may be read as implying that only humans have moral worth. But it might also be taken to imply a responsibility for other creatures in the natural world.

So the claim that the concept of a right is Westocentric or Eurocentric and that it is linked with the rise of capitalism is open to the above kinds of challenge. It might be responded, though, to the above points, that they are immaterial in the face of the power of imperial superpowers and the control they exert over postcolonial nations in particular. Moreover, there is a particular irony and moral problem with colonialism itself. How could it have been that the so-called 'liberal' powers treated colonial peoples so appallingly badly?[23] In particular, today, the power exercised by the United States gives the lie to any purported equality between nations in relation to the UN.

There is no doubt truth in the claim that there are nations, and in particular the United States, that are able to exert disproportionate power and force in the UN and in shaping some policies of the UN. However, it is important also not to go to the opposite extreme, which is what appears to be happening with the critics of the notion of a right and deny that it has any application at all outside the western context.

One might note, in that context, very large number of refugees and asylum seekers that exist in the present world – eighteen million according to a recent UNHCR report[24] – most of them outside the west and in developing countries. How does D' Souza's argument, as well as that of others, relate to them? If we removed the UN convention from the existing world, how would the world treat them? It is bad enough for them at the moment, with the increasingly hostile climate towards them in many parts of the world and with the extreme difficulty of gaining asylum in many western countries. But if there were no such system at all, would matters not be considerably worse for them? Moreover, the appalling failure to recognise the huge human rights violations, on the part of colonial nations towards the colonies, shows that there was a problem with those nations and not necessarily with the concept of a right.

I would like, at this point, to consider the argument of another writer who makes some connected points to those of D'Souza.[25] Costas Douzinas argues that the claim of human rights defenders like me that they are universal and cover the whole of humanity is 'a lie'. He writes: 'If that were the case, refugees, undocumented immigrants, the Guantanamo Bay prisoners who have no state or law to protect them should be prime beneficiaries of the consolations of humanity. They have very few. "Bare" humanity offers no protection and whoever claims to represent it lies.'[26] Once more however, the above point holds. If there were no rights at all, would any nation take in refugees? A further possible response to this is the one I have made a number of times: this shows not that there is a problem with the concept of universal human rights but rather that they have been improperly implemented by the colonial powers in the present world order and they may need to be substantially revised.

A further point made by D'Souza is that imperial and colonial regimes have exercised inordinate power in the expression of and defence of human rights.[27] Others have made similar claims. So, for example, Abdullahi An-Na'im- writes: 'The liberal scenario is paradoxical because it negates self-determination of poor countries in the name of protecting their human rights.'[28]

This relates to a further general claim of D'Souza's, the view that, as capitalism changes and develops, so does the discourse of human rights. Significantly, she argues, in the period of imperial capitalism, one of the themes of the discourse has been the imposition on postcolonial nations of the practice of monitoring elections. Postcolonial nations, she argues, struggled against imperial domination and they demanded not the 'legal right' to self-determination but rather the 'real thing' 'that the colonial powers pack up and leave'.[29] International election monitoring, she argues, has conflicted with the rights of postcolonial nations to self-determination. 'International election monitoring was resurrected in 1990 when the UN agreed to monitor elections in Nicaragua'.[30] IEM's (International Election Monitoring), she argues, turned the transitions from colonialism to independence on its head into international oversight over national independence. I'd like, first, to discuss the principle as D'Souza outlines it, and second to provide some examples of situations that may lead to a different conclusion from that drawn by her.

First, the principle which she puts thus: 'For the first time, in August 1989, the UN agreed to monitor elections held by a sovereign state.'[31] She argues that this represents a change from an early form of the charter, which prevented the UN from 'intervening in matters that are essentially within the domestic jurisdiction of a state'.[32] D'Souza argues that the move towards intervention in the affairs of sovereign states represented by this election monitoring 'was a fundamental shift in the two founding principles of international law: the sovereign equality of states and the principle of non-interference in the internal affairs of another state'.[33] The two principles, she claims, 'cut across the themes and values in classical liberal theory'.[34] The 'right to free and fair elections', she claims, actually does the opposite of what it purports to do and it in fact 'rolls back the rights to national self-determination, the basis for democracy in the third world'.[35] The IEM's, she suggests, were 'effectively initiatives in US led democracy promotion'.[36] She quotes Lenin on the need for national self-determination as a 'political claim'.[37] National sovereignty in the third world, she argues, derives from the anti-colonial struggles and functions differently from national sovereignty in the 'first world'. The 'third world' she suggests, developed a different model of statehood deriving partly from Mao's views on state formation and 'people's democracy'.[38] Sovereignty, in the 'third world' is based, she argues, on 'real political agreements between diverse races, tribes, nationalities, classes, religions and social groups'.[39]

I would like to raise a number of points about this, however. In general, the overall claim fails to recognise the inherent conflict that there is, at any time, between respecting the sovereignty of an individual state and respecting the basic rights of human beings. I will discuss her example – Nicaragua, once more – below. It seems to me that D'Souza veers too much, in her proper zeal to protect 'non-western' nations from interference from more powerful nations, in the direction of allowing such states to behave in unacceptable ways towards their citizens. She veers in the direction, moreover, of accepting anything that a 'third world' state might do, in their zeal to challenge the power of the United States, acting, she suggests, under the rubric of the UN or other international bodies, including the IMF, is acceptable. Because these various international bodies', including the LPG (Liquid Petroleum Gas) reforms worked together to undermine the 'third world' then D'Souza implies that anything 'third world' governments might do themselves to their citizens is implicitly acceptable.

One example of her doing the latter is the case of Nigeria. She writes that, in Nigeria, in opposition, this time to austerity programmes imposed by the IMF, local people went on strike. Then, in the wake of LPG reforms and in opposition to these, local people across four nations, including Nigeria, in 2002, formed Boko Haram, a movement that, as she puts it, 'viewed all western education as haram or forbidden'.[40] I will quote the following paragraph in full, for it encapsulates the core of my disagreement with her work, but also that of many others who make similar points in criticism of the concept of a right. She writes:

'Presumably in the absence of any other kind of knowledge or education, Western or otherwise, and where liberalism becomes synonymous with Western knowledge in the minds of the uneducated and disenfranchised poor, it was difficult for some at least to make sense of the re-scripted versions of rights and democracy that was being enacted in their name and in their nations. Boko Haram and others, most likely, relied on intuition to recognise something was not right in the theory and practices of rights and democracy when they declared Western education to be haram. If democracy was about the will of the people, why did their will matter so little?'[41]

I would like to make a few points about this. First, although D'Souza is not celebrating Boko Haram, she is not critiquing the organisation either. She is implying that human rights thinking is simply, by virtue of its association with the west and with western imperialism and capitalism, wrong. Correlatively she is valuing the opposite – in this case Boko Haram. She writes that they came to their views 'by intuition'. However, to quote other scholars from the field, Rasak Bamidele et al.:

Recently, Nigeria has witnessed a rise in the numbers of radical Islamic sects, notably among them is Boko Haram. These sects have resorted to the use of violence in a bid to realizing their ambitions of a wider Islamization of the Nigerian Population.[42]

To quote from a further piece on the Islamic fundamentalism of Boko Haram:

A curious feature of Nigeria is religious intolerance, especially in the Northern and the Middle Belt regions of the country. Religious fundamentalism in the Northern part of Nigeria has been hidebound and its spread is unbridled. For over two years, cities like Maiduguri, Bauchi, Damaturu and Gombe have worn a cloak of fear due to the Boko Haram insurgencies. Religious violence has been unleashed on many innocent citizens of this country.[43]

One problem, then, with instantly valorising groups that are formed in opposition to western imperialism is that the view fails to critique possible heinous acts committed by the groups themselves. It fails, also, to note that a group like Boko Haram was not formed purely from the seeds of innocent Nigerian soil. There were already, at the time of the earliest meetings of a group from which Boko Haram originated, at least two nations in the world and other groups that sought to label themselves nations that drew, as they did, upon principles of fundamentalist Islam. Indeed, a significant counter to her point that 'postcolonial nations' together drew on Marxism, is the case of Iran and other nations that seek to introduce sharia law. Instead of drawing on the Marxism of Eastern Europe, China or Cuba, Iran drew on fundamentalist Islam.

Let me reiterate with the utmost force that I am not celebrating imperial powers in making this point. As Derrida might have put it, it is all too easy to demarcate peoples into 'good' and 'evil' or 'friend' and 'foe'. D'Souza, perhaps inadvertently, appears to be valuing Boko Haram here, and devaluating the concept of a human right. I might be seen, by contrast, to be doing the opposite. It is difficult for me, as I have written previously, to critique Islam. Any critique of fundamentalist Islam could be turned, as Said put it, into 'a subtle and persistent prejudice against Arabo-Islamic peoples and their culture' and 'the aggressiveness necessitated by the colonial expansion of the European powers'.[44] I might be accused, therefore, by D'Souza and others, of defending an 'orientalist' perspective on Islam or a 'western' outlook. Many who demonise Islam also deny the great civilisations of the east when 'Europe slumbered in semi-darkness'.[45] The United States has, indeed, not only monitored elections in certain 'third world' nations but also condoned human rights abuses in other countries that it has supported – for example, Pakistan and Saudi Arabia.

I have a deep and abiding recognition of the atrocities committed by western powers, some of which are documented by D'Souza, and others take the form of further human rights abuses perpetrated by superpowers like the United States. The United States, indeed, is the only country in the world, apart from Somalia, not to have signed the UN Convention on the Rights of the Child.

However, that does not mean that we – people like me – who live in the west and who benefit from the relative democratic structures of the west, should not also critique some of the more horrific practices of Islamic and other religious fundamentalists.[46] According to one commentator, 'The word "fundamentalist" passed into English usage to describe those Muslims who seek, by whatever means, to establish an Islamic state'.[47] In Algeria and in Egypt, fundamentalists aimed to replace the 'sovereignty of the people with the sovereignty of God, as revealed through the Sharia'.[48] In Iran, a nation that has put fundamentalist Islam, through sharia law, into practice, according to Iranian women, gender apartheid has been the fundamental principle of the regime. At its heart, lies the principle of velayat-e-faqih. 'The role of the vali is like a child's guardian. There is no difference between the guardian of a nation and the guardian of a minor; their duties are the same'.[49] Quoting another 'women and men are equal in their human essence, but they are two different forms of humans, with two different sets of attributes and two different psyches'.[50] The notion that improperly veiled women are the source of sin is regularly promulgated in mosques and elsewhere.

The Iranian regime, since the 1979 Revolution, has sought to modify the UN Convention on the ground that it is a secular interpretation of the Judeo-Christian tradition. Muslims, it argues, should not accept the latter over the 'divine law of the country'.[51] Khomeini noted: 'What they call human rights is nothing but a collection of corrupt rules worked out by the Zionists to destroy all true religions.'[52]

It might be argued that a great deal has changed in Iran since 1979. However, it is important to note that, according to Amnesty International, these crimes continue apace. Amnesty International has condemned Iran on many occasions for extreme human rights violations. To take two examples: a 2004 report condemned the nation for 'hanging a 16-year-old for acts incompatible with chastity'[53] and in 2005 that, 'since 1990, 11 child "offenders" had been executed'.[54]

Boko Haram itself seeks to form an Islamic state. Contrary to D'Souza's view that the protagonists were acting on 'intuition', rather, according to a former governor of Niger, Dr Mu'azu Babangida Aliyu, in 1990, nine people went to a certain place in Niger, from outside the area, and claimed land from local village peoples. In a few years, their numbers had expanded to several thousand.[55] Boko Haram's nine-year-old fight to establish a hardline Islamic state has claimed at least 20,000 lives and displaced more than two million people.

Children have been targeted by the Islamists, who recruit boys and girls and indoctrinate them in order to replenish their ranks. In April, UNICEF claimed that over 1,000 minors had been abducted since 2013.

The military has been criticised by human rights organisations for conducting mass arrests of people suspected of ties with the group.

Amnesty International noted in a 2018 report that the military had held 'thousands of young men, women and children' in detention centres across the country.[56] In a very recent report in *The Guardian* UK, drawing on information from the Mines Advisory Group based in Maiduguri, that 'hundreds of people have been killed by landmines laid by Boko Haram'.[57]

Moreover, secondly, alongside the principle that D'Souza regards as an inappropriate extension of the powers of the UN, the following point was made by the then director general of the UN, Kofi Annan. He was recalling the failures of the Security Council to act in a decisive manner in Rwanda and the former Yugoslavia and he put forward a challenge to Member States: 'If humanitarian intervention is, indeed, an unacceptable assault on sovereignty, how should we respond to a Rwanda, to a Srebrenica, to gross and systematic violation of human rights that offend every precept of our common humanity?' The expression 'responsibility to protect' was first presented in the report of the International Commission on Intervention and State Sovereignty (ICISS), set up by the Canadian Government in December 2001. The Commission had been formed in response to Kofi Annan's question of when the international community must intervene for humanitarian purposes. Its report, 'The Responsibility to Protect', found that sovereignty not only gave a state the right to 'control' its affairs, but it also conferred on the state primary 'responsibility' for protecting the people within its borders. It proposed that when a state fails to protect its people – either through lack of ability or a lack of willingness – the responsibility shifts to the broader international community.[58] It may be relevant to note that Kofi Annan does not hail from a former colonial power. He is Ghanaian.

D'Souza herself is critical of the view that a set of principles has no pull on what she calls 'reality'. On a point of principle, then, if the UN Convention is to function at all as anything more than a set of concepts with no practical application, then it must have some ability to intervene in the affairs of a sovereign nation. I am not qualified, nor do I have the expertise or power, to consider the question of how this ought to happen. I am simply making the theoretical point that D'Souza may be wrong in her suggestion that the IEM cuts across themes and values in classical liberal theory. On the contrary, the UN was set up to protect the rights of individuals and sometimes this might entail monitoring the affairs of an individual state.

One example D'Souza gives of the inappropriateness of the procedures of what was effectively the United States, acting through the UN, is the case of Nicaragua. She writes: 'In February 1990 Nicaragua held the "election of the century".' For the first time, in August 1989, the UN, an international organisation founded on the legal principle of sovereignty of states, agreed to monitor elections conducted by a sovereign state.[59] Previously, the UN had refused to become involved in elections except when the elections formed part of the decolonisation project. The UN intervention in Nicaragua, she argues, violated the principle of the sovereign equality of states and the principle of non-interference in the internal affairs of another state. Now I have already suggested cases where these principles might, to all intense and purposes, be rightly seen to be open to challenge.

But to stick to the Nicaraguan case: this overseeing of national elections followed the failure of covert intervention in Nicaragua for many years. D'Souza points out that in 1984, the Republic of Nicaragua, under the Sandinistas, instituted legal proceedings under international law, in the International Court of Justice (ICJ), against the United States, arguing that the latter had illegally violated its sovereignty and political independence. D'Souza argues that the ICJ found that the United States had illegally violated the sovereignty of Nicaragua and ordered them to cease their activities. D'Souza claims, though, that the United States boycotted the proceedings and failed to respond to the Nicaraguan claims for reparations.

I would like to repeat the above theoretical point about this case. Even if it is accepted that the United States should not legally have been involved in the monitoring of elections in sovereign nations, and even if the above violation of the rights of Nicaragua was accepted as the wrong that they obviously are, this does not show that there is a problem with the language of rights. It shows, rather that there is a problem with power, with inequality and with the abuse of power. Even if, as is no doubt the case, in several places such as the justification for the war in Iraq, to take a different example, the discourse of human rights is used as a pretext for a war, that does not mean that the discourse of human rights is the problem. Indeed, a precisely parallel point might be made about the discourse of Marxism. Just because the discourse might or might not have been imperfectly applied in former Eastern Europe, this does not mean that Marxism itself is null and void.

But, to return to the Nicaraguan case, D'Souza argues that the Sandinista movement was both anti-imperialist and anti-authoritarian.[60] It was, she claims, a movement based on an alliance of diverse groups and classes against authoritarian rule.[61]

As a movement for postcolonial control from the US-backed Somoza regime, it is generally agreed that the Sandinistas succeeded against all odds, in gaining power from the brutal regime and its National Guards. The United States, under Carter, had taken a different view from that later pursued by Reagan and had argued, when pressed, that he should not interfere with the sovereign affairs of a foreign nation.[62] Indeed, the Carter regime gave aid to the Sandinistas in the early stages of their rule.[63]

The Sandinistas ruled Nicaragua from 1979 to 1990. They instituted a policy of mass literacy, devoted significant resources to health care and promoted gender equality but came under international criticism for human rights abuses, mass execution and oppression of indigenous peoples.[64]

D'Souza's claim that the Sandinistas were based on an alliance of 'diverse groups' though, is open to challenge. Another source claims that in the early years of their power they forced non-Marxists to resign from their cabinet.[65] After all, they had experience in guerrilla groups of many years, fighting the US-backed regime, of the need to maintain tight control over their units. It is important, therefore, just because they constituted a postcolonial nation, who had against all odds, come to power in South America, not to idealise either them or their achievements. Moreover, whatever the facts, D'Souza's claim that the US Congress approved, in the period of the election monitoring, a sum of 9 million US dollars to support the opposition candidate Violeta Chamorro, is again open to challenge from a different source. Kinzer claims that 'much of this wound up in the coffers of the Sandinista controlled Supreme Council'.[66] Moreover, according to Kinzer, the Sandinistas themselves officially had access to 6.4 million dollars, most of it from 'unidentified foreign donors'.

According to him, Violeta Chamorro, along with her husband who was assassinated in 1978, had run a newspaper that had relentlessly attacked the Somoza regime. She, along with her husband, had been an opposition activist and originally a Sandinista supporter. After the assassination of her husband, she became a powerful figurehead for the opposition movement against the Somoza regime. When the Sandinistas signed agreements in the early years of their time in power, with the Soviets, she disagreed with them and resigned her post in the government. So she was an unlikely figure for the CIA to devote huge resources to.[67]

In 1988, moreover, the country was in severe economic crisis. Perhaps these were in large part a result of the war but some would argue that they also resulted from Sandinista policies. There was massive currency devaluation, freezing of wages and prices and a huge desire for a change and for a new government. Leading radio commentators were regularly denouncing the Sandinistas.[68] Moreover, a further matter that is not mentioned by D'Souza is that with the demise of former communist Eastern Europe in the late 1980s, Nicaragua lost all but Cuba and North Korea of their former allies.

This period was devastating for their ally, Castro in Cuba, but it was even more so for them. They had to liberalise their regime or lose all hope of aid or trade from anywhere in the rest of the world. Chamorro, according to Kinzer, because she was not a member of any political party, was able to unite factions from different political groups. Kinzer claims, moreover, that the Sandinista leadership wanted the UN to monitor their election because they wanted it to be seen as legitimate by the rest of the world. According to Kinzer's sources, 55 per cent of the population voted for Chamorro, including Sandinista soldiers, and she promised to build a democratic republic as she and her husband had always dreamed of doing. To describe the first woman leader in the Americas, a lifelong opponent of Somoza's regime and a former Sandinista herself, as merely 'pro-US', as D'Souza does, seems somewhat unfair to her. Her movement comprised a coalition of forces and it included communists.

The Sandinistas were produced, at least in part, by western imperialism and colonialism. They came into being as a reaction to US imperialism and to the Contras interference in their country – Nicaragua.[69] They used guerrilla tactics to fight the Contras and, for a while, appeared to succeed in their aim of becoming the major power in Nicaragua. Whether or not the government they instigated was a force for good remains a moot point. There were some significant achievements and some failures. But they were real – the Sandinistas had their own agency and it would be inappropriate to hold US Imperialism or the UN Convention responsible for all of their acts. Similarly, to reiterate the point, it is inappropriate to deny any application at all for the concept of a right in a non-western context.

In this chapter, I have challenged a number of key claims that amount to a critique of the concept of a right, as they appear in a book by Radgar D'Souza. I have referred to other sources where relevant, that make similar claims to hers. I have suggested that, while it is obvious that there is a power imbalance among nations in the world and this gives UN members unequal power and, in particular, more power to the United States, it is important not to imagine that everything done by nations that are opponents of the United States is thereby immune from any criticism. It is important, to make a further general point, that attributing all pervasive causal power to imperial and colonial nations, over others, is to do what Chetan Bhatt, a postcolonial theorist, has suggested, and that is to deny causal agency to postcolonial powers and postcolonial peoples. It is overly one-sided to fail, in the cases outlined in this chapter, to attribute causal responsibility to, for example, Boko Haram or the Sandinistas, for their acts. Doing so, indeed, may lead either to despair about the possibility of challenging this super power or to idealisation of the postcolonial world. I would now like to move on, in chapter 7, to critique the views of another critic of the concept of a right – Saba Mahmood.

NOTES

1. See, for a number of examples: S. Prakash Sinha, "Human Rights: A Non-Western Viewpoint," *ARSP: Archiv für Rechts- und Sozialphilosophie/Archives for*

Philosophy of Law and Social Philosophy 67, no. 1 (1981): 76–91; Hakimeh Saghaye-Biria, "Decolonizing the 'Universal' Human Rights Regime: Questioning American Exceptionalism and Orientalism," *ReOrient* 4, no. 1 (2018): 59–77; Sebastian Bonnet, "Overcoming Eurocentrism in Human Rights: Postcolonial Critiques – Islamic Answers?" *Muslim World Journal of Human Rights* 12, no. 1 (2015): 1–24 (this is a critique of the liberal individualist focus of much human rights literature and a consideration of whether or not Islamic human rights might counter this. An edited collection Human Rights in Africa: a cross cultural perspectives (eds.) challenges the claim that human rights are Eurocentric).

2. Radgar D'Souza, *What's Wrong with Rights? Social Movements, Law and Liberal Imaginations* (London: Pluto Press, 2018).

3. Ratna Kapur, "The Radical Intellectual Legacy of Saba Mahmood," *Radical Philosophy* 2, no. 5 (Autumn 2019).

4. Ibid., 40.

5. One critic who challenges her as a cultural relativist is Sindre Bangsted, "Saba Mahmood and Anthropological Feminism After Virtue," *Theory Culture and Society* 28, no. 3 (May 2011).

6. D'Souza, *What's Wrong with Rights?*, 208.

7. Ibid., 46.

8. Ibid.

9. Ibid., 9.

10. Ibid., 16.

11. See, for example Cassirer.

12. Descartes, *Meditations*.

13. See Parekh 2000.

14. For a useful discussion of refugee rights issues, see Ahsan Ullah, *Refugee Politics in the Middle East and North Africa* (London: Palgrave Macmillan, 2014).

15. Elisabeth Grosz, *Volatile Bodies: Towards a Corporeal Feminism* (Bloomington, IN: Indiana University Press, 1994), 181.

16. Sahgal 2014, 67–83.

17. Bhatt 2006, 98–115.

18. Afia Zia, *Faith and Feminism in Pakistan* (Brighton: Sussex Academic Press, 2018).

19. See Michael Freeman, *Human Rights: A Very Short Introduction* (Cambridge: Polity Press, 2002), 35.

20. See Johannes Morskink, *The Universal Declaration of Human Rights* (Philadelphia, PA: University of Pennsylvania Press, 1999) and the papers on Human Rights and Columbia University. Universal Declaration of Human Rights. Final authorized text. *The British Library*, September 1952, Retrieved August 16, 2015.

21. Some of this is material sourced from https://en.wikipedia.org/wiki/Drafting_o f_the_Universal_Declaration_of_Human_Rights, accessed July 11, 18.

22. *Universal Declaration of Human Rights* (Article. 1), adopted by General Assembly resolution 217 A (III) of December 10, 1948, Printed at United Nations, Geneva, June 1996.

23. See, for example: Abdullah An-Na'im, "Human Rights and its Inherent Liberal Relativism," *Open Democracy*, August 25, 2014.

24. UNHCR 2014.

25. Costas Douzinas, "Human Rights and the Paradoxes of Liberalism," *Open Democracy*, August 7, 2014.

26. Ibid., 1.

27. There are a number of critiques related to this one – those who suggest that human rights are linked to colonial power. See, for example: An-Na'im, "Human Rights and its Inherent Liberal Relativism." Indeed, in a powerful piece on France and West Africa, Alice Conklin considers how it was possible for powerful colonial nations to subjugate colonies, using state sanctioned violence, at the same time as appearing to believe in liberal values. Alice L. Conklin, "Colonialism and Human Rights, A Contradiction in Terms? The Case of France and West Africa, 1895–1914, Colonialism and Human Rights, A Contradiction in Terms? The Case of France and West Africa, 1895–1914," *The American Historical Review* 103, no. 2 (April 1998): 419–442. Once more, though it seems to me that this illustrates a problem with the colonial nations and their failure to recognise the immorality of their practices, rather that with the concept of a right itself.

28. An-Naim, "Human Rights and its Inherent Liberal Relativism," 1.

29. D'Souza, *What's Wrong with Rights?*, 77.

30. Ibid., 82.

31. Ibid., 90

32. Quoted in Ibid. and taken from the UN Convention, Article 2(7).

33. De Souza, *What's Wrong with Rights?*, 90.

34. Ibid.

35. Ibid., 75.

36. Ibid., 82.

37. Ibid., 77.

38. Ibid., 79.

39. Ibid.

40. Ibid., 27.

41. Ibid.

42. Rasak Bamibele et al., "Fundamentalism, Boko Haram Movement and Socio-economic Development in North-Eastern Zone of Nigeria," *The Nigerian Journal of Sociology and Anthropology (NASA)* 16, no. 2 (2018): 93–111.

43. See Mashood Omotosho, "Dynamics of Religious Fundamentalism: A Survey of Boko Haram Insurgency in Northern Nigeria," *Journal of Philosophy, Culture and Religion* 4 (2015), www.iiste.org, ISSN:2422-8443, accessed December 31, 2019.

44. Edward Said, *Orientalism* (New York, NY: Pantheon, 1978).

45. Ali 2002, 101.

46. I am discussing the Islamic form of fundamentalism here since it is relevant to the discussion of Boko Haram. However, I could equally discuss Hindu or Christian fundamentalism both of which are on the rise at the present time.

47. Malise Ruthven, *Fundamentalism: The Search for Meaning* (Oxford: OUP, 2004), 5.

48. Ibid.

49. Chitsas, quoting Khomenei 2000.

50. Motahhari, quoted in Chitsas 2000.

51. See, for example, Littman 2003; also for a discussion of this, see Danesh 2018.

52. See Rieffer-Flanagan 2013 quoted in Danesh 2018.

53. Amnesty International Report 2004.

54. AI 2005 Report.

55. See http://dailypost.ng/2018/07/09/babangida-makes-shocking-revelations-or igin-boko-haram-nigeria/.

56. See https://www.news24.com/Africa/News/nigerias-army-releases-children -suspected-of-boko-haram-ties-20180709-2.

57. *The Guardian*, September 23, 2018, 17.

58. See www.un.org/en/preventgenocide/adviser/responsibility, Outreach Programme on the Rwanda Genocide and the United Nations: www.un.org/prevent-genocide/rwanda, Published by the Department of Public Information, March 2014.

59. Ibid., 89–90.

60. D'Souza, *What's Wrong with Rights?*, 90.

61. Ibid.

62. See Stephen Kinzer, *Blood of Brothers: Life and War in Nicaragua* (New York, NY: David Rockefeller Centre Series on Latin American Studies, Harvard University, 1991), 40.

63. See Ibid., 87.

64. See Amnesty International Reports but these were also critiqued as biased, see *The Morning Star*, February 26, 2019. Amnesty turns truth on its head in Nicaragua, report by Louise Richards.

65. Kinzer, *Blood of Brothers*, 61 and elsewhere.

66. Ibid., 390.

67. Ibid., Chapter 22.

68. See Ibid., 380.

69. See ibid., 388.

Chapter 7

Saba Mahmood

I have responded to critiques of essentialism and universalism from the perspective of the metaphysical theory developed at the beginning of the book. In a number of places apart from this book, I have defended a universalising perspective about humanity, a view that suggests that there are political and moral imperatives deriving from the fact of our universal humanity. I have argued that there are reasons why all groups, including feminists and those who are critical of the forms of need a perspective of universal humanity.

Chapter 4 responded to critiques of essentialism and universalism from the perspective of the metaphysical theory developed at the beginning of the book. I have also replied to some critics of the concept of a right in previous chapters. I would like, in this chapter and in chapter 8, to offer a response to one very specific and influential critique of universalism, secularism and the concept of a right and that is the work of the brilliant theorist, Saba Mahmood. Her work is finding considerable favour with many people including, especially, those who are sceptical about secularity. Indeed, as Afia Zia has pointed out, her voice is linked, alongside that of others, with a field of study – Islamic feminism.[1] Because of the influence of her subtle critique of the concept of a right, I would like to devote a couple of chapters to her work. In this chapter, and in chapter 8, I will engage with her books *Religious Difference in a Secular Age: A Minority Report* and *The Politics of Piety*.

Mahmood's work lies in a trajectory, deriving from the significant work of Foucault and Judith Butler, that is familiar at the present moment: this is one that decries the conception of human rights and the UN Declaration. as western and partial, as implicitly racist and sexist. Indeed, she goes further, to suggest, in Foucauldian vein, and like D'Souza, that the discourse of rights is produced by imperialism and colonialism. She adds to this, in

Religious Difference in a Secular Age, two further distinct claims: first that 'secularism' is directly connected to the formation of nation states and that, in former colonies, it cannot be disconnected from colonialism. Secondly, she claims that secularism and the twin notions of minority rights and the public/ private distinction implicitly ferment hatred of minority religious groupings. Moreover, the pretence of universality on the part of purportedly secular nations and their very claim to *secularity* disguise their actual commitment to a majority religion.

It is important to note at the outset of the chapter that Mahmood's brilliant writing represents the pinnacle of a body of work that challenges prominent western forms of binary framings of women's agency in majority Muslim nations. To take one example of such framings from another theorist, Abu-Lughod showed how the United States deployed the persecution of Muslim women by the Taliban, making their 'rescue' a justification for the invasion of Afghanistan.[2] There is no doubt that 'Orientalism' and racism against Muslims remain in these contexts. But the postcolonial lens that holds a pow- erful all-pervasive 'west' responsible for all the ills of these contexts is open to challenge. It is especially open to challenge in the contemporary context, where, as noted elsewhere in the book, the 'western, liberal imaginary' is itself under threat. Indeed, there is a specific threat in these Muslim-majority country contexts where religious norms prevail as the 'opposition' to the western imaginary. Some women, who use the 'rights discourse' in this con- text, have been termed 'immoral' in the Egyptian and other Middle Eastern contexts.[3] Moreover, it is not only Mahmood and some of her followers in the west who label human rights as 'western'. Ayesha Khan has pointed out, in her magisterial tome on the history of the women's movement in Pakistan, that women's rights activists in that country were labelled as 'westernised and corrupt' by 'the religious lobby, the mainstream press and educated classes'.[4] This was in the context of the Islamisation of the nation, under the regime of Zia-ul-Haq and where human rights activists were protesting against such things as women receiving sentences of stoning for 'adultery' (which was often rape) or discriminatory laws against women.

Indeed, as Mariz Tandros and Ayesha Khan put it; 'there are some glar- ing similarities in the binaries that have emerged in Western-based feminist post-colonialist literature and those that are deployed to counter the gen- der equality agenda within Southern contexts'.[5] Tandros and Khan are not claiming that western postcolonial feminists collude with fundamentalists in the Middle East, but rather they note that there are similarities in the two discourses.

In parallel to Mahmood's discourse there is also an alleged link between colonialism and the under-valuing of the environment. Ariel Salleh wrote: 'Eco-feminist politics .... is an ecology because it reintegrates humanity with nature; it is a postcolonial discourse because it focuses on deconstructing Eurocentric domination'.[6] Dominant forms of production, Salleh argues, are both Eurocentric and anti-life in all its forms. She critiques Marx and Engels's account of liberation through technological development. One aspect of her thinking that may resonate with that of Mahmood is that, like her, she critiques 'western' feminism, which she describes as white and middle class. She also, like Mahmood, saw western feminism as being aligned with Enlightenment thinking, which, she argues, downgrades women in general as well as postcolonial peoples and nature. Indeed, there is a strand of eco-feminism, which both values the body of humans, as I do, but that also celebrates what Shiva[7] described as 'indigenous' spiritual views that she viewed as marginalised in western knowledge.

Some aspects of these eco-feminist views have been critiqued as homogenising 'indigenous' cultures and peoples and exaggerating the extent to which women's activities as carers, which were also valued by some earlier eco-feminists, downplay the oppressive aspects of these practices. Moreover, if the concept of a right is reconstructed along the lines I have been suggesting in this book then it could involve a reconstructed conception of post-colonialism, of feminism and of environmentalism – rights to land, for example – for landless peasants. The natural world also, as I argued earlier, would be viewed as continuous with humanity rather than being viewed dualistically as radically other than the human.

In order to mount a further defence of the notion of a right, in this chapter and in chapter 8, I will engage in detail with the specifics of Mahmood's argument.

In her *Introduction* to her book, *Religious Difference in a Secular Age, A Minority Report*, Mahmood suggests, in support of her general claim, that the norms of European nations, which were purportedly universal and a-religious, were in fact substantively Christian. She quotes two sources in partial support of this latter claim: Habermas, on the one hand and, on the other, the decision of the European Court of Human Rights (ECHR): that upheld the right of Italian public schools to display the crucifix in classrooms. The latter reads as follows:

'Looking beyond appearances, it is possible to discern a thread linking the Christian revolution of two thousand years ago to the affirmation in Europe of the right to liberty of the person and to the key elements of the Enlightenment, namely the liberty and freedom of every person, the declarations of the rights of man, and ultimately the modern secular state. It can therefore be contended that in the present-day social reality the crucifix should be regarded not only as a symbol of a historical and cultural development, and therefore of the identity of our people, but also as a symbol of a value system: liberty, equality, human dignity and religious toleration and accordingly also of the secular nature of the state'.[8]

Clearly, given the argument of chapter 5, I would suggest that there is
another possible story about the origin of the concept of a right. However, I
would like also to respond to Mahmood on her own terms. I will therefore
continue, for now, with her argument. In the above context, she argues that
the fact of the majoritarian religion in much of the Middle East and in Egypt
in particular being Islam, should neither be seen as indicating that the east
improperly upholds secularism nor that Egypt is, in the respect to its actual
intertwining of religion and secularism, any different from the west. Egypt
is different from the west in that it is a postcolonial state and a state that
is therefore shaped in part by its colonial past, and it is also a state that is
informed by the principles of Islam. But the general similarity Mahmood
sees between west and east in regard to secularism is that in all cases, it is
the principle and practice of certain secular principles, themselves shaped
by Christian values, that has significantly shaped the treatment of minority
religions. She suggests that there is an important parallel between the treatment of Jews in Europe and that of the Copts in Egypt. Secular principles
did not help the Jews in Europe,[9] and, she argues, they have contributed to
the marginalisation of the Copts in Egypt. Germany, in the 1930s, deployed
largely Christian norms and values in the public sphere and these shaped its
implementation of Enlightenment liberal secular values. Egypt is a majority
Islamic nation and yet, Mahmood argues, its values are shaped by its colonial
and Christian history. Upholding the colonial Christian and 'liberal secular'
principles, in Egypt today, Coptic Christians must follow, in public, the
secular and Islamic codes of the nation, while in private they can theoretically practice their religion. This privatising of their religion contributed to
destroying their cultural heritage. Ironically, then, it is implicitly Christian
values, according to Mahmood, that contributed to undermining Christianity
in Egypt.[10] Specifically, as she puts it, in a deeply significant section of her
book on the history of colonial influence on the formation of national groupings: 'The political imaginary of Copts and Muslims alike at the turn of the
twentieth century had become saturated with European depictions of Islam
and Christianity. Just as the European discourse on race and eugenics under-
girded the Coptic claim to racial purity, the western portrayal of Islam as a
barbaric and uncivilised religion was the foil against which declarations of
Muslim glory were crafted'.[11]

Mahmood quotes Marx in *On the Jewish Question* and endorses his suggestion that Jews will only be fully emancipated when religion is no longer the
spirit of civil society.[12] She supports his claim that the hidden Christian religi-
osity of many nation states disguises and masks the actual inequalities between
religious identities when it presents all citizens as equal before the law.

Mahmood sometimes claims that she is not necessarily critiquing secularism as a set of ideals, but she is rather engaged in an ethnographic study of

the way in which secularist principles have shaped the life of modern day nations and of Egypt in particular. She argues that the birth of the concept of religious liberty as well as the concept of 'minority rights' is bound up with the establishment of the principle of state sovereignty. For example: 'In modern Egypt the demand for minority rights (or opposition to it) has always been entangled with the struggle for national sovereignty, and never autonomous of the concepts, practices and policies that Western powers promoted'.[13] Christian European states, she suggests, used their authority, with the demise of the Ottoman Empire in the nineteenth century, to force Muslim-majority states to grant special privileges to non-Muslims that were not reciprocated in majority Christian states. She implies that, in the earlier period of dominance by the Ottoman Empire, that empire, despite it being forged upon a high degree of inequality, did not force non-Muslims to convert to Islam, unlike Christian states that compelled non-Christians to covert.[14] She argues that the principle of political equality, when it was applied in the former Ottoman Empire, came alongside a decline in communal autonomy when non-Muslim minorities were forced to proclaim allegiance to the newly formed nation states. In the nineteenth century, furthermore, Protestant missionaries made 'Orientalist' assumptions about Christian minorities in the Middle East and regarded them as in need of redemption from the weight of custom and tradition. In this process, they deployed the notion of an individual right to religious liberty.

She argues that this colonial Christian evangelical root in human rights discourse continues into the twentieth century. Article 18 of the UDHR deploys a conception of religious liberty that was the result of a campaign by American evangelicals and European missionaries.

It is, as noted, two specific secular principles Mahmood objects to. One is the concept of individual religious liberty and alongside this is her parallel critique of the notion of a minority grouping. She quotes Hannah Arendt who states that the concept of a minority did not exist outside the recently formed conception of the nation state.[15] Mahmood argues, indeed, following others, that the concept of a minority is a complex and paradoxical notion. 'For a minority to draw attention to its plight it must necessarily highlight its difference from the nation, exacerbating the fissure that produces the groups exclusion in the first place'.[16] The concept presupposes that the group subjectively 'embraces a shared sense of collective discrimination'.[17] If the minority, she suggests, is to assimilate into the dominant national collectivity, then that would presuppose the attenuation or abandonment of values that are crucial to the identity of the dominant grouping.

A very important component of Mahmood's argument, then, is that it is the twin discourses of 'minority rights' specifically to religious identity and of the 'public' and the 'private' domains that, rather than ameliorating already existing tensions and inequalities, in fact exacerbated them. In modern Egypt, the demand for minority religious rights is inextricably entangled with the struggle for national sovereignty and western discourses and powers were tied up with this latter struggle. The political discourse, she argues, of Egypt was entangled with European conceptions of Islam and Christianity. European claims about racial purity affected Coptic and other perceptions of Christianity in Egypt while views of Islam were coloured by European depictions of it as barbaric and primitive.

To take an illustrative example: these two secularist discourses functioned both to exclude Copts from their requested (in 1919) positions on government bodies on the ground that Egypt was a 'majority' Muslim country and also narrowed previous normative religious identity to purely private and family matters. A particularly astute example of this is a Coptic leader in the Wafd party in the early twentieth century, who claimed that he was a Muslim by country and a Christian by religion.

This chapter will continue with some critical discussion of Mahmood's thinking in this seminal text of hers. In the chapter following, I will engage, in more detail, with *The Politics of Piety*. In the latter book, Mahmood celebrates Muslim women who re-discover, in a critical engagement with western liberal conceptions of agency, the values of piety and submission. She challenges, in light of these women's practices, the 'secular' 'progressive' values of what she sees as the western and liberal feminist movement.

CRITICAL DISCUSSION OF MAHMOOD – ANOTHER READING OF THE HISTORY

It is possible, and indeed necessary, to challenge Mahmood's reading of history. Her work moves in two directions. One the one hand, as a good anthropologist, she is careful to suggest that she is investigating only one particular cultural grouping – the Copts in Egypt. Yet, on the other, she is clearly providing a general historical overview and critique of the history of colonialism and imperialism and of the Christian root of purportedly secular principles and her work has certainly been read in this latter manner.

Mahmood offers a convincing historiographical account that holds 'secularism' and its Christian root as significantly responsible for the treatment of the Copts in Egypt. However, there is a risk that this kind of account, while it is a clearly a major component of the history, underplays the agency of some of the figures who were partially produced by this colonial history, in similar fashion to the underplaying characterised in the last chapter of the Sandinistas in Nicaragua. It also leaves a crucial question unanswered. Mahmood notes, '(Secularism) entails a re-ordering and remaking of religious life in

accordance with specific norms' and 'the secularist hope that a truly secular-
ised state will deliver us from religious conflict and prejudice is premised on a
fundamental misunderstanding of what exactly the state is (or can be) neutral
towards'.[18] This is fine, but it leaves open the question of what Mahmood
sees, normatively, as the alternative to secularism? Secular principles that at
least in theory advocate tolerance and the rule of law, are surely precondi-
tions for engaging in further struggle for greater levels of equality. When we
see the reactions of some dictatorial governments in the world today, towards
individuals and groups who advocate greater equality and receive at best a
severe prison sentence and at worst get killed, is secularism not preferable?
Moreover, perhaps Mahmood did not live to see the kinds of extreme threats
secularist principles have undergone in recent years.

I concur with Marx's claim, quoted above, as a statement of an ideal.
However, it seems to me, by contrast to Mahmood, that secular principles
of human rights constitute a precondition for this kind of dramatic change.
As the former British MP Rory Stewart recently wrote: 'The assumptions of
liberal democracy that seemed so solid as recently as the Obama presidency,
are shattered'.[19] He writes that this seems to be a global phenomenon. If they
are shattered will religion not take over their role? Mahmood suggests that,
in fact, secular principles have been shaped by their Christian underpinning.
But would not religious principles without their secularist clothing be worse?

A BRIEF ACCOUNT OF THE HISTORY OF A
DIFFERENT MUSLIM-MAJORITY NATION

I would like to begin the critical discussion of Mahmood's work by outlining
the work of a theorist whose work I have referred to earlier in the book and
also earlier in this chapter – Ayesha Khan. She, like Mahmood, is discussing a postcolonial, majority Muslim, country. However, in contrast to the
work of Mahmood, not only does Khan not hold the 'secular' principles of
human rights responsible for the ills of Pakistan, but she sees them as key
to challenging many of the problems in her nation. As noted, in her book,
The Women's Movement in Pakistan, Activism, Islam and Democracy, Khan
offers a detailed and comprehensive history of what she calls the 'women's
movement' in Pakistan. Unlike Mahmood's women, however, throughout her
book, the women celebrated by Khan comprise a secular, human rights-based
minority movement. Again unlike Mahmood's 'pious' women, the WAF in
Pakistan (Women's Action Forum) critiqued and opposed the creation and
the extreme practices of the Islamisation movement of General Zia-ul-Haq
(who ruled Pakistan from 1977–1988) and some of his followers. The women
wanted to resist such fundamentalist practices as the imposition of sharia

law, which, for example, led to the persecution of non-Muslims, through the blasphemy laws. In relation to the distinction much critiqued by Mahmood, the public/private distinction, Khan writes, 'The 1979 policy (of Zia) upheld the division of public/private and gender roles but placed extra emphasis upon women as "guardians of tradition, culture and morals" in opposition to "an immoral, threatening and intrusive west". Women became the markers of "national" morality.'[20] Women therefore, through the Islamic regimes interpretation of the public/private distinction, were construed as being more unequal than they would be in western contexts. Moreover, in Khan's account, it was not the oppositional Muslim women who celebrated Islam against a regime that deployed concepts from the misguided western human rights discourse, but it was rather the Islamic regimes of Pakistan, and particularly that of Zia, that set out to inculcate a suspicion of the west.[21] Indeed, when we get to a later period in Pakistan's history, according to Khan, in 2002, when there was an religious alliance of various 'Muslim' groups, under Musharraf, these groups 'used a rhetoric of "us", a moral community of pious Muslims who followed their interpretation of religion, ritual, dress and distaste of arts and culture, versus "them", a shifting, nebulous group of non-Muslims and/or bad/Muslims'.[22] This was, ironically but perhaps not surprisingly to those who understand these things, at the same time as the various Islamic parties were 'allies of the Americans'. Indeed, Khan argues that Zia earlier had gone so far as to 'infuse' textbooks in schools, 'with a deep suspicion of science and secular knowledge which worked well with a growing distrust of the west and its immorality'.[23] Rather than, as with Mahmood, the feminist women rejecting western notions, instead the women's movement in Pakistan challenged (bravely and in ways that were often at extreme risk to themselves) the Islamisation of Pakistan which warned them to 'beware the pernicious influences abroad'.[24] This became more difficult for them under Musharraf. His alliance of Muslim groups, including the majority group Jamiat-Ulema-e-Islam, whose *madrasas* had trained the Taliban, instituted such measures as 'blackening out women's faces on billboards', 'banning male doctors and technicians from performing ultrasounds on women' and 'in some areas, banning women from working in public call offices because they aroused immoral urges in men who saw them'.[25] Indeed, Khan points out that it was particularly difficult for them during the 'reign' of Musharraf whose 'fundamentalism' (my word) was less apparent than that of Zia. On one occasion, Musharraf was under pressure from the United States to reign in the Taliban and al-Qaeda. One way in which Musharraf attempted to do this was to streamline the *madrasas* that he believed were fermenting intolerance. So the army killed the insurgents and broke up their secret tunnels. But the *madrassas* fought back, sometimes using women and children as shields. Clearly there was sympathy within Pakistan for the militias in the *madrassas* fighting the army. But WAF had to remind people of what had been happening in the *madrasa* where children were taught anti-state ideology and were given military training.[26]

Khan does note that there were women activists in WAF, who were wary of rejecting Islam altogether and who initiated conversations about the compatibility of human rights discourse and Islam. But she argues that the primary focus of WAF remained that of campaigning in Pakistan for human rights, even if these rights had to be adapted to the local context. It is also important to point out that there are, in Pakistan's constitution, unlike that of more extreme Islamic states, provisions for individual liberty and the prohibition of slavery. The constitution requires a two-thirds majority to change any of the provisions, though, which made it difficult for Benazir Bhutto's government to repeal some of the more fundamentalist clauses. It also led to some of the more ostensibly bizarre incidents where a group of women, under Musharraf's rule, dressed in full black nikab came out into the streets to force music shops to close as 'un-Islamic'. Along with male colleagues, they abducted three Chinese women from a massage parlour and formed their own 'department of vice and virtue'. They issued full dress codes and instructed the government to introduce full sharia or they would commit suicide.[27] The WAF women and others obviously reacted against this, however.

FURTHER CRITICAL COMMENTARY ON MAHMOOD

Khan offers an alternative history of a Muslim-majority nation from that of Mahmood. A different point that it is important to make is that each one of Mahmood's 'constructivist' arguments – to the effect that there is a one way causal influence – analogous to Butler's argument about compulsory heterosexuality giving rise to the notion of woman – can be critiqued theoretically as overly one-sided. Each one of us, and each historical period, comprises many different elements – at least biological, cultural, religious and social. Given that, according to the argument of this book, each one of us is a vital material, desiring being, comprising many intersecting and conflicting forces, there is always room for resistance and challenge to the causal processes outlined by Mahmood. As she points out, the Copts were shaped and influenced by the colonial history. Yet they, as well as Muslims in Egypt, are also shaped by other influences as well as by their own agency.

In accordance with this point, Mahmood underplays the role of agents created by the context she outlines in Egypt: recently, the Muslim Brotherhood is known to have incited their followers to attack Christians and their churches have been looted and torched.[28] Mahmood's subtle and significant analysis remains normatively one-sided. While colonialism, the imperfect application of secular principles and Christianity are significantly normatively responsible for the situation in Egypt today, the individuals and groupings created by this history have their own agency and their own responsibility for some of the horrors we have seen in Egypt in recent years.

Mariz Tandros has documented some of these. In her book, *The Muslim Brotherhood in Contemporary Egypt: Democracy re-defined or Confined*,[29] she offers a contextual history of the Muslim Brotherhood. She describes it as being concerned (like the case of Pakistan) with the 'Islamisation of society' which would serve as a precursor 'for the establishment of an Islamic state'.[30] In its turn, the latter would be based not on normative precepts that are subject to change and development but rather on the will of God. She claims further that when the Muslim Brotherhood came briefly to power, it attempted to modify its discourse under a nominal liberal outlook but that this was undermined by its more significant commitment to norms governed by a divine power. Although her analysis has been challenged, for example in a review by Gerasimos Tsourapas,[31] some facts are more difficult to challenge.

In a piece in *Open Democracy*,[32] Tandros writes:

On 9 April 2017, in the second largest church in the city of Tanta, a suicide bomber approached the alter and blew himself up. At least 29 people were killed and 71 injured, some gravely. Three hours later, a suicide bomber tried to enter St Mark's Church in Alexandria where Pope Tawadros, head of the Coptic Orthodox Church, was presiding over a service. The man was stopped by police, and detonated his bomb outside. At least 18 people died, with 35 wounded.[33]

She notes that there had also been attacks previously, in 2011 for example. But she argues that the bombings in Cairo, Tanta and Alexandria were different from previous attacks in significant ways – and they were each preceded by threats from the ISIS.

She further writes: 'Again the December 2016 and April 2017 bombings of churches mark a new shift in the religious targeting of Copts that is qualitatively different. The actors, ways of striking and intended outcomes of attacks have all expanded. ISIS has vowed to pursue a campaign of annihilating the Copts and with every bloody terrorist attack they believe they are progressing towards that goal'. 'We are no longer dealing with local Salafi groups obstructing Copts from praying in a local church or fanatical mobs burning Christian homes and property or even a state that resorts to divide and rule policies to detract attention from its governance failures. ISIS is not a national entity – it has cells across borders'. 'It is a global actor, well-networked and resourced with a wide array of splinter cells across borders'.[34]

It might be argued though that it is misleading to associate the Brotherhood with these attacks since the latter were inspired by the ISIS rather than by the Muslim Brotherhood. The Muslim Brotherhood, by contrast to ISIS, has publicly committed itself to a non-violent Salafist ideology. Yet, according to the Counter-Extremism project in the United Kingdom, the two groups share a 'vision of a global caliphate governed by Islamic law'.[35]

Recruiters to violent Islamist groups also frequently use Brotherhood literature and ideology as a part of their religious indoctrination programme for potential recruits, who then easily transition to overtly violent jihadist groups such as al-Qaeda and ISIS.[36]

One might argue, along Mahmoodian lines, that the behaviour of the Brotherhood is ultimately rooted in the rejection of the imposition of secular principles upon countries including Egypt. So, according to this argument, the Brotherhood arose in part because of secularism. This point is made by Stephen Cowden and Gita Sahgal in their piece *Why Fundamentalism?* quoting Bruce Lawrence, who 'has argued in his 1987 book *Defenders of God: the Fundamentalist Revolt against the Modern Age* that while … (fundamentalist) movements exist within Christian, Jewish and Islamic traditions, they can be collectively characterised as 'fundamentalist' on the basis of their common rejection of the legacy of Enlightenment reason and a corresponding belief in the 'morally corrosive' impact of modernity'.[37]

Bruce claims that the Enlightenment and modernity, 'rather than being a specifically Christian or Western experience, have impacted on Jews and Judaism within Europe and on Islam through the colonisation of Asia, Africa and the Middle East'.[38]

Further, Chetan Bhatt claims that the view that fundamentalist Hinduism as well as fundamentalist Islam were both hermetically sealed from 'contamination by the west' is a claim made both by fundamentalists and by 'orientalist' assumptions about the east. He suggests that the fact that the notions mirror one another, signifying positively on the one hand and as a sign of inferiority and backwardness in the latter, points to religious fundamentalism itself being a product of modernity.[39] Bhatt notes that while the two 'fundamentalist' movements *Hindutva* and the *Jamaat-e-Islami* both emerged from different faith traditions, both developed in India in the first half of the twentieth century and appealed in very similar ways to the 'fundamental truths' of the Vedas or the Qu'ran, rejecting secularism as 'Western'.

It is highly probable, then, that the fundamentalism of the Brotherhood is, as noted earlier, partially a product of western and Enlightenment values. However, it doesn't follow from this either that secularism is itself at fault or that the Muslim Brotherhood does not have its own agency. Even if secular values, read through the lens of Christian colonialism, partially gave rise to the forms of fundamentalist religion described above, it doesn't follow that those values themselves are misguided or wrong any more than the fact of the Brotherhood being a reaction to imperialism shows that its values are right or good. The implementation of secular values in Egypt might have been partial or misguided. However, to proclaim that, in the above case, the Egyptian Muslim Brotherhood holds no responsibility for the attacks on Copts is to treat the Brotherhood as lacking in agency in a way that Mahmood herself, following her desire to re-evaluate the agency of the very different pious women of Egypt, in *The Politics of Piety*, would reject.

Continuing in the same trajectory, a further radically different historical account of the roots of attacks on minority groups from that of Mahmood is given by Mark Sedgwick in his book *Against the Modern World*.[40] Rather than holding secularism responsible for some of the worst tragedies of the twentieth century, Sedgwick suggests that it is the very challenge to secularist ideals that is responsible for these events. The book provides a powerful and interesting history of 'Traditionalism' – a body of ideas stemming from the work of a philosopher, Guénon – who was working in the early twentieth century and whose work combined a very specific reading of Hinduism, reducing it to the Vedanta, with some insights from Marsilio Ficino. The latter was a medieval priest who combined Platonism and Christianity.

Guénon used the concept of 'inversion' to describe aspects of what he saw as the decline of the modern world. Like Mahmood, Guénon critiqued the 'illusions' of reason, progress and change. He wanted to avert what he saw as the 'extinction' of the west. The 'extinction' was to be avoided by 'receiving traditional teaching by the restoration of oriental doctrines so as to push the west towards the restoration of traditional civilisations'.[41] He was specifically critical of such 'western' practices as (to use contemporary examples) 'youth fashions as opposed to self-restraint'. 'Western' civilisation was materialistic and had lost values that stem from the European Middle Ages.[42]

A key period in Guénon's intellectual development, according to Sedgwick, took place in Egypt. In 1930, Guénon moved from Paris to Cairo, and it was in this phase of his life that 'traditionalism' became a movement.[43] In the 1930s Cairo was not a particularly Islamic city but there were a number of pious Muslims who were not westernised and their lives were not much touched by modernity. In Cairo, Guénon lived as a pious Muslim and a Sufi. According to Sedgwick, he neither had little contact with 'traditional' Egyptian Muslims nor did he have much to do with intellectuals in the city at the time. But his period in Egypt, practising as a pious Muslim, contributed significantly to his 'idealisation of tradition'[44] and gave him some direct experience to inform his early idealised picture of the East. Just as Mahmood stresses in her book *The Politics of Piety*, the significance of religious practice in daily life, so too did Guénon recognise and appreciate that fact from his period living in Egypt.

Sedgwick traces the influence of 'traditionalist' ideas on European fascism and on the Islamic Revolution in Iran, among other areas. He is careful to note that the influences of these various thinkers on particular political movements

were not direct. However, he notes a number of connections between traditionalist thinkers and fascism. Sedgwick's book discusses various attempts,
over the course of the twentieth century, to put Guénon's project into action
– to restore 'traditional civilisation' to the west.[45]

Although Sedgwick does not make this point, it is worth pointing out that
the period when Guénon lived in Cairo was the period when the Muslim
Brotherhood began operating in Egypt. The Brotherhood in fact had strong
ties in the period with the Nazis and they are reported to have disseminated
copies of *Mein Kampf* as well as copies of *The Protocols of the Elders of
Zion*. These texts were seen as contributing to negative views not only of
Jews but of 'western' societies more generally.[46]

The Brotherhood not only pointed to the corrupting influence of 'Western
culture', but advocated avoiding Western dress, 'neckties, laughter, the use
of Western forms of salutation, handshakes, applause', discouraging but not
forbidding other activities such as sports, ideally limiting the Muslim public
space to 'the family and the mosque'.[47]

In the final chapter of his carefully researched book, Sedgwick notes that
Guénon's ideas, while not original, synthesise a number of elements in a
somewhat unusual way. One of the themes for which he became known is
the view that Wisdom originates somewhere in the east, as opposed to the
west. Hinduism and Perennialism (represented by Ficino) were the specific
ingredients of Guénon's philosophical outlook, but others deployed elements
from Sufism and Taoism. Sedgwick argues that 'traditionalism' has something in common with 'Orientalism' as developed by Said. It is, Sedgwick
suggests, the flip side of the coin of Orientalism. Said showed how much
western understanding of 'the east' owed more to the self-understanding of
the west than to anything that actually existed. Traditionalism, Sedgwick
argues, is the counterpoint of Orientalism. It is the inverse of Orientalism
in that while Orientalism downplays the east, traditionalism, drawing on the
same somewhat mythical idea of the East, applauds the latter. He writes:
'Traditionalism contrasts a West characterised by modernity, materialism and
mere technical skills to a Middle East of tradition, spirituality and wisdom.
This understanding of the East is arguably no more accurate than that of the
classic Orientalist'.[48]

Sedgwick suggests that there were many who might be described as 'traditionalists' who did not adopt any of the dubious political ideas outlined above.
But, he notes: 'The entire field of contemporary religious studies (of which
he himself is part) bears the imprint of Eliade's (another follower of some
of the aspects of the above thought) "soft traditionalism" and "many leading
scholars have been traditionalists".'[49] Sedgwick also suggests that many of
the critics of traditionalism, including the original referee of Guénon's PhD,
who failed it, have not treated them as serious scholars. He suggests, also,

that their work has much in common with postmodernism, in their respective rejections of modernist ideas of 'science, rationalism and objectivity'.[50]

On the one hand, therefore, Mahmood's criticisms of secularism have much in common with the thinking of Guenon and Evola. This is not, of course, to claim that she herself was linked to fascism or fundamentalism , but her thesis, insofar as it challenges the notions of 'Enlightenment reason' and 'rights' has much in common with that of the thinkers mentioned above. Moreover, on the other hand, while there may be something in some of her claims about the notion of a 'minority' religion, it seems farfetched to blame the treatment of the Copts wholly on secularism as a set of practices and principles rather than also and more significantly on the more clear-cut and well-documented acts of some of the fundamentalists in the country. In their turn, then, a significant influence upon these fundamentalists was not only a reaction to the Enlightenment form of secularism but also these Nazi- and fascist-inspired ideas. Extending Sedgwick's analysis, from the cases he discusses, to other parallel cases would suggest that a major component of the cause of the mistreatment of the Copts in Egypt, then, according to this alternative reading of the history from that of Mahmood, was therefore the circulation of ideas within the Muslim Brotherhood and therefore within Egypt more widely that connect with Fascism and Nazism. Secularism, on this alternative reading, then, not only was not primarily responsible for the treatment of the Copts but rather provided something of a counterweight to the circulation of ideas that had a much more sinister focus.

SOME FURTHER CRITICAL
DISCUSSION OF MAHMOOD

I would like, additionally, to challenge some of the particular arguments of Mahmood's. In her chapter *Religious and Civil Inequality*,[51] she claims that the poor treatment of the Bahai peoples in Egypt is a direct result of the secular distinction between 'public' and 'private' rather than being due to the implementation of sharia law. She claims, in partial support of this, that exactly the same treatment is meted out to representatives of minority religions in Christian-majority nations. Her argument runs as follows: 'The Bahais in Egypt combine monotheistic and non-monotheistic beliefs and their views run counter to a state that recognises only monotheistic religions. They constitute only about 1% of the population of Egypt. Securing public order, she argues, allows states to restrict the basic rights of citizens when they are deemed to 'threaten the moral and legal cohesion of a given society'.[52] She argues that this power is deployed equally in states such as Egypt and European states. In the specific case of the Bahais, their religion, as noted, is not formally recognised. Yet, when they complete a national identity card, they are required to complete a section that asks them to state their religion. Publicly, Mahmood notes, their religion is not recognised, and yet they are required to have this card and required to complete this section of it. She quotes various rulings both for and against them being required to mention their religion in this context. One ruling required Bahais to complete this section of the card precisely in order to recognise their *inequality* in the eyes of Egyptian society which is majority Muslim. A later ruling overturned this and prevented the Bahais from listing their religion but this time on the ground that the law *prohibited* the expression in public of this non-Muslim and non-monotheistic religion. The ruling, she argues, is Islamic but the discriminatory notion depends upon the secular notion of the right to enforce public order.

Mahmood suggests that there is a precisely parallel treatment of a minority religion when a dual Finnish and Italian citizen in 2011 argued in Italy, that the compulsory display of crucifixes in schools violated her son's rights to freedom of conscience, thought and religion proposed in Article 9 (1) of the ECHR. The woman lost her case (although one court did support her) and the grounds used were that the public order clause allowed the display of 'majority' religious symbols in public. Schools were allowed to 'perpetuate the traditions and culture' of the nation, in public.[53]

I would like to make a number of points about this. First of all, Mahmood has chosen to focus on the 'public/private' distinction in order to support her case. She might, however, equally have chosen to concentrate on the religious aspects of the rulings. Even if we allow that a factor in the decision was the distinction between public and private, it is still the religion that superimposed on the secular. So it is odd to blame *secularity* for the rulings. The public order rulings favour a majority *religious* culture. A truly secular state would have tried harder to get rid of Christianity in the Italian case and Islam in the Egyptian instance.

Furthermore, and this is a very important point: the notion of a public order defence was outlined by J. S. Mill to prevent serious disruption in public. To quote from *On Liberty*:

'An opinion that corn-dealers are starvers of the poor, or that private property is robbery, ought to be unmolested when simply circulated through the press, but may justly incur punishment when delivered orally to an excited mob assembled before the house of a corn-dealer, or when handed about among the same mob in the form of a placard'.[54]

It is farfetched to claim that the Bahais, at 1 per cent of the population of Egypt and by requesting a legitimate identity card, posed a threat to public order. So using the public order defence in this way does not indicate a problem with secularism. Rather it suggests an inappropriate application of

the public order defence. The Italian case is not parallel – there is no preven-
tion of a minority religious action using the public order defence. The only
parallel between the cases is that both involve the use of purportedly secular
principles to defend a majority religion. So again, it is odd to claim that the
problem is secularism. Overall, then, it seems that Mahmood may sometimes
be reading history with a predisposition to see a problem with secularity,
when in fact the problem, is, as many other scholars have pointed out, much
more plausibly read as a problem with the majority religion imposing itself
on culture in general.

Saba Mahmood writes, as previously noted, as an anthropologist. This
is both her great strength and her weakness – it is a strength because she
engages in relative depth with a particular group of people, a group of
Coptic Christians in Egypt and attempts to draw general conclusions from
this. It is a weakness, though, for these two very reasons: from the point
of view of some subgroups within the cultural and religious community
of Coptic Christians, she may not engage deeply enough with them and
from a more general and abstract perspective her overall view may be too
influenced by the particular case, or by her reading of that particular case.
These are similar to criticisms that have been made of the work of one of
her mentors – Michel Foucault.

It is possible, in many of the cases mentioned in the previous section, to
suggest that if the purported secular 'universalising' principles were not universal enough, then those principles need revising. I have made this kind of
argument in detail elsewhere. If, to make the point in relation to Mahmood's
work, the concept of a minority right is being used in Egypt to accentuate
their minority status, then this means that the concept has not been properly
implemented and that it needs constantly to be challenged. The notion of a
minority right, after all, was not developed to emphasise the notion of *minority*, rather it was the intention to make sure that every group has equal rights.
The same kind of point, but in a different context, could be made about the
notion of black rights in contemporary United States. The intention is not
to give black people *minority* rights. It is rather to give all people the same
rights and there is a need to focus on black rights precisely because black
people have not been treated as equals. Mahmood does recognise this point.
However, she may underplay the positive value of the notion.

It is important to make the point, that it is possible, to a degree, to abstract
oneself from one's culture and heritage. Normative ideals are precisely
important because they represent perspectives that challenge taken-for-
granted assumptions. Our ends and values are subject to revision and re-
formulation. We can constantly revise what constitutes a good and a valuable
life. If we were wholly formed through our cultural, religious and national
ends and values, then this revision would be impossible.

There are other ways, moreover, than Mahmood's, of thinking about secularism. Freedom of choice, to take one important concept that is implicit in the liberal and 'secular' tradition, is a precondition for engaging in any project at all. We can all think of examples of states, in the modern world, which deny their citizens freedom of choice – to adopt a religion, to express a dissenting opinion and so on. The concept of a minority right is one expression of the notion of freedom. While it may be true that the Copts in Egypt faced some additional problems that stemmed from the notion of their minority status, one can only imagine the situation they would have faced, had they been banned altogether from upholding their religion.

Mahmood makes the claim that the Ottoman Empire was actually more liberal in its tolerance of a range of religious views than the Christian states that succeeded it. While this may or may not be true (it is perhaps difficult to make this comparison), it is also important to point out that the founders of what might be described as liberal enlightenment thinking were themselves ostracised and their lives threatened by the power of the Catholic Church.

Mahmood is critical of the purported 'imposition' on postcolonial nations of the public/private distinction. However, alongside her relative silence on what she believes is a preferable alternative form of governance to that of human rights, she does not discuss the pre-Enlightenment historical period in Europe. Nation states after all, were partially formed, in Europe, at the time of the early Protestant reformers, in order to counter the power of the Catholic Church, which, in the medieval period, had power over the kings and queens of the various states. Luther's proclamation of the right to private interpretation of the scriptures was a counter to the power, the greed and the corruption of the medieval Catholic Church. Insofar as she rejects secularism, is she suggesting that the pre-Enlightenment period in Europe was preferable to this period? But those states today, like their pre-Enlightenment precursors, that deny any minority the right to uphold their religious beliefs are surely worse than those who attempt, in convoluted and complicated ways, to uphold the right to a minority religion.

While it is impossible to deny that all of us are embedded in our cultures, traditions, societies and, in the modern period, our nation states, it is possible, to different degrees, to abstract oneself from these. One set of possible abstractions from ones' cultural context is the deployment of secular discourses to challenge existing norms and practices and to do this in a way that is positive and productive for minority and oppressed groupings. As O'Neill writes: 'Abstraction is a matter of bracketing but not of denying predicates that are true of the matters under discussion. Abstraction in this sense is unavoidable theoretically and practically important.'[55]

It is possible to abstract, for example, the principle of 'minority rights' from its partial and imperfect application in many of the cases described by Mahmood and to deploy it in a different way. The concept of minority rights has been deployed, in other contexts, as a principle, to increase overall equality rather than, as in Mahmood's case history, to decrease this. So it is at least arguable that granting minority language rights, to take Kymlica's[56] famous case, enhanced rather than eroded the culture of the Canadian Quebecois. Indeed, granting them minority rights seems to have strengthened their cultural identity.[57] It is arguable that these 'minority' rights went the other way and gave too much power to the French language in relation to other language-speaking groups who entered Quebec. But this is a different point.

Mahmood claims that secularism entails a re-ordering of social life in accordance with specific norms. Secularism, put into practice in specific ways, does indeed entail a re-ordering of social life. Mahmood claims that this re-ordering is either useless, as in the case of the Jews in Europe, or positively disadvantageous for the group in question. However, there are cases where the 're-ordering' has had positive consequences for oppressed groupings, as for example, in allowing victims of domestic violence, all over the world, to seek legal redress for specific harms experienced.[58] Secular discourses have also been deployed, in positive ways, to work for the rights of individuals to gain citizenship or refugee status in particular nations, when it has been unsafe for them to remain in their countries of origin.

Mahmood's work, insofar as it claims a generalised critique of secularism, from her detailed ethnographic study, makes a strong relativist claim. She writes:

> One might argue that I have painted too bleak a picture of secularism, in which it is nothing more than the exercise of state and (neo) colonial power and that I have ignored its more promising and liberatory dimension: the protection it extends to individuals and religious minorities to hold and practice religious beliefs freely without state or social coercion; or it's guarantee that a citizen's religious affiliation is inconsequential to her civil and political status in the eyes of the law; or that it allows believers and non-believers to speak their mind without fear of state or social discrimination.[59]

She writes that these are not negligible freedoms. However, as noted above, she argues that secularism also entails the re-ordering and re-making of religious life according to specific norms. She argues that it generates exclusions, hierarchies and, indeed, forms of violence. However, as I pointed out earlier, while there are no doubt 'forms of violence' exercised by many states that claim to be secular, it may not be 'secularity' itself that is responsible for this. The Muslim Brotherhood, in the case she discusses, has expressly committed itself to violence against minority religions. Moreover, as Abou-Odeh notes in her review, *Secularism's Fault*, of Mahmood, in *Feminist Dissent*, 2017, 2.:

> If the alternative to secularism were to prevail, then, secularists like me would have had their *own* lives upended instead and in ways that the specific interpretation of the principle of no separation in our state would dictate. We may have to veil in public. We may have to be shepherded to mid day prayers in our work places. We may have to lie to public enforcers about not fasting in Ramadan. Many terribly un-secular things, 'foreign to the lives' of us secularists would have to take place and we won't like it one bit.[60]

Mahmood emphasises what she calls a 'failure of imagination' in relation to the context she describes. Perhaps one inspiration for this aspect of her outlook is the work of Richard Rorty, another thinker in the relativist tradition outlined above, but who, as we have seen earlier, advocated replacing the ideal of Reason, developed in the Enlightenment, with that of imagination as a way of escaping one's culture and tradition. It is imagination, according to Rorty, that allows us to distance ourselves from our cultures and traditions and speculate about something better. But it seems that there is a dimension of Mahmood's thinking to the effect that implementation of these ideals, in all the cases she considers, has been coloured by implicit colonial and Christian presuppositions.

Once again, a very different view of the question of cultural relativism is given by Ayesha Khan who argues that activists in Pakistan led the charge against the cultural specificity of the defence of traditional institutions, many of which discriminated against women. It was not, of course, an easy matter to defend universal human rights but they argued that sometimes cultural specificity and the Islamisation project were used to consolidate the power of those already in power and human rights language was necessary to counter this.[61]

Mahmood argues that the twin concepts of minority rights and the private/public distinction are necessarily embedded in a set of cultural and social traditions that, in her case, importantly include the power of colonialism and its shaping of the context she describes. The discourse of human rights is, she argues, ineluctably bound up with misguided and oppressive colonial practices. It is difficult, therefore, for her to suggest that she is not critiquing the ideals of secularism. If all the illustrative examples of the effects of secularity show it in a poor light then it is difficult to hang on to anything positive about it.

ANOTHER BRIEF CASE HISTORY

A different but in some respects analogous argument to that of Mahmood was made seventy years ago by Horkheimer and Adorno in *The Dialectic of*

Enlightenment.[62] Their work has already been mentioned in this book but I would like to make a different point about it here.

First published in 1944, the authors described what they saw as the domination of mass culture over the individual. Putting it briefly, they argued that Enlightenment reason effectively collapses into myth and, in the form of the culture industry, standardised cultural forms are produced that manipulate people into docility and conformity. These ingredients, they suggested, form the ground on which the seeds of totalitarianism are able to germinate.

The argument of these two thinkers is different from that of Mahmood, but they have in common a strong critique of secularism and Enlightenment reason.

However, one thinker frequently quoted by Mahmood in support of many of her claims, in fact challenges the overall perspective of Horkheimer and Adorno. It is significant that Hannah Arendt, writing in the same period as Horkheimer and Adorno, makes the following point: 'Terror becomes total when it becomes independent of all opposition: it rules supreme when nobody any longer stands in its way'.[63] Arendt's work, indeed, suggests a different understanding of what could be meant by the distinction between the public and the private. It also gives further support to the view that the root of concepts critiqued by Mahmood is not the Enlightenment colonial period, but at least the Ancient Greeks. Indeed, some would go further than this and suggest that its true root is earlier still, as noted in chapter 5, in the Persian Empire. Insofar as the root of concepts like the 'polis' is ancient Greece, this history influenced early Islam as well as Christianity. I will elaborate on this further in chapter 8.

Arendt suggests that genuine activity of human beings, as opposed to mere labour or mere work, involves challenging taken-for-granted assumptions. Truly to engage in politics is to move beyond what she calls mere 'labour' and mere 'work'. The former is the business of survival – the basic processes required to sustain life – like the production of food and the conditions for shelter. The latter is a notion that produces something that survives a little longer like items of clothing. But neither of these function to characterise true humanity or proper action. Genuine political activity, for Arendt, involves abstracting oneself from these processes. Political activity involves following principles, and these must involve moving beyond taken-for-granted cultural assumptions. Political activity is carried out by people collectively and in conditions of freedom. I have suggested, in previous chapters of the book, the significance of the need for essentialising categories, derived not from Enlightenment reason, but from a 'new' materialism that has seen the human to be continued with the rest of the animal and the natural world. It is possible, in strong contrast to the view of Mahmood, to see the notion of a right, in the sense of a right to freedom, a right to food and shelter, as deriving from the common vitalist biological core of humans. Even though, in fact, some of these rights were implemented by the UN Convention, it is possible to see them as expressing these core aspects of humanity, the core aspects that are, in accordance with the argument of previous chapters, undergoing constant change and development, but which in certain cases, remain such that humans would be unable to act at all were they removed. Far from certain of these rights being exclusive to Enlightenment colonial thinking, they are, by contrast, necessary for the continued existence of humanity as a whole. They are also, in other forms, in the contemporary unequal and capitalist world, vital for defending the rights of those without citizenship, to food, shelter and other simple requirements of life.

In her major work, *The Human Condition*, Arendt suggests that every time we really act as a free person we perform something new; we engage with the world in radically different ways, as if we are being reborn. For her it is the notion of *natality*, of *beginning*, that makes for real political activity, this is 'the central category of political [...] thought'.[64] Genuine political activity takes place in her version of the 'public' sphere. Mass culture, as Horkheimer and Adorno had noted, tends to normalise individuals. People therefore require a public space, which she calls the 'polis', in which they are truly able to act together. Action of this kind involves thought that challenges taken-for-granted cultural assumptions. Freedom, then, is not just the possibility of making choices, but rather the potential to act. 'With word and deed we insert ourselves into the human world, and this insertion is like a second birth [...] This insertion is not forced upon us by necessity, like labour, and it is not prompted by utility, like work [...] its impulse springs from the beginning which came into the world when we were born and to which we respond by beginning something new on our own initiative'.[65] Indeed, Arendt, following her mentor Kierkegaard, praises a key Enlightenment thinker, Descartes. She extols the universal characteristic of Cartesian doubt and suggests that Kierkegaard used Cartesian tools to critique taken-for-granted religious assumptions.[66] Her critique of Eichmann exemplifies that he demonstrated a failure to take doubt seriously and a failure to think clearly and deeply about his actions.

I would like, at this point, to mention another brief but important critique of the work of Horkheimer and Adorno. In her book, *Axel Honneth: Reconceiving Social Philosophy*, Dagmar Wilhelm argues that the project of Horkheimer and Adorno 'seemed to foreclose any possibility of emancipatory action and is suspicious of the sciences to a degree that renders an interdisciplinary project almost impossible'.[67] Like Mahmood's work, Horkheimer and Adorno's text had a huge reception but it was one that made social analysis and action much more pessimistic. A further parallel with Mahmood's work is that, according to Wilhelm's critique, it was the very tool

– reason – that is the means of emancipation that is, according to Horkheimer and Adorno's analysis, the source of domination. Emancipatory thinking and action, then, on the view, becomes impossible. Similarly, although in a less extreme way, with Mahmood's work, the tool of tolerance – a recognition of the normative importance of human rights to making any further changes in society – becomes itself the problem.

Returning to Arendt, the possibility of doing any critical work on religious and other assumptions that may not be justified requires a public sphere where, like Socrates, individuals can question authorities; they can question the established order. This, in turn, as noted, requires freedom,[68] a notion that is core to a certain conception of action, and therefore of humanity.

In the present period, to take a few examples, following the election of one of the most misogynistic and racist presidents of the United States, there has been extensive opposition to his policies. The women's marches, organised at very short notice, after his election, and the marches all over the UK when he visited, illustrate the power that people, coming together across continents and cities, can bring to bear to counter the developments in the early weeks of Trump's presidency. One could make the same kinds of point about oppositional politics, for example, in Pakistan, in Iran, in Turkey and in India. Where it is possible to do so, and where individuals and groups overcome their fear of acting, as in India in opposition at the end of 2019, to Modi's proposed citizenship law, change is possible. Nowadays there are multiple sources of information. There are many individuals with the ability, at very short notice, to organise a demonstration (in countries where this is possible and even in countries where the risk to life is extraordinarily high); there are many lawyers who are prepared to challenge racist policies that may violate the constitution of an individual nation. Moreover, the hugely powerful 'tech' industry, including the ubiquitous 'Google' with its ability to shape how information is disseminated, tweeted 'resist' 'No Ban; no Wall' 'Make America Sane again in response to the various policies of the new president of the United States.[69]

It is the liberal state, with its partially 'enlightenment' inspired commitment to universal human rights and to the rule of law, that makes some of these things possible and that is desired by many in countries where it does not exist. First, liberal democratic states have recourse to the law: it is possible to use the law to challenge such things as Holocaust denial and even to challenge the president of the United States or the prime minister of a billion-strong state like India. Second, liberal democratic states allow people like me to express opinions like these without (at the moment) risking arrest. There is still in these states a rudimentary commitment to the principle of freedom of speech.

When there is a risk, therefore, of some of these hard-won human rights being undermined, it is vital that those of us who believe in challenging sexism, racism, anti-Semitism, homophobia, anti-trans behaviour, racism against Muslims and all forms of discrimination, recognise the deep significance of these secular rights – rights to freedom, to the rule of law and so on. It is vital, indeed, that we recognise these rights in order to be in a position to act in the fashion outlined by Arendt.

The concept of a right, indeed, if it is genuinely and properly universal, need not be encumbered with Enlightenment forms of liberalism that either implicitly or explicitly exclude certain groups, nor need it be associated with any legal system that does the same thing. Paul Gilroy's[70] work, for example, demonstrated that slavery was in fact part and parcel of the Enlightenment ideal. But this need not lead to a dismissal of universalism. Rather it ought to encourage the comment that the form of purported universalism was not universal at all. So any pretence at universalism that excludes women, LGBT people or, at the other extreme, a purported 'terrorist' from the domain of the law is not a proper universal system. To reiterate an earlier claim, if the concept of minority rights has accentuated already existing inequalities, then that represents a poor application of the notion.

So when critics, like Mahmood and others, of 'liberalism' claim that the self is encumbered, and not atomised and isolated as it appears to be in some forms of Enlightenment thinking, a universalist secularist can agree, and suggest that one form of encumbrance is precisely our universal humanity and indeed, our deep connections with the rest of the animal and natural world. But she would not agree with Mahmood that the self cannot abstract from the particularities of her situation.

The UCHR is one imperfect and partial attempt at an expression of this universal humanity. It is indeed partial and imperfect but it has served many valuable purposes. Mahmood's ethnographic study is precisely that. It is one particular case study. But one case study, however valuable, should not lead us to dismiss overall either the concept of a minority right or 'secularism' more broadly. Indeed, as I have suggested here, if secularism is rejected and, in its place we are offered some vague commitment to a religious discourse, the danger is that the outcomes could be far worse.

I would like to end the chapter by referring to an important point made by a feminist who is sympathetic to restoring a notion of a right in a Muslim-majority state like Egypt. Elsadda writes: 'The pursuit of rights, similar to the pursuit of justice, must not only be contextualised, but must also be understood against the background of possibilities, struggles and achievable aims, rather than with reference to ideal worlds and abstract concepts'.[71] I agree that the concept of a right has to be contextualised. But I disagree with Elsadda that this means that we cannot also talk about 'ideal worlds' and 'abstract concepts'. Without the abstract concepts we cannot develop contextualised versions of them. So long, also, as the theoretical 'ideal' underpinning the concept of a right is seen to be exclusively European and colonial, then there will continue to be the risk of any 'contextualised' use of the concept itself wearing these clothes as well.

NOTES

1. See Zia, *Faith and Feminism in Pakistan*, Chapters 1 and 2.
2. L. Abu-Lughod, *Do Muslim Women Need Saving?* (Boston, MA: Harvard University Press, 2013).
3. Mariz Tandros and Ayesha Khan, "Challenging Binaries to Promote Women's Equality," *Feminist Dissent* 3 (2018): 13.
4. Ibid., 104.
5. Ibid., 3.
6. Ariel Salleh, *Eco-feminism as Politics: Nature, Marx and the Post-Modern* (London: Zed Books, 1997), 192.
7. See for example. V. Shiva, "Women's Indigenous Knowledge and Biodiversity," in *Ecofeminism*, eds. Maria Mies and Vandana Shiva (London: Zed Books, 1993).
8. *Italian Administrative Court's Judgement*, March 18, 2011, quoted from Saba Mahmood, *Religious Difference in a Secular Age: A Minority Report* (Princeton, NJ and Oxford: Princeton University Press, 2016), 7.
9. See Ibid., Chapter 1.
10. See Ibid., Chapter 2.
11. Ibid., 72.
12. Ibid., 14.
13. Ibid., 72.
14. See Ibid., Chapter 1.
15. Ibid., 57.
16. Ibid., 67.
17. Mahmood, *Religious Difference in a Secular Age*.
18. Ibid., 21.
19. Rory Stewart Comment Columns, *"I Weekend" Saturday and Sunday*, December 21–22, 2019.
20. Tandros and Khan, "Challenging Binaries," 129.
21. Ibid., 172.
22. Ibid., 174.
23. Ibid., 128.
24. Ibid., 129.
25. Ibid., 175.
26. Ibid., 183–88.
27. Ibid., 180.
28. https://www.thedailybeast.com/the-muslim-brotherhoods-war-on-coptic-ch ristians, accessed July 22, 2018.

29. Mariz Tandros, *The Muslim Brotherhood in Contemporary Egypt: Democracy Re-Defined or Confined* (London: Routledge, 2012).

30. Ibid., 5.

31. Gerasimos Tsourapas, "Polyvocia," *The SOAS Journal of Graduate Research* 5 (2013).

32. Mariz Tandros, "Copts of Egypt: from Survivors of Sectarian Violence to Targets of Terrorism," *Open Democracy* 50 (April 2017): 50.

33. Ibid.

34. Ibid.

35. https://www.counterextremism.com/content/muslim-brotherhood%E2%80%99s-ties-isis-and-al-qaeda, accessed July 29, 2018.

36. Gov.UK.

37. Bruce Lawrence, *Defenders of God: the Fundamentalist Revolt against the Modern Age* (Columbia, SC: University of South Carolina Press, 1987) quoted in Stephen Cowden and Gita Sahgal, "Why Fundamentalism?," *Feminist Dissent* 2 (2017): 13.

38. Lawrence, *Defenders of God*, 1997, quoted in Cowden and Sahgal, "Why Fundamentalism?," 13.

39. Bhatt 1997, 79.

40. Mark Sedgwick, *Against the Modern World: Traditionalism and the Secret Intellectual Heritage of the 20th Century* (Oxford: OUP, 2004).

41. Ibid., 26.

42. René Guenon, *Orient et Occident*, trans. Mark Sedgwick (Paris: Payot, 1934).

43. See Sedgwick, *Against the Modern World*, Chapter 4.

44. Ibid., 79.

45. See Alison Assiter, "Review of Mark Sedgwick, Against the Modern World: Traditionalism and the Secret Intellectual History of the Twentieth Century," *Feminist Dissent* 3 (2018).

46. See, for example, Jeffrey Herf, *Nazi Propaganda for the Arab World* (New Haven, CT and London: Yale University Press, 2009).

47. See Sedgwick, *Against the Modern World*.

48. Ibid., 266.

49. Ibid., 271.

50. Ibid., 264.

51. Mahmood, *Religious Difference in a Secular Age*, Chapter 4.

52. Ibid., 150.

53. Ibid., 167–68.

54. J. S. Mill, *On Liberty* (Yale, MI: Yale University Press, 2003), Chapter 3.3.1.

55. O'Neill 1996, 40.

56. Kymlica 1989, 1995.

57. It is arguable, of course, that this is not necessarily in the interest of all Quebecois, especially those whose first language is English.

58. See, for example, Gill Hague and Ellen Malos, *Domestic Violence: Action for Change* (Cheltenham: New Clarion Press, 1993).

59. Mahmood, *Religious Difference in a Secular Age*, 20.

60. Lama Abou-Oddeh, "Secularisms Fault," *Feminist Dissent* 2 (2017): 151.

61. Tandros and Khan, "Challenging Binaries," 159–67.

62. M. Horkheimer and T. Adorno, *Dialectic of Enlightenment*, trans. Edmund Jephcott (Stanford, CA: Stanford University Press, 2002).

63. Hannah Arendt, "Ideology and Terror: A Novel Form of Government," *The Review of Politics* 15, no. 3 (July 1953): 310.

64. Hannah Arendt, *The Human Condition* (Chicago, IL: University of Chicago Press, 1998), 9.

65. Ibid., 176–77.

66. Ibid., 275.

67. Dagmar Wilhelm, *Axel Honneth: Reconceiving Social Philosophy* (London: Rowman and Littlefield, 2019), 15.

68. Arendt 1958.

69. See *The Evening Standard*, February 18, 2017.

70. Gilroy 1993.

71. Elsadda, quoted in Tandros, 20.

Chapter 8

The Politics of Piety

Mahmood draws on and develops the work of Judith Butler and Foucault, in fashioning her concept of agency in *The Politics of Piety*.[1] Butler, following Foucault, argued that the law produces *both* sanctioned heterosexuality and transgressive homosexuality. The drag queen, to take one example, both draws attention to and demonstrates that what appears normal, natural and taken for granted – heterosexuality – is not this at all. In her turn, Mahmood suggests that it is imperialism that has, partially, produced the liberal, secular autonomous subject of rights and effectively imposed this on those who may wish, to use Mufti's words, 'to embrace docility, submission, conservatism, patriarchy and even Islamism'.[2] Mahmood discusses how difficult it is for working women in the mosque movement she investigated to embrace the virtue of 'modesty' in the face of challenges from those who set out to disrupt their practices.

Mahmood challenges what she saw as western normative assumptions effectively imposed on would-be pious Muslim women in Egypt. In *The Politics of Piety*, she writes: 'The on-going importance of feminist scholarship on women's agency cannot be emphasised enough, especially when one remembers that Western popular media continues to portray Muslim women as incomparably bound by the unbreakable chains of religious and patriarchal oppression'.[3] She questions what she labels the 'liberal' 'western' feminist conception of agency that she sees as deriving from a person making autonomous self-willed choices that are not shaped by custom, tradition or patriarchal norms. She argues that the concepts of positive and negative freedom (developed in fact not by any feminists, as she claims, but by Isaiah Berlin[4]) have shaped much of feminist theory and practice. Positive freedom, she claims, informs studies that examine women's self-directed action and negative freedom shapes those that explore aspects of

women's life that set out to escape the influence of men. Mahmood argues
further that the twin notions of positive and negative freedom as understood
within feminism add up to a view of autonomy as involving the ability to
make choices without the person's will being shaped by any force external
to this.

Mahmood claims that while it is true that feminist critics of the liberal
notion of the subject, that itself draws on a conception of a transcendent self
that is disconnected from its environment and its body, have challenged some
aspects of this liberal notion of autonomy, feminists in general have equated
agency with challenging patriarchal norms. She wants to revive a conception
of agency that allows that women might choose very differently. Her alternative view of agency sees it as the capacity to 'realize one's own interests
against the weight of custom, tradition, transcendental will, or other obstacles
(whether individual or collective)'.[5] She writes: 'Despite the many strands
and differences within feminism, what accords the feminist tradition an ana-
lytical and political coherence is the premise that where society is structured
to serve male interests, the result will be either neglect, or direct suppression,
of women's concerns'.[6] Viewed in this way, she argues, what may appear to
be a case of deplorable passivity and docility from, what she calls, a 'progres-
sivist' point of view, may actually be a form of agency 'but one that can be
understood only from within the discourses and structures of subordination
that create the conditions of its enactment'. 'In this sense, agentival capacity
is entailed not only in those acts that resist norms but also in the multiple
ways in which one inhabits norms'.[7]

She writes that, in the 1970s, there was a proliferation of writings that
expressed surprise that 'modem Egyptian women' have returned to wearing
the veil. She argues that these studies suggested that women might wear the
veil to avoid sexual harassment or to express opposition to the hegemony of
Western values. She herself expresses surprise, however, that their authors
paid so little attention to the Islamic virtues of female modesty or piety and
she hoped 'to redress the profound inability within current feminist political
thought to envision valuable forms of human flourishing outside the bounds
of a liberal progressive imaginary'.[8] Given the stringent demands of their
desire to abide by high standards of piety placed on them, these women
often had to struggle against the secular ethos that permeated their lives and
made their realisation of piety somewhat difficult. One of the mosque women
Mahmood quotes, called Amal, said,

I used to think that even though shyness [al -*hayaa'*] was required of us by
God, if I acted shyly it would be hypocritical [*nifaaq*] because I didn't actually feel it inside of me. Then one day, in reading verse 25 in Surat al Qasaas
['The Story'] I realized that *al-hayaa* was among the good deeds [*huwwa min
al...af!mal al...al*], and given my natural lack of shyness [*al-hayaa*], I had

to make or create it first. I realized that making (*sanaa*) it in yourself is not hypocrisy, and that eventually your inside learns to have al-hayaa too.

Here she looked at me and explained the meaning of the word *istihyaa*: 'It means making oneself shy, even if it means creating it.'[9] Here we see exemplified Mahmood's original idea of the performative creating of the emotion of shyness.

Mahmood quotes, 'Nama, a single woman in her early thirties', who had been sitting and listening, (and who) added:

> It's just like the veil (hijab). In the beginning when you wear it, you're embarrassed [*maksufa*] and don't want to wear it because people say that you look older and unattractive, that you won't get married, and will never find a husband. But you must wear the veil, first because it is God's command [*hukm allah*], and then, with time, because your inside learns to feel shy without the veil, and if you take it off, your entire being feels uncomfortable [*mish raadi*] about it.[10]

Mahmood's subtle extension of Butler's work has her suggesting that practices inform desires and emotions rather than the other way round. Her argument is that through repeated bodily acts one's memory is trained. Wearing the veil is a critical mark of piety. Shyness in the secular feminist literature Mahmood critiques is understood as the subjection of women's bodies to patriarchal norms. She admits that *Al haayaa* does embody a masculinist understanding but far more is at stake. Instead, we have an entire conceptualisation of the role the shy body plays in the making of the self. Modesty is a divinely ordained virtue. Modest bodily form is the means by which virtue was acquired. The acquisition of ethical virtue depends upon the proper enactment of certain behaviours.

In line with the overall argument of the book, it is important to qualify this view of Mahmood's. Butler's claim that the discourses of compulsory heterosexuality produce the notion of woman is open to challenge and so too are these views of Mahmood. The pious women are shaped by their own desires, by their religious faith, by biological forces and by a complex of other forces internal to each individual as well as by western feminist beliefs and attitudes. The liberal notion of autonomy that was circulating, according to her, in the arenas in which the pious women operated were surely counteracted by the women's own "vital materiality" – their own desires, thoughts and wishes. Moreover, on a different point, 'western' states have supported and promoted purported 'Islamic' values as well as those that stem from a so-called 'liberal' ethos. In the case of Afghanistan, the US state, backed by Pakistan, supported the use of 'jihadi' ideology during the anti-Soviet struggle of the 1980s.[11] Moreover, as several scholars have pointed out, the Pakistani state, supported by western powers, has 'consistently side-lined moderate Islamic *ulema* and academics'.[12]

Ethics, Mahmood understands, in Aristotelian vein, as a set of embodied practices relative to a particular tradition. The ethical subject is formed within the limits of a historically specific set of formative practices and moral injunctions are delimited in advance – what Foucault characterizes as 'modes of subjectivation'.[13] Foucault's work encourages us to think of agency: (a) in terms of the capacities and skills required to undertake particular kinds of moral actions; and (b) as ineluctably bound up with the historically and culturally specific disciplines through which a subject is formed. Mahmood gives the illustrative example of the pianist whose agency is conditional upon her ability to be taught.

In turn, the political efficacy of the mosque movement is a function of the work they perform in the ethical realm – those strategies of cultivation through which embodied attachments to historically specific forms of truth come to be forged. Their political project can only be understood through an exploration of their ethical practices. This requires that we rethink not only our conventional understanding of what constitutes the political but also what is the substance of ethics.

CRITICAL COMMENTARY ON MAHMOOD

As noted above, it will be obvious, by now, that I believe, as noted previously, that Mahmood's work is very important in its challenge to what may be seen as 'western' normative assumptions about some Muslim women's agency. One respect in which I might be sympathetic to her argument lies in its challenge to some aspects of the individualism of the 'conventional' liberal tradition. But there are ways of challenging the framework without reverting to the dualism of 'western feminist' – and 'pious Muslim woman', subject to patriarchal norms.

Ethical subjects, to my way of thinking, are not exclusively formed within the limits of particular social practices and historical traditions. Instead, ethical subjects, I have been arguing throughout this book, are significantly a result of recognition of our universal embodied and material humanity which gives rise to a set of needs that, in its turn, produces rights and obligations on each of us. Appreciating this universal aspect of our ethics need not involve full abstraction from our communities and traditions, but simply some level of abstraction from these. I would like to quote from a piece written by Charles Eisenstein, during the present pandemic, (May 2020) that offers a very different kind of thought along the above lines. He wrote: 'Covid-19 is showing us that when humanity is united in common cause, phenomenally rapid change is possible. None of the world's problems are technically difficult to solve; they originate in human disagreement. In coherency, humanity's creative powers are boundless. A few months ago, a proposal to halt commercial air travel would have seemed preposterous. Likewise for the radical changes we are making in our social behavior, economy and the role of government in our lives. Covid demonstrates the power of our collective will when we agree on what is important. What else might we achieve, in coherency? What do we want to achieve, and what world shall we create? That is always the next question when anyone awakens to their power'.[14] There is a universal and embodied humanity. Eisenstein notes the potential power this universal humanity has to create a very different kind of world from the one may of us saw as the 'normal' prior to COVID-19.

Further, I think it is important to note that while Mahmood does accept that she is not outlining all forms of 'western' feminism, she suggests that feminism in general 'in the west' is dominated by a focus on freedom. I would like to note, though, that this focus, in much so-called 'western' political theory in general, is countered by a notion to which Mahmoud attaches less weight, and that is a desire for equality. The 'western' feminists she is referring to, particularly liberal feminists as opposed to radical or Marxist feminists, desired a society where all individuals would have an equal opportunity to pursue their own interests. This is a second-order claim and is different from the desire to pursue individual autonomy.

Indeed, one irony for the subtle and intriguing thesis Mahmood develops about the women in the mosque movement in Egypt, is that it is some of the second-order liberal assumptions, that are precisely those that are under attack in much of the world at the present time, that are necessary in order for the women to practise the form of piety that she examines in her work. It is precisely where norms deriving from non-liberal assumptions are developed for whole societies or nations that the ability to attempt to develop the form of piety Mahmood celebrates is under threat.

Moreover, most early western feminists challenged the conception that Mahmood sees as key to all forms of feminism and that is the conception of autonomy she outlines. Alison Jagger, for example, who was one of the earliest socialist feminists, in her work *Feminist Politics and Human Nature*, challenged the 'pure liberal feminist' focus on individual autonomy, for its mistaken individualism and its dualism about the mental and the physical domains.[15] So it is not historically accurate for Mahmood to characterise 'western' feminism as normatively liberal in character nor is it fair to describe it as focusing primarily on the conception of autonomy she outlines. Simone de Beauvoir, whose text *The Second Sex*[16] is hailed as inaugurating the 1960s 'liberal' tradition of feminist thinking, explicitly challenges the above, largely Kantian notion and develops a view of autonomy that requires interaction both with bodily desires and with the emotions and actions of others. Indeed, a careful reading of de Beauvoir on autonomy would no doubt lead to some similarities between her notion and that espoused by the 'subjects' of Mahmood's research. De Beauvoir challenged conventional femininity and faced hostility for so doing; Mahmood's women challenged what she describes as liberal norms but that I would suggest may not have been these at all. Rather, they were masculinist assumptions – in this case against Islamic piety and the wearing of the hijab – about the women's agency.

Mahmood's work lies in a trajectory of cultural relativist thinking. Her analysis is of a piece in some respects with that of, for example, Alasdair MacIntyre's[17] on morality. Indeed she refers to his work alongside her celebration of Foucault and Butler. MacIntyre argues that Enlightenment theorists set out to displace cultures, traditions and authorities and to appeal, instead, to genuinely universal theories and ideals. Modernity, in contrast to the premodern, purports to establish an individual who is able, in theory, to detach themselves from tradition and authority and judge that outlook from a position that is, to a degree, outside it. In fact, MacIntyre argues, this outlook is illusory. Instead our normative standards are always formed within a particular tradition, culture and outlook.

However, the force of a normative moral theory is that it provides one with a standard against which to judge the value of a particular set of cultural assumptions. No doubt the women in the mosque movement in Egypt believed that they had this standard – the standard came from their reading of the Koran and their view of the nature of God's will. So their particular set of beliefs was not wholly informed by a set of cultural practices that were unique to them. Perhaps one might imagine them giving a justification along the following lines: there are objective moral facts and God provides the best explanation of the existence of objective moral facts. Mahmood does after all claim that the mosque movement presupposes a divine plan and that the women recognise moral codes through the invocations of divine texts.

However there are two difficulties with this kind of explanation. First, there is a standard objection to such a theory – namely the conundrum – is this right because God wills it or does God will it because it is right? If the former, then we don't necessarily know that the act is right and if the latter then it is right anyway, independently of God's will. But also, the difficulty with providing this kind of an overall justification for Mahmood's celebration of the piety movement is that their practices presumably only apply to fellow Muslims who accept their particular interpretation of the Koran and it is not therefore a moral practice which would be generalizable outside the remit of their own grouping. This differentiates their practice from the ethical system celebrated by MacIntyre. The latter was making a radically different kind of point from that made by Mahmood. She reads Aristotle through Foucault:

'Foucault's conception of positive ethics is Aristotelian in that it conceives of ethics not as an Idea, or as a set of regulatory norms, but as a set of practical activities that are germane to a certain way of life'.[18] MacIntyre's claim, in *After Virtue*, however, takes a radically different form. It is that morality is in disarray following the Enlightenment because the type of moral theory developed by thinkers as diverse as Kant and Kierkegaard mistakenly detracts from Aristotle's broadly correct teleological theory of human development – namely that there is a purpose or an end to the life of human beings. As MacIntyre puts it in *After Virtue*: 'Within (Aristotle's) moral scheme there is a fundamental contrast between man-as-he-happens-to-be and man-as-he-could-be-if- he-realised-his-essential nature. Ethics is the science, which is to enable men to understand how they make the transition from the former state to the latter. Ethics therefore on this view presupposes some account of potentiality and act, some account of the essence of man as a rational animal and above all some account of the human *telos*'.[19] To refer to the quote from Eisenstein once more, humanity, acting collectively, has the power to make changes that could benefit all as well as the world on which we all depend.

In a sense Mahmood goes along with this view of MacIntyre, for she is describing a group of people who set out to recover a sense of purpose in their lives. But she also wants to decry, along Foucauldian lines, any attempt at developing a general moral theory, from her story, that applies to humankind overall.

FURTHER CRITICAL COMMENTARY

Mahmood herself, as noted, was very careful to claim that her work should be read as an ethnographic study of the Egyptian Copts and the Egyptian mosque piety movements, but it has been taken, by many, to be a general critique of liberal secular principles. Moreover, she does accept in the opening chapter of her *The Politics of Piety*, that the women's mosque movement 'is part of the larger Islamic Revival or Islamic Awakening (al..Sabwa al.. Islamiyya) that has swept the Muslim world, including Egypt, since at least the 1970's'.[20]'Islamic Revival' is a term that refers not only to the activities of state-oriented political groups but more broadly to a religious ethos or sensibility that has developed within contemporary Muslim societies. This sensibility has a palpable public presence in Egypt, manifest in the vast proliferation of neighbourhood mosques and other institutions of Islamic learning and social welfare.[21] It is important, once again, to mention a significant part of this context which is very much played down by Mahmood, and that is the Islamic Revolution in Iran, which took place in 1979, and which instituted a form of sharia law in that country that made it very unlikely that women would be able to exercise anything like the kind of agency outlined by Mahmood. It is also important to note the similarities in the form of sharia adopted between Iran and its rival, Saudi Arabia and also the Islamisation project instituted around this time, in Pakistan. As noted previously, in a country, like Iran, where not wearing a hijab is an offence punishable by imprisonment, it would be very unlikely that women would be in a position to have the kind of debate or agentic trial about the effect on their emotions of the performative behaviour of the trying out of the wearing of the veil.

Moreover, Mahmood's work, *The Politics of Piety*, has, according to Afiya Zia, for one, inspired a popularised notion of pietist agency among many Muslim women in the post-9/11 period.[22] Some activists, Zia notes, in Pakistan as well as elsewhere 'borrow, extend and model Mahmood's theory of the docile Muslim female agent as an alternative discourse to liberal feminist aspirations in general'.[23] According to Mufti, 'the new ethnography of Islam and *The Politics of* Piety is now hugely influential and even canonical in this regard – is in active agreement with Islamism itself when the latter thinks of itself in revivalist terms as a return to the true tradition of Islam'.[24] Zia notes, quoting another source, that some have argued that there is an invitation, in Mahmood's works, to read 'agency as even substitutive for women's rights in Muslim contexts'.[25]

In a comment on the binary 'western secular' and 'local religious', another writer on the Pakistani context has argued:

> One of the detrimental effects of this binaristic approach has been to perpetuate the notion that feminism is a Western import and that an 'authentic', culturally sensitive and hence more effective approach to gender-based development interventions must operate within a religious framework.[26]

This framework, it is argued, romanticises the notion of the pious subject and fails to recognise the 'messiness' of identities as they are practised in everyday life.[27] It also fails to recognise and appreciate the power of human rights thinking among women activists in this contemporary Muslim context.

As will be apparent again, I concur with Judith Butler and Saba Mahmood's view that human capacities are not foundational in the sense they were seen to be by some Enlightenment theorists. Similarly I would concur with the ascription to Mahmood by Bautista[28] – that no concept 'has a causal determinist role to the reality it claims to represent'. The relationship between concepts and 'reality' is not like that, since, as I have argued in earlier chapters, human beings, along with animals and plants, are part of this 'reality' and the concepts they produce arise out of the reality of which they are part. On the other hand, just as I contested Butler's view that 'inter-sexuality' is wholly produced by discursive practices that are cultural in form, so too do I contest Mahmood's view that rights are wholly produced by the 'discursive practices' of imperialism and colonialism or that religious identities are as pure and unsullied as Mahmood sometimes implies.

Far be it for me to set out to defend the myriad of liberal, secular rights that proliferate in the contemporary world – property rights, rights to religious beliefs and so on. However, in line with the points made in earlier chapters, human beings are embodied beings, and as embodied beings they have needs – for water, food, shelter – in order to survive. These needs, I have suggested, are grounded in powers or capacities. So some rights, deriving from needs – for water, food and shelter and then for the ability to make some kinds of choice about how to live one's life – at the very least, are core to our humanity and essential for the well-being of all of us. Moreover, these rights can be adapted and modified in particular cultural contexts. In Pakistan, once again, despite the accusations from some quarters that these practices are 'western and retrograde', women activists, as we have seen, have drawn on a universal secular rights-based discourse and adapted it for their own purposes. In 2002, for example, according to Mirza, the number of reserved seats for women in the national and local assemblies was increased, precipitated by Musharraf's strategy of promoting 'enlightened moderation'. This 'facilitated the passage of a series of women-friendly pieces of legislation in subsequent years, including laws related to honour killings, acid attacks and harmful customary practices'.[29] As Khan and Kirmani put it: 'WAF (Women's Action Forum), which spearheaded the modern rights-based women's movement, was established in 1981 as a platform to organise against Zia's Islamisation programme. WAF maintained a publicly ambiguous position vis-à-vis its position on religion out of political necessity throughout the 1980s. However, they largely chose to work within a universalistic rights-based framework'.[30]

Women activists have organised campaigns for land rights for landless women peasants.[31] It is important to point out, once more, that Khan and Kirmani argue that we should move beyond what they see as a false binary, between 'western' rights-based discourse and local religious language. No doubt it is the case that the universal language invariably has to be adapted according to context. Yet it remains significant that this is the language that is being used.

In line with the argument of chapter 5, it may be an assumption that the discourse of rights began in the European Enlightenment and there is an alternative account that sees them originating in ancient Persia. So the very idea that they are 'western' may itself be an ideological construction that holds sway throughout the world. Moreover, to reiterate the above point, the view that all 'rights' are produced by the discourses of imperialism and colonialism is to miss the vital point that some rights are so important to the survival of each one of us that they form a deeper core of humanity than even imperialism or colonialism could reach. They are not produced by the Enlightenment, by any US president, by any official of the UN, by any law or by any performativity of any feminist grouping, rather they arise out of our biological core, that is, as argued earlier, shared with the rest of the natural world. This biological core, again to reiterate earlier points made in the book, is not fixed and essential, but dynamic and changing and interconnected with the environment but it is none-the-less a biological dimension of our humanity that ought not to be denied or decried. Moreover, there was a moral intention behind the setting up of the UN Declaration that ought also not to be denounced or decried as western since the Declaration was set up to protect all humans from atrocities like those committed by the Nazis. Most of the people, indeed, whose fundamental rights and needs were denied at the time – Jews – were western.

When it comes to the desire on the part of some Muslim women to prefer 'subjugation over autonomy', there are different arguments that need to be brought into play. I would like in the next few paragraphs to challenge Mahmood's notion of agency from a different perspective. Mahmood refers to the 'performance of gendered Islamic virtues'.[32] She wants to remove references to 'emancipatory politics' and 'uncouple the notion of self-realisation from that of the autonomous will'.[33] Mahmood seems to see 'emancipatory politics' as linked to 'left liberalism'. However, the tradition of Marxism is surely more significant here than liberalism. Moreover, as Zia points out, 'patriarchy is also a very valuable anti-emancipatory tool that enables many men to "Flourish" but to suggest that political critique of this should be suspended while analysing its cultural and religious situatedness is hardly a definition of the critical engagement and unsettling that Mahmood herself demands of secularists and feminists'.[34] Zia also argues that the idea that Islamic laws will 'provide sanctuary to women relies on a paternalistic and infantilised notion that prescribes only protective laws for Muslim women'.[35]

Another important point made by Zia is the following: 'She argues, in the Pakistani context, that it is in part state policy that has contributed to promoting gender segregation and that when the state actively promotes women's professionalization, even in traditional female roles, this has a positive impact upon their levels of autonomy and agency'.[36] In the Islamisation years of Zia-ul-Haq women in employment were indeed described as liabilities to Islam. So if their agency is increased by being employed, then the opposite is the case where their abilities to engage in such way are reduced. Moreover, many groups enforced 'religious mores' in that period thus shedding doubt on the idea that the concept of piety was an innocent, if also performative choice, at least in the Pakistani context, of many women.

Just as Nira Yuval Davis and Floya Anthias[37] documented the role of women in promoting certain forms of nation state, so too have women played a significant role 'across the site of religious nationalisms, Islamic extremism and popular culture in Pakistan'.[38] Zia also suggests that the faith-based agency of women 'is not just innocuously adopted for non-liberal, non-feminist ends nor as a willing embracement and celebration of gender inequality only but increasingly to actively support a patriarchal Islamic agenda'.[39]

The competing appropriation of the female body, according to Zia, 'by both extremist and fundamental/nationalist articulations suggests that women's bodies continue to act as repositories of religious and nationalist identity in Pakistan'.[40] Moreover, in a counterclaim to the view that human rights develop and thrive with capitalism, Appiah points out that 'Islamisation' in this context has also served the ends of capitalism. Appiah writes: 'The new Islamisation of society in Pakistan is commoditised and thrives in and by expanding the market'.[41] Appiah continues: 'What we have seen in the US is not secularisation – the end of religions – but their commodification, and with that commodification, religions have reached further and grown – their markets have expanded – rather than died.'[42] In the Pakistani context, 'a body of work on the intersection of consumerism, capitalism, women and the Islamic culture industry demonstrate that Muslim women believers navigate and consciously engage in Islamic practices through various modalities of capitalism'.[43]

A FURTHER SET OF POINTS – A BRIEF LOOK AT SOME IRANIAN CASES

I would like, at this point, to consider a very different case and contrast it with Mahmood's work. This is the case of women in Iran who, rather than performatively setting out to become pious or shy, are rather protesting against being forced to wear the hijab. Perhaps the comparison would be unfair, if, as Mahmood herself might have intended, her account of the performativity of the Egyptian mosque women was taken purely as a description of the agency and the practices of that grouping. But, as noted above, both her own account and the way her work has been used, have taken it far beyond that. Her own account is not simply a description of the mosque women, but it is also a stringent critique of the values underlying the feminist movement from the 1960s onwards. It is not surprising therefore, that her work has been taken to have a much wider reach than that simple disclaimer which, as the good anthropologist she was, she made at the outset of her significant work.

To return to the Iranian case: in 2018, according to Amnesty International:

A warning by Iranian police that women could be jailed for up to a decade for joining protests against compulsory veiling has put dozens at immediate risk of unjust imprisonment and represents an alarming escalation of the authorities' violent crackdown on women's rights. More than 35 women have been violently attacked and arrested in Tehran alone since December 2017 for taking part in on-going peaceful protests against the discriminatory and abusive practice of compulsory veiling.

As Amnesty International further puts it:

In compelling women and girls to cover their hair, the Iranian authorities have violated women's human rights in Iran for decades and also deeply hurt women's dignity. Rather than threatening women with jail terms for claiming their human rights, the authorities should immediately abolish the discriminatory, abusive and degrading laws and practices of compulsory veiling.[44]

Using Mahmood's language, we might ask: how might these women be performatively enacting their desire not to wear the hijab? How might they performatively handle the prison sentence they risk getting and what effect might it have on their agency and their identity?

It might be argued that this is unfair on Mahmood and unfair on the women whose experiences she describes. Mahmood argues in her work that we should avoid the denunciation of the piety movement in Egypt. It does not seek to become a state or a theocracy. The project of feminism needs to be continually re-thought, she claims, within specific contexts. One context, though, that contrasts vividly with her Egyptian women in the piety movement is the case of women protesting in Iran against being forced to wear the hijab. Maybe Mahmood would have accepted such a case, but it does suggest, if she had done, that it is not possible to offer a ubiquitous critique of the notion of a human right, since the above women were using the concept to critique the Iranian regime.

ANOTHER IRANIAN CASE STUDY

Pertaining to the case of Iran, I would like to make one final and very different point on performativity. I would like to connect the work carried out by Saba Mahmood in rehabilitating the piety movement from its critics on both left and right to another case of a group of women. This is a group of exiled Iranian women who are part of an Islamic socialist, Iranian opposition group that is based, as I write this, in Albania where they were relocated after their previous 'homes'– Camp Ashraf and then Camp Liberty, in Iraq – were heavily attacked. The group was branded a 'terrorist' group for many years, but the label was removed by the EU Council of Ministers in 2009 and, by the

United States, through Hilary Clinton, in 2012.[45] Accessed 18 July 2018. The MEK, I note, is committed to rejecting the Islamic Retribution Law in Iran, adhering to the UN Declaration on Human Rights and abolishing the death penalty (Iran carries out more executions per capita than any other country in the world and it also executes children).[46]

I am not, I would like to say at the outset, expressing any view as to whether or not the MEK is a cult, or whether its members are brainwashed, as many critics of the organisation claim. The point is simply to suggest a direct comparison between the work of Saba Mahmood and the following claims made by Sara Hassani about press coverage of the MEK.

Sara Hassani begins her brilliant piece of writing with the following words: 'Feminist scholars the world over are increasingly aware of the importance of analyzing popular discourse, especially regarding women's involvement in proscribed violence.'[47] She writes powerfully and movingly of the way in which the MEK have been depicted in the popular press, worldwide as 'irrational actors incapable of autonomous political participation'.[48]

While the members of this group are long-standing female resistors, they are depicted, argues Hassani, as 'maniacal slaves', mindless actors who exhibit violence as a symptom of their ideological and sexual slavery.

As Hassani puts it: 'The exemplary case of the MEK decenters the familiar face of political resistance, complicating our most basic understandings of gender, political agency and proscribed violence. The scope of this article (hers) cannot, and therefore does not, attend to the validity of the discourse in question; rather, its aim is to problematize the rhetorical patriarchy informing the representation of women's involvement in armed struggle'.[49]

Founded by university students in 1965 in opposition to Iran's shah, the MEK later began to oppose the theocratic regime headed by Ayatollah Khomeini following the 1979 Islamic Revolution. As Hassani puts it, the MEK set out 'to develop systematically a modern revolutionary interpretation of Islam – an interpretation that differed sharply from both the old conservative Islam of the traditional clergy and the new populist version formulated in the 1970s by Ayatollah Khomeini'.[50] The organisation is the largest Iranian resistance movement with thousands of members in exile, nearly half of them women (US Dept. of State, 2011). The leadership of the organisation is comprised entirely of women. This is in a context, writes Hassani, in Iran, where male-only polygamy is allowed and where a prescribed Islamic dress code is mandatory for women.

Hassani examined the coverage of the MEK by eight distinct major news outlets between the years 2003–2013, with a total of 263 articles. Using a combination of qualitative and quantitative analysis, Hassani examined articles from the United States –the *New York Times* and the *Washington Post* as well as articles published in France in *Le Figaro* and *Agence France*

Presse. She also examined Iranian media coverage of the organisation in both English and Farsi. She tested for the typology of Mothers, Monsters and Whores across these various press outlets.

Her findings suggest that the women's voices themselves are systematically distorted over all these media outlets and re-transcribed in the tropes of victims, monsters and whores. In Hassani's case study, rather than simply being caricatured as 'docile and passive' as the critics of the women's piety movement characterised them, women are caricatured using a combination of the language of victimology and, alongside this, the language of whores and monsters. I would like simply to note, in what follows, Hassani's characterisation of the contrast between the women's own words describing their views and their behaviour, and the reportage in various media outlets of these women's testimony. Did these women not also, to use Mahmood's words once more: '(seek to) realize one's (their) own interests against the weight of custom, tradition, transcendental will, or other obstacles (whether individual or collective)'.[51] But, rather than seeking to become 'docile' against 'western modernity', they seek to fight against an extreme form of Islamic fundamentalism using the language of human rights. They seek their right to express their views and the right to institute a democratic system in Iran based on the principle of human rights.

Instead of focusing on the MEK women's expressed political aims, the media outlets referred to by Hassani portray the women, first of all, as victims of supposed patriarchal power, much as Mahmood's women in Egypt were portrayed by western feminists. 'By heavily relying on binaries of masculine power and feminine subordination, hysterectomies are portrayed as evidence of women's forceful captivity: "Hysterectomy, Latest MKO Cult Strategy." (2008) In so doing, this discourse disavows women's expressed political goals while emphasizing the patriarchal fixations undergirding the media's expectations of fecund and prolific femininity'.[52]

The women, moreover, in extreme forms of misogynistic depiction, are also portrayed as sexual slaves. According to Hassani, the press articles claim 'that female resistors are all married to the organization's former Secretary General', female resistors are portrayed as sexual slaves and reduced to the status of patriarchal appendages. Similarly, male resistors are often implicated in the promise of women's subservience through a reliance on hearsay, which assumes the validity of recruiting tactics ascribed to the MEK. Quoting one such 'hearsay' media report, Hassani writes:

'A Mujahedeen recruiter spotted [two young Iranian men] sleeping on the streets, so hungry he couldn't think anymore. ... He enticed them to join with an offer to earn money in Iraq while simultaneously fighting the cruel Iranian regime. What's more, he said, you can marry Mujahedeen girls and start your own family'.[53] Hassani notes, 'In fact, in many instances western portrayals of the MEK are virtually copied and pasted from state-run newspapers in Tehran'.[54]

One of the most disturbing instances quoted by Hassani from one source is the following:

'One of the most disturbing encounters I had in Ashraf was with Mahnaz Bazazi, a commander who had been with the Mujahedeen for 25 years. I met her in the Ashraf hospital. Bazazi was probably on drugs, but that didn't explain the natural intoxication she was radiating, despite – or perhaps because – she had just had her legs amputated after an American missile slammed into the warehouse she was guarding. The doctor told me he never heard her complain. "Even in this way, she's confronting the Mullahs," he said. Bazazi interrupted him. "This is not me personally," she said in a soft high voice. "These are the ideas of the Mujahedeen. It's true I lost my legs, but my struggle will continue because I have a wish – the freedom of my country." At the foot of her bed, surrounded by candles, stood a large framed photograph of Maryam [Rajavi, the leader of the group] in a white dress and blue flowered head scarf'.[55] Rather than enacting the roles ascribed to her by the press reports, then, in a very strong sense, therefore, Bazaxi is 'performatively creating' her role as a fighter and a defender of freedom in her country.

Hassani continues: 'Likening Bazazi's image with that of a sedated psychiatric patient, the author [of one of the press reports caricaturing her actions] blithely suggests that the subject had a loose grip on reality'.

Hassani further continues: 'This draws the autonomy of Bazazi's testimony into question, implying that she is incapable of rationalizing her own involvement in political resistance. Casting her stated political aspirations in the shadows of an otherwise simple display of iconography, the author sensationalizes her role as a victim of indoctrination. One cannot help but wonder whether this same imagery could have been legitimated if the subject of Rubin's reporting had been a man hospitalized in a war zone?' The same article employs the rhetoric of 'drugged' intoxication to portray female resistors as an 'army of Stepford wives' while revelling in hypersexualised tales of love and celibacy.[56]

It may seem to many in the west, and in the east as well, hard to believe Hassani's report of the MEK members' words. Hard as it might have been for Mahmood to persuade anyone that the women of the Mosque Movement were genuinely expressing their own agency, it is much harder still to persuade anyone who has not directly experienced the commitment, bravery and conviction of members of the MEK, to believe that the kind of stories documented by Sara Hassani might be true.

Another case mentioned by Hassani is the following. It pertains to the decision, made by the group in the late 1980s, to commit themselves to celibacy. She writes: 'I asked Sima, a woman in her late twenties, whether she ever regretted making that celibacy commitment'. "'When I feel that I'm getting closer to my goal," she shouted in English against the wind, "it's a more beautiful feeling than anything else. It's love." And what was her goal? "I have to teach the women in Iran to feel like I feel inside and rebuild what Khomeini destroyed. He is killing the soul of every person".'

The contrast between the press portrayal of these MEK women and their own expressed agency is stark. Hassani notes that many of the press pieces that have appeared in the west are direct replicas of the pieces that appeared in the press inside Iran. Just as the case of the mosque women is surely complex and multilayered and there is no doubt some link between their expressed commitment to piety and the views of others in the Islamic world, so too are there some complex influences on the views of these MEK women. But we might consider taking their expressed views as genuine rather than, what is commonplace in the press, the dismissal of their agency.

This case is not one that Mahmood herself would wish to draw to the attention of the world, particularly since the expressed view of the Mujahedeen is, as noted, the development of a regime in Iran that upholds basic human rights. She is rather concerned with portraying a group of practising Muslims whose faith was, in her view, distorted and denigrated by western feminists as well as by western-influenced cultural assumptions across Egypt. She wanted to valorise the agency of these women. What I have suggested, however, is that it is not only groups of religious women, whose aim is to become pious and modest, whose agency is denied and distorted by culture and custom. To the contrary, this case study has documented the case of another group of women whose agency is also distorted and misrepresented. But this group of Muslims is setting out, so the women say, to defend the very values that Mahmood rejects. Indeed, they are prepared to go to what many would describe as very extreme lengths in order to make their voices heard.

CONCLUSION

This chapter and chapter 7 have engaged with the brilliant and influential work of Saba Mahmood. In this chapter, I have critically engaged with her text *The Politics of Piety* and thrown some doubt upon three claims of hers: (i) that the sort of feminism she decries is 'western' and 'liberal' in a bad sense; (ii) that there is little influence of fundamentalist forms of Islam that are political and theocratic in intent on some of the new revivals of Islam and religion more broadly and (iii) that the religious movement is purely a cause for celebration for women. In the final section of the chapter, I have drawn attention to a case study of another group of women whose agency is widely decried and denied, but who, rather than challenging human rights thinking as western and imperialist, seek to use it in their majority Muslim country, to replace the fundamentalist form of Islam there. They claim that they seek to establish a liberal form of government that is compatible with the UN Convention on Human Rights.

NOTES

1. Saba Mahmood, *The Politics of Piety: The Islamic Revival and the Feminist Subject* (Princeton, NJ: Princeton University Press, 2011).

2. Aamir R. Mufti, "Why I Am Not a Post-Secularist," *Boundary 2* 40, no. 1 (2013): 7–19, in Zia, *Faith and Feminism in Pakistan*, 39.

3. Mahmood, *The Politics of Piety*, 7.

4. See Isaiah Berlin, "Two Concepts of Liberty," in *Liberty* (Oxford: Clarendon Press, 2002).

5. Mahmood, *The Politics of Piety*, 14.

6. Ibid.

7. Ibid., 15.

8. Ibid., 155.

9. Ibid., 156.

10. Ibid., 157.

11. See for example R. Dreyfuss, *Devil's Game: How the United States Helped Unleash Fundamentalist Islam* (New York, NY: Holt Paperbacks, 2005).

12. See Ayesha Khan and Nirda Khirmani, "Moving beyond the Binary: Gender Based Activism in Pakistan," *Feminist Dissent* 3 (2018): 153.

13. Mahmood, *The Politics of Piety*, 28.

14. Charles Eisenstein, *The Coronation*, https://charleseisenstein.org/essays/the -coronation/, accessed May 31, 2020.

15. Alison Jagger, *Feminist Politics and Human Nature* (New York, NY: Rowman and Littelfield, 1988), 40–44.

16. Simone de Beauvoir, *The Second Sex*, trans. H. M. Parshley (London: Penguin, 1972).

17. Alisdair MacIntyre, *After Virtue: A Study in Moral Theory* (Notre Dame, IN: University of Notre Dame Press, 1981).

18. Mahmood, *The Politics of Piety*, 27.

19. MacIntyre, *After Virtue*, 50.

20. Mahmood, *The Politics of Piety*, 3.

21. Ibid.

22. Zia, *Faith and Feminism in Pakistan*, Chapter 2.

23. Ibid., 38.

24. Mufti, *Why I Am Not a Post-Secularist*, 12.

25. Sadia Abas, "The Echo Chamber of Freedom: The Muslim Woman and the Pretext of Agency," *Boundary 2* 40, no. 1 (2013): 155–89, quoted in Zia, *Faith and Feminism in Pakistan*, 39.

26. Khan and Kirmani, "Moving beyond the Binary," 154.

27. Bangstad 2011, Ibid., 164.

28. Julius Bautista, "The Meta-Theory of Piety: Reflections on the Work of Saba Mahmood," *Contemporary Islam* 2 (2008): 75–83. I would like to add one qualification here. I am assuming that Bautista is reading "causal influence" in a determinist fashion here rather than in the rather different sense of self-causation I have developed in early chapters of this book.

29. Naeem Mirza, "Seven Pro-Women Laws in Seven Years," *Legislative Watch* 38 (2011): 1–4.

30. Khan and Kirmani, "Moving beyond the Binary," 157–58.

31. Ibid., 169.

32. Mahmood, *The Politics of Piety*, 203.

33. Ibid.

34. Zia, *Faith and Feminism in Pakistan*, 42.

35. Ibid., 48.

36. Ayesha Khan, *Women's Empowerment and the Lady Health Worker Programme in Pakistan*, Paper for the Collective of Social Science Research, Karachi, 2008, quoted in Zia, *Faith and Feminism in Pakistan*, 71. s.

37. Nira Yuval Davies and Floya Anthias, eds., *Woman, Nation, State* (Basingstoke: Macmillan, 1989).

38. Zia, *Faith and Feminism in Pakistan*, 86.

39. See also Haq 2007, Ahmad 2009.

40. Zia, *Faith and Feminism in Pakistan*, 93.

41. Appiah, in Ibid., 106.

42. Appiah, 144 in Ibid.

43. Zia, *Faith and Feminism in Pakistan*, 107.

44. https://www.amnesty.org/en/latest/news/2018/02/iran-dozens-of-women-ill-treated-and-at-risk-of-long-jail-terms-for-peacefully-protesting-compulsory-veili, accessed July 18, 2018.

45. https://www.nytimes.com/2012/09/22/world/middleeast/iranian-opposition-group-mek-wins-removal-from-us-terrorist-list.html.

46. https://www.iranfocus.com/en/index.php?option=com_content&view=article&id=32884:how-mek-would-protect-human-rights-in-iran&catid=50&Itemid=137, accessed July 18, 2018.

47. Sara Hassani, "Maniacal Slaves: Normative Msogyny and Female Resistors of the Mujahadin-el Khalq, Iran," *International Feminist Journal of Politics* 19, no. 3 (2017): 281–95, 1.

48. Ibid.

49. Ibid., 2.

50. Ibid., 3.

51. Mahmood, *The Politics of Piety*, 14.

52. Ibid., 7.

53. Hassani, "Maniacal Slaves,"quoting Rubin 2003, Ibid., 3.

54. Ibid., 8.

55. Rubin 2003, quoted in Hassani, "Maniacal Slaves," 5.

56. Ibid., 6.

Conclusion

In this concluding brief chapter, I would like to return to the subject matter of the Introduction. I wrote that in the summer of 2019. I am now writing on New Year's Day 2020. The last decade, as noted in the Introduction, has been a tumultuous one globally, with the rise of far-right populism across the world. In the winter 2019, there have been huge protests right across the vast Indian democracy, against a proposed new citizenship law that would deny citizenship, among certain potential immigrant groups, to Muslims. In the United States, impeachment proceedings have begun against Donald Trump. In the UK we saw a spectacular defeat in the first general election for years to take place just before Christmas, for Jeremy Corbyn's Labour Party. The interminable war in Syria continues to rage and the number of refugees globally continues to mount. Indeed, in January 2020, we saw the assassination of the right-hand man of Khamenei in Iran, Soleimani and the fall-out from that across the Middle East.

Furthermore, as I mentioned in the Introduction, I had not submitted this manuscript when we were hit globally by the coronavirus pandemic that placed many of us, in many nations of the world, in lockdown, with thousands dying in isolation, from this illness. As I mentioned in the Introduction, the draconian legislation that has been necessary globally in order to deal with this pandemic must not be allowed to continue indefinitely and, if anything, there is a greater need for defences of human rights than there was prior to the pandemic.

In May 2020, Amnesty International published a special issue[1] on *Coronavirus and Human Rights*. It argued, 'Human rights must be at the centre of government actions everywhere'.[2] The article pointed out that the measures that have been taken worldwide to protect health have disproportionately affected the 'low paid, those in precarious employment, at the front line of social care, teachers and health workers on whom privileged lives depend'.[3] It is those whose rights are least protected who often face the greatest threats – migrants, refugees, minority communities – not only from the disease but also from increased deprivation, discrimination, scapegoating and violence. The article moreover points out that while the measures taken to protect overall health are justified, they must not be disproportionate.

During the pandemic, the far-right has claimed that authoritarian regimes are better at dealing with the disease than democratic ones.[4] In fact, so far, and the time is now June 2020, the picture is mixed. While some autocracies, like Singapore, have done well; others, like Iran, have fared badly. Cuba developed a sophisticated, if draconian, procedure for 'actively screening' all households on the island and medical students have been deployed to walk round areas, checking door to door for signs of the illness. While the numbers dying from the disease are very low indeed, on the other hand, people who refuse to wear face masks can be jailed.[5] Countries where there are far-right leaders whose regimes have been labelled 'totalitarian' such as Brazil, have fared very badly. But so too have countries, such as the United States under Trump and the United Kingdom under Johnson, which are ruled by right-wing conservatives. Democracies such as South Korea and Taiwan have done well.[6]

Indeed, it is also important to point out that while religious belief is no doubt helpful for some in dealing with such a crisis, it is also noteworthy that some of the guidance that has been issued, often by far-right religious leaders, has been unhelpful. Trump, for example, made remarks about ingesting bleach that had to be rapidly countered by health workers and companies making the substance. Some members of Modi's nationalist party in India hosted a party to drink cow's urine as a potential antidote.[7] In the United States, right-wing religious preachers have encouraged people to congregate to come to services to pray to ward off the virus. Further, the *New York Times* reported: 'In Myanmar, a prominent Buddhist monk announced that a dose of one lime and three palm seeds – no more, no less – would confer immunity. In Iran, a few pilgrims were filmed licking Shiite Muslim shrines to ward off infection. And in Texas, the preacher Kenneth Copeland braided televangelism with telemedicine, broadcasting himself, one trembling hand outstretched, as he claimed he could cure believers through their screens'.[8] Some of these sources may be unreliable but the number of claims, covering most of the main religions, suggest that they may have some reliability.

On the other hand, though, as Charles Eisenstein points out: 'Covid-19 is showing us that when humanity is united in common cause, phenomenally rapid change is possible. None of the world's problems are technically difficult to solve; they originate in human disagreement. In coherency, humanity's creative powers are boundless. A few months ago, a proposal to halt commercial air travel would have seemed preposterous. Likewise for the radical changes we are making in our social behaviour, economy and the role of government in our lives. COVID demonstrates the power of our collective will when we agree on what is important.[9]

Eisenstein also points out that the numbers who have died from the virus, while each unnecessary death is shocking, are no way near the numbers who die each year from starvation, close to five million. Many more suffer each year from malnutrition. The scale of the changes the pandemic has brought about indicates the power of humanity, overall, acting collectively, to make changes for the better for our shared world.

On this note, we have seen the rise, on a global scale, in the last decade, of movements to challenge the climate crisis the world is facing. These concern a topic of this book, the right to life of future generations of humans as well as of animals and plants. We have also seen demonstrations across the Middle East, in Iraq and in Iran, against the fundamentalist regimes there. Some of the women demonstrators couched their slogans, as they remove the hijabs they are forced to wear in Iran, in terms of the 'right to do what they want with their bodies'. We saw in earlier chapters, as well, how protestors in Pakistan have used the concept of a right to make their case. The example from India, given in the opening paragraph of this conclusion, also reveals the importance of the concept of a right. The right fought for here was the liberal right to citizenship. This is a right, according to the protestors, that should be available to all potential immigrants into India, independently of their religious beliefs.

The concept of a right, it must be noted, is limited in its efficacy. Liberal democracy is not the most just form of political system. However, a limited democratic system based on human rights is a precondition for engaging in deeper change that may, one day, challenge the deep inequalities of the capitalist system.

In this book I have articulated a metaphysical theory that I have described as a version of 'new materialism'. I believe this theory is important as it stresses, in Darwinian fashion, the continuity of the human race with the rest of the animal and the natural world. This kind of theory is particularly important given the threats to the natural environment we are seeing at the present time. I have drawn, in support of this theory, on a number of philosophers, particularly Bergson and Schelling and others as well, but also on Darwin and some contemporary biologists. I have attempted, in chapters 1 to 3 of this book, both to articulate such a theory, to explain why I believe it is important and also to defend it against some of the most common alternative accounts. My 'new materialist' metaphysic is one that sees humans as emerging from a reality that precedes them; one that sees the world as primarily comprising 'processes' or powers as opposed to static things.

I have suggested that a metaphysic of this kind links with a non-anthropo-centric ethical theory. In the course of defending such a theory, I drew, for inspiration, on the work of Hans Jonas. He is important for me, in seeing eth-ics as applying not only to existing humans but also to future people as well and also to the animal and the natural world.

Some might argue that, given these premises, they would expect me to defend a theory of animal rights or of the needs of animals for fair treatment. While I believe that this is very important thing to do, I have chosen, in this book, to do something different. I have focussed instead on responding, in the latter part of the book, to some prominent critics of the concept of a right. It seems to me to be important to do this, as a precursor to the former task. If rights in general are regarded as obsolete – as associated, as some of the crit-ics have argued, ineluctably, with capitalism, individualism, colonialism and imperialism – then there would be no point in defending the rights of animals. So my task, in the second half of the book, has been to defend the notion of universal humanity from its many detractors. Indeed, some of these detrac-tors, as noted, have not merely critiqued the concept of universal humanity, as well as the concept of universal woman, but they have rather denigrated it as a 'non-starter' and as hopelessly tied up with Eurocentrism, colonialism, sexism and many more 'isms'. While I have recognised that some of these critiques are important, I have also argued that some of them miss their target. In their zeal to decry some 'partial' attempts at outlining universal humanity, some that are indeed racist or sexist, to give just two examples, they have thrown out the baby with the bathwater. Instead of properly recognising that the accounts are wrong because they mistake the nature of universal humanity, they have claimed, rather that the problem lies with the notion of universality itself. I have, in the book, challenged this notion and defended a processual version of universal humanity, one that recognises the impor-tance of the biological body but that challenges the European Enlightenment account of universality.

I then moved, in the second half of the book, to defend the concept of a right. I have suggested two other potential sources, than the European Enlightenment, for the concept – one is Aristotle in the ancient Greek world and the other is Cyrus, the leader, for a while of the ancient Persians. To reiterate, I am not suggesting that this account has more plausibility than the view that associates rights with the European Enlightenment. I am rather sug-gesting, instead, that it is an account that deserves not to be ignored, as it has largely been, in the literature.

In the final sections of the book, I have chosen to focus on some prominent contemporary critics of the concept of a right, as Eurocentric, imperialist and inevitably tied up with colonial power. The main critic on whose views I have focussed, in chapters 7 and 8, is the work of Saba Mahmood, since her critique has been finding huge support among academics in postcolonial studies, religious studies and elsewhere. I believe, therefore, that her work deserves not only to be applied and applauded by other academics but also to be – as rigorously as possible – critiqued. I hope I have gone some small way, in this book, towards doing this.

NOTES

1. *Coronavirus and Human Rights*, Amnesty, Summer 2020, Issue, 205.
2. Ibid., 14.
3. Ibid., 15.
4. https://www.americanprogress.org/issues/security/news/2020/04/06/482715/authoritarin-regimes-seek-take-advantage-coronavirus-pandemic/.
5. See "Covid Success in Stark Contrast to Region's Failures," *The Guardian*, June 8, 2020, 25.
6. https://carnegieendowment.org/2020/03/31/do-authoritarian-or-democratic-countries-handle-pandemics-better-pub-81404.
7. https://www.dw.com/en/hindu-group-hosts-cow-urine-drinking-party-to-ward-off-coronavirus/a-52773262.
8. https://www.nytimes.com/2020/03/22/world/middleeast/coronavirus-religion.html, accessed April 2020.
9. https://www.northatlanticbooks.com/blog/the-coronation-an-essay-by-charles-eisenstein/, accessed May 2020.

Index

Abu-Odeh, Lama, 134–35
abstraction, from cultural context, 133–34
Abu-Lughod, L., 118
Adorno, T., 135–36
Afghanistan, 145
After Virtue (MacIntyre), 149
Against the Modern World (Sedgwick), 128
Agamben, Giorgio, 5
Akeley, Lewis Ellsworth, 16
Alderwick, Charlotte, 30
Algeria, 109
Aliyu, Mu'azu Babangida, 109
Allison, Henry, 49, 50
Amnesty International, 109, 110, 116n64, 153–54, 161
An-Na'im, Abdullahi, 105–106, 115n27
Annan, Kofi, 110
Anthias, Floya, 152
appearance, significance of, 8
Appiah, Kwame Anthony, 153
Aquinas, Thomas, 89
Arendt, Hannah, 86, 98–99n23, 121; on freedom, 137, 138; on minority, 121; on political activity, 136, 137; on public/private distinction, 136
Aristotelianism, 85

Aristotle, xviii, 83–84, 149; on animals, 84; on soul and living things, 84; on women, 85, 98n16
Aryanpoor, M., ix
Assiter, Alison, 21n4, 46n37, 47n62, 47n65, 60n3, 141n45
autopoiesis, significance of, 40, 41, 47n82, 73; critique of, 42–43; machines and, 43
Avesta Fargard (Bleeke), 88
Axel Honneth (Wilhelm), 137
Ayer, A. J., 16

Badiou, Alain, 5
Bahais, in Egypt, 130–31
Baker, Gordon, 22n14
Bamidele, Rasak, 107
Bangsted, Sindre, 114n5
Barad, Karen, xiv, xv, 2, 4, 20, 26
Battersby, Christine, 34
Bauch, Leo, 81
Bautista, Julius, 150
Being (*Ein Wesen*), 31
Being and Worth (Collier), 51
Bennett, Jane, 1, 26, 27, 35, 36, 84
Benton, Ted, 51
Bergson, Henri, 1, 3, 16, 22n15, 26, 74; on humans, 6; on life, 28; on

www.ingramcontent.com/pod-product-compliance
Lightning Source LLC
Chambersburg PA
CBHW021817270326
41932CB00007B/229